1 4

To Ride the Mountain Winds

A history of aerial mountaineering and rescue

To Ride the Mountain Winds

A history of aerial mountaineering and rescue

Leslie Symons

SANDSTONEPRESS
HIGHLAND | SCOTLAND

First published in Great Britain in 2011
Sandstone Press Ltd
PO Box 5725
One High Street
Dingwall
Ross-shire
IV15 9WJ
Scotland

www.sandstonepress.com

Editor: Robert Davidson

The publisher acknowledges subsidy from
Creative Scotland towards this volume.

ISBN: 978–1–905207–60–2

Jacket design by Gravemaker + Scott, Paris.
Typeset in Linotype Sabon by Iolaire Typesetting, Newtonmore.
Printed and bound in Poland.

To Gloria
and to
the rescuers who risk their lives to save others,
whether by sea, air or land

Contents

Acknowledgements

A large number of people have given freely of their time and expertise to help in the writing and preparation for publication of this book. In particular I should like to thank the librarians who have patiently sought to meet many requests, often difficult to fulfil. Help extending over several years has been generously provided at the libraries of the École Nationale de Ski et d'Alpinisme (ENSA) and the municipal library at Chamonix; by Christine Boesiger, archivist of the Swiss Museum of Transport (Verkehrshaus) Luzern and at many public libraries in Switzerland, France and Italy. In Britain I am indebted to Brian Riddle, librarian, and other staff of the Royal Aeronautical Society; Ministry of Defence DASA; the Air Historical Branch, Royal Air Force; the Royal Naval Air Service; H.M Coastguard especially Mark Clark and John Bentley; the Alpine Club; the British Mountaineering Council, especially Tony Ryan; the National Library of Wales; the Mitchell Library, Glasgow; the British Library of Political and Economic Science, London School of Economics; and several public libraries, especially in Shropshire, Dorset and Inverness and the Carnegie Library, Kendal. I am no less grateful for the help generously given by the personnel of HMS Gannet, Prestwick, especially Mike Paulet; the Peloton de Haute Montagne (the Gendarmerie) at Chamonix; Philipp Keller, Communications, Rega, Zurich; and members of staff, past and present of aviation firms, notably AgustaWestland; Air-Glaciers; Air Zermatt, Pilatus Aircraft Ltd, especially Chalid Baumann, Chamonix Mont Blanc Helicopters, and from staff of the Swiss Tourist Office, Editions

Glénat, Grenoble and the Forest Fire Control Branch, Ontario. I have also received many helpful comments from pilots and aircrew members, instructors, mountain guides, doctors and others involved in the mountain rescue services, from the Air Accident Investigation Branch, Farnbrough; the National Transportation Safety Board, Washington DC, and the International Civil Aviation Organisation, Montreal. Special thanks for helpful comments and supply of information and photographs are due to Robert Davidson, John Allen and the members of the Cairngorm Mountain Rescue Team, Colin Cruddas, David Gibbings, Chris Sanger-Davies of Lindstrand Hot Air Balloons Ltd., Mark Radice, Ruth Tyers, Stephen Elliott, Frank Card, Alister Haveron, Roy Wheeler, Dr. James Begg, Richard Meredith-Hardy, Patrick Roman, Regina Bittel, Anne Françoise Lee, Alan Blackshaw, the late Mike Holton, Georgina Hunter-Jones of *Helicopter Life*, John Russell, Richard Royds, Anne Sauvy and John Wilkinson, Dennis and Gwen Greenald, Nick Thoennissen, Bruno Jelks, Beat Perren and Geoff Wood; and thanks and apologies are offered to the many others who have helped though not specifically mentioned.

Most of all I owe debts of gratitude, extending over the years, to my wife, Gloria, without whose inspiration this book would never have been begun, though sadly she has not lived to see its completion, and to my daughters Alison, who has helped tirelessly through the most difficult stages, and Jenny and her husband Raymond. Without the help of all of them it is safe to say that this book would never have been completed and published.

Finally, Robert Davidson has proved to be a paragon of an editor beyond the reasonable expectations of an author, patiently reading, correcting, monitoring and offering suggestions and encouragement throughout the past year.

It is to try to advance some way towards remedying the deficiency in perceived awareness of the work of all those courageous flyers and mountaineers, whose interests have come now so close together, and to widen understanding of the long process that has led to the present level of achievements, that this book has been written. Readers will also be reminded of some of the exploits of aviators and climbers now forgotten, or perhaps known only to relatively few people.

Apologies are made for any errors or important omissions, and comment on these, via the publisher, will be most welcome with the hope that corrections and thanks may be made in future editions. Every endeavour has been made to obtain copyright permissions and to avoid causing offence to any person, living or dead, but if I have failed or transgressed I apologise most sincerely.

Note: The metric system is preferred for the altitudes of mountains as well as for distances and most other measurements. However, in quotations and references to historical material in which Imperial measures were used as was normal at the time, these are retained. Furthermore, aeronautical data are usually quoted following normal practice in aviation, i.e. altitudes in feet, except where, in the context, this would confuse matters. Flying distances are given, as is normal, in kilometres. (The lengths of runways are usually expressed in metres.) Speeds are usually quoted in kilometres per hour, occasionally in knots (nautical miles per hour), as they also are used in the aviation world and in meteorology. A knot (kt) is one nautical mile per hour. One nautical mile is one minute of latitude, normalised as 1,853m/6,080ft. Aviators tolerate these complications because having altitudes and distances expressed in different units can actually avoid confusion in verbal communications, though some crews relatively unfamiliar with 'English' measures naturally find them difficult to deal with. For the convenience of readers, mountain altitudes are also sometimes given in feet, either as a reminder of the equivalents or where this was the usage of the author cited. Temperatures are stated in degrees Celsius.

List of Illustrations

Drawings

P12 Seedpod of the Southeast Asian climber *Zanonia macrocarpa* (Alison Symons)

P13 Artist's impression of the Dunne D.3 glider (David Gibbings)

Photographs

1. Spelterini preparing balloon 'Stella' at Jungfraubahn-Station Eigergletscher, 1904.
2. Monte Rosa and glacier confluence taken from Spelterini's balloon.
3. Georges Chavez preparing to take off in his Bleriot XI at Brig in 1910.
4. The DH50 in which Cobham flew to India to survey the projected airship route. Cobham is seen here with Arthur Elliott (flight engineer) on his right, Sir Sefton Brancker (Director of Civil Aviation) on his left, and the Maharajah of Datia.
5. A philatelic cover flown by Charles Lindbergh in a De Havilland DH4M, as shown on the special stamp, on the inaugural mail flight by Robertson Air Transport.
6. An airmail cover flown from Valparaiso to Santiago, then by Jean Mermoz over the Andes to Buenos Aires.
7. Powered by a supercharged Bristol Pegasus 9-cylinder engine, the Houston-Westland approaches Everest over the mountains of Nepal in 1933.
8. Westland Whirlwind over Cwm Idwal in North Wales.

9. A Westland Whirlwind makes a landing at high altitude in Austria, 1961.
10. Westland Wessex on mountain operations.
11. RN Westland Sea Kings deployed in the Norwegian mountains.
12. The Pilatus P4 first flew in 1948 and was used as an ambulance and for parachuting rescuers, search dogs and supplies.
13. Pilatus SB-2 Pelican, STOL design, predecessor of the Porter.
14. Pilatus PC-6 Porter 'Yeti' supplied to the Dhaulagiri expedition.
15. The De Havilland DH50 piloted by Alan Cobham on the survey flight to India in 1924 as depicted on a contemporary magazine cover.
16. Austers of Mount Cook Airways, New Zealand, 1950s.
17. A Cessna 180 of Mount Cook Airways with skis retracted, being prepared for a tourist flight from the Mt. Cook airstrip 1960.
18. A Pilatus PC-6 Porter on an Alpine glacier.
19. PGHM rescuers with an Alouette III in the Mont Blanc range.
20. A Eurocopter EC145 poised for a rescue on a glacier in the Mont Blanc range.
21. A rescuer with search dog boarding a Rega Agusta A109.
22. A rescuer on a longline descent from a Rega Agusta A109.
23. A Rega Da Vinci helicopter being signalled to a landing on a Swiss glacier.
24. Rescuer with stretcher landing from a Rega Da Vinci helicopter.
25. A Rega Da Vinci swoops down over the Bietschhorn, a peak in the Bernese Oberland to the southwest of the Jungfrau.
26. A Eurocopter Lama heavy-lift helicopter of Chamonix Mont Blanc Helicopters, showing the fuselage construction which helps operation in high winds.

Front cover image
A Rega A109 rescue helicopter passes in front of the Matterhorn (Rega Photo Service)

Credits for Photographs

The author and publishers express their appreciation for the use of the photographs included in this book:

Introduction

On a blustery autumnal day in the Highlands of Scotland above Blair Atholl, north of Perth, some four years after the Wright brothers made in America what is generally recognised as man's first sustained aeroplane flight, a surprising experiment was bearing results. A strange contraption of wood, fabric and wire rose briefly into the mountain air. It was one of the first manned flights by a heavier-than-air machine in the British Isles, for although this flight was for only a fraction of the time that pilots were now making frequently in the USA and France, there had as yet been no sustained flight made in Great Britain. In the context of this book it is especially interesting because it was one of the first attempts in the world to seek to benefit from the winds that sweep mountain slopes. Although a hilltop launch was the normal requirement for launching a glider into the air, to take the machine to mountain terrain for this purpose was certainly not normal.

Every detail of the preparations and the flying attempts were recorded night by night by the light of a flickering candle in a draughty tent, notes that would be read by few but would be preserved in official records and intrigue aviation historians decades later. It is hoped that the brief summary, which will be found in Chapter 1, will therefore be of interest.

There are now thousands of books in many languages and countless articles in magazines and journals on mountains and on flying. There are, however, not a great many books that examine the relationships between mountains and aviation, or mountaineers and aircrew. There seems to be, particularly, a notable lack of them in English, as compared with French or German. Books and journals specialising in mountaineering usually refer to aircraft only when they are directly involved with climbing – mostly either in support activities, such as getting to the nearest available landing place for the approach to the climb, or in mountain rescue work. These publications rarely elaborate on the aeronautical aspects, while, for pilots, mountains are mainly of interest for the problems they pose; their scenic aspects and opportunities presented for employment and sport.

In modern times, aviation circles feel even less need than formerly to refer to mountains, which now do not offer the obstacles or, in general, the dangers, to flight they once did. Again, most references to mountains in aviation literature today are concerned only with accidents and survival. The relationships and interwoven threads between aviators and mountaineers are, however, intriguing, and deserve exploration. Flying among the mountains has produced many acts of enterprise and daring that compare with those of mountaineers, though rarely calling for the output of long sustained physical effort and serious discomfort that are constant accompaniments of mountain climbing.

Flyers and climbers share the same challenges in many of the emotions they experience, notably in the need to subject themselves to the discipline of long and complicated training, meticulous attention to detailed planning, constant alertness when facing the inevitable hazards of their environment and the ability to make instant responses. Perhaps above all they must overcome fear when faced with acute danger and remain calm in the face of adversity. They also share constant involvement with weather and climate and the need to understand the vertical structure of the atmosphere. Often they must travel without being able to see beyond the grey, damp environment of enveloping clouds and cope with winds of high velocity and sudden and deceptive air currents. For the mountaineer wind is almost always an adversary to be feared, threatening and debilitating. For the aviator air currents may be either foe or friend. For some it provides the essential ingredient in a successful enterprise. Both climbers and air travellers can also enjoy and frequently become enraptured by the beauty of their cloud worlds and the vast horizons of their outlook, enjoying similar spectacles of mountain ranges spread before them in all their variety and immensity.

For the pilots of modern aircraft *en route* high above the mountains, there is little involvement with the terrain below – only in keeping safe altitudes, very different from the heroic days of aviation. There are, nevertheless, many present-day aircrew whose daily work involves them with the hills and mountains – in rescue work, in supply of high-altitude huts and hotels, in scenic flights and in local passenger transport, to give but the most obvious instances. Many of them are mountaineers as well as flyers. There is also a growing number of mountaineers who are also pilots, especially in the sporting branches of aviation, which now offer great variety of opportunities and experiences at modest cost and are expanding all the time.

For most mountaineers the object is to get to the top of a peak, or to get there by a special route, though sometimes the route is almost all that matters and the summit is given a miss. For balloonists and early aeroplane pilots the aim was simply to pass over them, usually from one area of lowland to another where there would be a reasonable chance of a safe landing. Then came the solving of the challenge of how to land aeroplanes safely on glaciers and to take off again in the mountains, where altitude as well as terrain added to the problems by reducing the effective power of engines, often inadequate even at low altitudes.

Mountaineers have often gone to the help of crashed aviators; now the reverse is a daily part of the worldwide mountain scene with mountain rescue, wherever possible, relying on helicopters to get rescuers to the scene of an accident followed by the evacuation of casualties. Sporting flyers, including the devotees of gliding, hang-gliding, paragliding and parachuting, have all found the mountain environment conducive to their enjoyment. Thus the worlds of mountaineering and flying have become inextricably entwined.

There have been interesting differences in the way mountaineers and flyers have gone about writing up their adventures. Mountain travellers were writing of their experiences centuries before the prospect of flight became practical. A Chinese report in 37 BC referred to the Great and Little Headache Mountains and sickness at high altitudes of both men and their animals. (Gilbert, 1983, quoted by Ward, 1990–91, 191) True, such people were travellers rather than mountaineers, and were reporting, above all, the unusual aspects of the countries they had explored. They tended to make light of their problems, being used to hardships, though the headaches and related problems of lack of oxygen at altitude – 'thinness of the air' as it was called – received much comment and speculation from travellers in the high mountains of Asia in the 16th, 17th and 18th centuries. (Ward et al, 1995) Whether deliberately or not, mountain travellers contributed substantially in many other ways to scientific as well as geographical knowledge.

In the 18th century, the Age of Enlightenment, serious mountaineering began with the first ascent of Mont Blanc, five years after man's flight began with the launching of hot-air balloons by the Montgolfier brothers followed within months by hydrogen-filled balloons. The balloonists and the mountaineers learned from each other about the physics of the atmosphere but soon the balloonists were flying far higher than the mountains. In their turn, they also learned of the additional hazards they faced once they dared to penetrate mountain regions.

The idea of mountains as places of peace and stimulation of the mind and of religious belief was expressed by a few thinkers and wanderers much earlier. One such was Francesco Petrarch, who ascended Mont Ventoux (1909m, 6263ft) near his home at Avignon in the 14th century. A few renaissance artists introduced distant mountains as backgrounds of pictures, such as Leonardo da Vinci in his *Madonna of the Rocks*.

Much later, artists found that mountain detail provided some of the most remarkable subjects for their talents and many mountaineers developed their artistic skills to illustrate their adventures or commissioned artists to do so. In the case of

Edward Whymper, instigator of the first ascent of the Matterhorn in 1865, it was as an illustrator that he first went to the Alps and succumbed to the lure of climbing them. He would not ever have wished to have been presented with the material that came his way on that most famous of 19th century alpine excursions – the picture of five of his colleagues, still flushed with victory, suddenly plunging to their deaths as they began the descent.

At that time, the art and science of photography was making rapid progress and soon it was practicable for mountaineers to record in photographs the superb scenery they encountered and specialists combined climbing and photography in a new profession, as in the case of the Abraham brothers in the English Lake District, in the 1890s and early 1900s. Those of Vittorio Sella, who, in the same period, produced photographs of the Himalaya and other distant ranges, are still regarded as among the best ever made, though the cameras and plates available to the early photographers were incredibly cumbersome and heavy. For the balloonists who began the adventures of flying over the Alps, photography enabled them to record images previously barely imaginable, such as those recorded by Spelterini and Falke, whose views of glaciers and peaks deserve comparison with Sella's. Photography helped mountaineers to plan ascents and photographs taken from the air became instrumental in the planning of some major ascents, such as those of Brad Washburn, using his own Alaskan pictures. Air photographs taken in the 1930s and 1940s were used in the early stages of planning the first successful ascent of Mount Everest, the world's highest mountain, in 1953.

Throughout the 19th century and into the twentieth, exploration and geographical discovery were necessarily limited to travel by land and sea. Some explorers and geographers climbed mountains and made notable advances in the exploration of the Himalaya, the Andes and Africa. In Europe, the Alps had already become, in Leslie Stephen's terms, the 'playground of Europe.' (Stephen, 1871) Alpinists published books that excited public imagination as they wrote of how they grappled with rock, snow and ice. For decades there were surprisingly few fatalities, the routes undertaken being mostly just within the abilities of the exploring amateurs and the capabilities of their guides and the equipment they had developed. When the readily available mountains had been ascended by the most obvious routes, enterprising climbers sought out ever more demanding alternatives and developed new techniques to deal with the new problems encountered. As each 'last great problem' was solved a new one filled the gap. Excuses of scientific discovery, as being the objectives and reasons for ascents, were put aside, the sporting challenge was dominant and it was now freely admitted to be so. Explorers in the Arctic and Antarctic regions had to cope with mountain ranges and months of hazards and agonies imposed by low temperatures, winds and storms.

Conquest of the air had been in the minds of men from the earliest times. Envious of the flight of birds, man's imagination had roved freely over such mythical achievements as the escape from their captor of Daedalus and his son, Icarus, who flew too near the sun, so that its heat melted the wax that secured his wings and he fell to the sea. When winged flight was at last achieved, it was by men who concentrated on acquiring scientific knowledge and engineering skills and had little time for literary invention. Sir George Cayley in England and Otto Lilienthal in Germany pioneered the way towards flight with wings by constructing gliders. Lilienthal found the Rhinower Hills west of Berlin provided excellent sites for launches. When the Wright brothers in America achieved the first brief powered flights in 1903, it was, however, on the coastal lands of Kitty Hawk.

Aeroplane flight was gradually improved, especially in France, and in 1909 Louis Blériot flew across the English Channel. The very next year saw adventurous pilots attempting mountain crossings. They were not mountaineers looking for easier ways to ascend the peaks, but aviators intent on extending the envelope of flight and showing that they could make links between places separated by high mountains as well as those divided by seas. It was in the Alps, where mountaineering had been born, that the mountain flying techniques also were first advanced, though in the case of flying there was not the same pioneering input from the British and Irish that there had been in mountaineering. It was in a French aeroplane – a Blériot mono-plane – that the first crossing in the air above an alpine pass was made, by a Peruvian living in Paris, unfortunately with a tragic ending. The achievement by Chavez of that first trans-Alpine flight, described in Chapter I, is often passed over by aviation historians but for Gustav Hamel and Charles Turner, whose important treatise on flying was published in 1914, it was a most significant flight:

> Although he [Chavez] sacrificed his life, the moral effect of that tremendous victory was incalculable, for it showed that the mightiest strongholds of the air are conquerable. (Hamel and Turner, 1914, 16)

There was, however, little direct contact between mountaineers and aviators and their thoughts and writings proceeded along different lines. Mountaineering during the pioneer days was mainly an activity with two classes of participants. Amateurs, mostly men with some wealth and leisure, sought achievements for their own sake and relished the excitement – and even the fear – that came inevitably with their adventures in the mountains. Their guides were local men, peasants with little education, who helped them achieve their objectives in return for modest payment. Many of the former wrote books and articles about their climbs, whereas few of the latter were capable of, or desirous of, putting their thoughts on paper.

In aviation it was different. The men who first aspired to 'conquer the air' were comparatively well educated tradesmen (like the Wright brothers) or professional engineers but their writings were mainly of a technical nature, concerned with explaining their achievements in aeronautical terms. Flyers soon, however, attracted an enormous amount of public interest. Journalists, poets and novelists, as well as the politically-minded writers who commented on the rapidly evolving scene, put their thoughts to their readers in France, Great Britain, Germany, Italy and the USA, to mention only those countries most involved in the race to command the skies.

After the early, mainly quite separate, adventures in challenging the mountain and aerial environments, the possibility of any connection between the two great ways of seeking access to the realm of the clouds was made drastically less likely by the advent of the First World War. The prospect of aerial attack had caused public alarm as soon as the Channel had been crossed by air. Lord Northcliffe's *Daily Mail* lost no time in calling for the country to 'wake up' to the urgent need to develop air power to add to its dominance of the seas, and the prizes he offered for ambitious air races brought aerial competition to England, though it did not result in the crowds of public spectators that had become common in France.

In contrast to the peaceful and highly personal activity of mountaineering, aviation attracted warlike thoughts. F. T Marinetti, a novelist and poet, found in aviation the key to developing his futurist outlook. He went to North Africa in 1911 and saw aircraft being used to support the Italian troops in the fighting against the Ottoman forces at Tripoli. Whereas many intellectuals, such as H.G. Wells and John Galsworthy, foresaw the horrors of aerial warfare and bombardment and warned of the prospect of death and destruction raining from the skies, Marinetti relished the possibilities that aerial power could bring to Italy to overcome its enemies, notably the Austrians. He even imagined deliberately attacking thousands of women who were trying to block the troop trains going to the front. They would be killed by the wings of the aeroplane that he envisioned in his poem, *Le Monoplan du Pape*, which he completed in the trenches. (Wohl, 1994, 142). There could have been no greater contrast with the ideals of many mountaineers, even if not all would have shared the idealist views of Geoffrey Winthrop Young, alpinist, poet and author of the standard text, *Mountain Craft*, who in the war served with the Friends Ambulance Unit on the battlefields and lost a leg in the process – but still managed to return to climbing with an artificial limb of his own design.

From the time that a major war seemed inevitable, aviation received attention and investment on a scale that it could never have attracted in peacetime. It also meant that aesthetic and spiritual ideas that may have been found by aviators in a way similar to the inspired thoughts of many mountain travellers had little opportunity of flowering in the war-torn skies. Oswald Boelcke, the first of the German flyers to gain fame as an 'ace' pilot was, indeed, a skier and climber who was at home on steep precipices, and said, according to his father (also a mountaineer), 'It was when danger threatened that his young soul leaped with joy.' (Perthes, 1916, 11, quoted by Wohl, 1994) Boelke had the sensitivity to recant on the 'joy' he had first expressed on seeing his opponent crashing to his death over Flanders, but his successors, such as Manfred von Richthofen, most famous of all the aces, had no qualms in identifying with the ruthless killing that was accepted without question in the land and sea conflicts. Richthofen had come to flying from a 'sport' but it was that of hunting, and he described how the hunter's approach was part of the calculating and merciless technique that lay behind his phenomenal success in aerial combat. (von Richthofen, 1917, quoted by Wohl, 1994, 226)

Except in the eastern Alps, mountaineering was an irrelevant sporting pastime, which clearly had to be put aside by combatants during hostilities. On the Italian-Austrian front, however, ordinary troops on both sides suffered dreadfully from cold, frostbite and avalanches while mountaineers performed incredible feats in defence of their fortifications and in pursuit of the foe – inevitably also, many pilots on reconnaissance and attack flights found disaster among the peaks. Once the war had ended, mountaineering took on wholly new dimensions with the beginnings of the assault on Everest and other Himalayan giants, and the introduction, again in Europe, of aggressive new techniques in climbing. Aided by the use of pitons (metal pegs) and advanced rope techniques, the new generation showed that they could overcome technical problems that had been far beyond the reach of earlier climbers, who had been restricted by traditional methods. Though risks could be limited to acceptable levels by new precautionary measures, it became increasingly common for mountaineers to push themselves to new levels of danger. The technical problems they sought to overcome and the associated objective and environmental dangers, such as exposure to the physiological risks of high altitude, climatic dangers and avalanche hazards, demanded the acceptance of increasingly greater risks.

Interestingly, the opposite trend ruled in most branches of aviation as the pressures mounted to make flying commercially viable, which necessitated being safe enough to attract wealthy patrons, and, eventually, the general public. Nevertheless, many of those passionate about flying did not limit their personal activities by being overly cautious. By the time the war ended, aeroplanes had levels of performance and load-carrying capacity that had been beyond dreams before the war and the challenge for ambitious pilots now became to fly to all parts of the world and to set up and constantly break records for speed, range and altitude and to make any number of impressive point-to-point flights. For others who struggled to make their living in aviation, war surplus aircraft offered a start with only a little capital needed. Barnstorming and air circus pilots and test pilots were among those who seriously risked their lives in every flight, many times a day. In his National Aviation Days (1932–35), Sir Alan Cobham's displays reached over 250 in a summer season, often two programmes a day, every pilot making many display flights in each. (Cobham, 1978)

All the pioneer pilots who flew airmails accepted the dangers inherent in getting the mail through in often virtually impossible weather, by night and over hostile terrain, and casualties were common. Such airmen were often cast as heroes in books and films. As late as 1939 the film *Only Angels have Wings* highlighted the dangers faced by the mail pilots, picturing an unsuccessful attempt to fly through bad weather over an Andean pass of 14,000ft. (Wohl, 2005, 145) The reality of that kind of flying could be much worse in discomfort and danger than fiction depicted, typified by the experiences of Antoine de St. Exupéry and his fellow pilots of Aéropostale. They faced capture after forced landings in the desert among hostile tribesmen and incredible hardships in the mountains, as highlighted in the description of Henri Guillaumet's fight for life after a forced landing in the Andes, described here in Chapter 2. Yet the pilots were passionately proud of their airline, as were many of their contemporaries serving other airlines or flying independently.

Whereas mountaineering in its earlier days had been justified by scientific enquiry, such reasons and excuses were advanced in the 1920s only for major, expensive expeditions, such as those to the Himalaya, especially, for the British, Mount Everest. For many of the new breed of rock climbers, the climb itself was all that mattered. Such climbing was, however, seized upon for propaganda purposes by the fascist regimes that came to power in Europe. The German and Austrian climbers who made the first ascents of great north walls, such as those of the Matterhorn and the Eiger, were given medals and, in the latter case, photographed alongside Hitler. To die in the pursuit of conquests that would redound to the honour and fame of the Reich was held to be a worthwhile risk. Similarly in the air, it was considered that the probability of death was an essential ingredient of the devotion of pilots to the domination of the air by their own country. Italian pilots wrote of their joy in seeing the panic-stricken flight of the helpless hordes that they attacked in the campaign mounted by Mussolini in North Africa. Mussolini had become an enthusiast for aviation when he was a journalist before the First World War, claiming in 1909 that a new heroic age, distinguished by speed and movement, had arrived:

'Movement toward the icy solitude of the poles and towards the virgin peaks of the mountains, movement toward the stars and toward the depths of the sea.' (quoted by Wohl, 1994, 287, after Guido Mattioli in *Mussolini aviatori*, L'Aviazione: Rome, 3rd edn. 1938, 20–21)

When he came to power in 1922, Mussolini made the development of air power a cornerstone of his fascist government.

During the 1920s and early 1930s aviation was still at the

stage where those who practised it were very much in the public eye and the most successful of them, who pioneered the long intercontinental flights and competed in breaking records, were looked upon as heroes and were as famous as great movie stars – though not in the same league financially. Aviators also ran great risks with their lives, though no longer dramatically greater than those accepted by mountaineers. Except for the relatively small number of expeditions to the Himalaya, mountaineers did not receive the attention from the public that record-breaking flyers did. The loss of George Mallory and Andrew Irvine on Everest in 1924 did really attract public interest in Britain and America and has remained an event that some members of the non-climbing public recognise today, but it was an exceptional case. Nobody could see in mountaineering the possibility of value to other people, as could be distinguished increasingly in aviation. Even though few except very wealthy travellers and senior politicians as yet could experience flight as passengers, the advantages of rapid transport of intercontinental mail could be widely appreciated. So flying gradually progressed from being an activity in which only daredevils would actually participate, to a romantic and exciting way of making a career or of simply finding satisfaction and enjoyment.

As the capabilities of aircraft increased, it became inevitable that they should become employed in overcoming the problems of exploration and transport in increasingly hostile territories, over oceans, deserts and mountains – sometimes all three in one area, as in the Arctic and Antarctic regions. Flights of long duration in these areas necessitated mastering the techniques of landing and operating from ice and in the worst of weather. The techniques learned were interwoven with those of pilots in more temperate mountain regions and it was in the Alps that techniques of glacier flying were refined and pushed to the limits on steep and highly crevassed icefields. Now the time had come for these techniques to be applied to rescue work, with dramatic intervention in the case of accidents to other aircraft, including airliners, which came to grief when aiming to fly over the mountains. Specialised air rescue services were started and, increasingly, aircraft came to the aid of mountaineers, not only when they were in trouble but also when they perceived the advantages of aerial transport for access to the peaks and conveyance of supplies. Co-operation between mountaineers and flyers was born and some talented persons became experts in both fields, like Brad Washburn and Terris Moore in North America, and many mountaineers in the Alps.

Meanwhile other sportsmen had found new challenges in the mountains. Advancing designs of gliders had made possible soaring flight, which could take pilots over alpine passes and peaks. As they became masters of harnessing the air currents that had been serious hazards for the pioneer flyers, glider pilots extended the range of their flights to include complex multi-sector competitive flying over hitherto unimaginable distances and altitudes. As the 1970s rolled into the 1980s, hang-gliders, microlights and paragliders enabled new generations to link inexpensively their desire to fly with their enthusiasm for the mountains. The development of the modern hot air balloon brought more new possibilities, including taking passengers up to revel in the spectacle of the great mountain landscapes.

It is a great advantage of all forms of gliders, parachutes and balloons that they are virtually silent and hence do not disturb the environment through the creation of noise, a common complaint about motorised aircraft. The purpose of a machine may be the rescue of a person in danger, whether injured or not – but it still makes a noise that disturbs the peace of the mountains. That is one of the elements of the price that must be paid as part of the overall cost of modern mountain rescue by helicopter, which includes not only monetary and environmental costs; but also the risks accepted by the pilots, technicians, guides and doctors that fly the mercy missions.

The change in the roles and in the public perception of aviators on the one hand and mountaineers on the other has been accompanied by a change in their involvement in literature. Mountaineering has always produced a steady flow of books. If you climbed a mountain, or tried to climb one, that had not been climbed before, you would expect to write a book on the subject and the public would enjoy reading about the struggles, successes, disappointments and disasters experienced on the high peaks. The number of flyers who wrote successful books for the general public never reached similar proportions, though some, like Sir Alan Cobham, published many first class accounts of their long exploratory flights, and Antoine de Saint Exupéry entered the portals of the great in literature. St Exupéry is one of the very few aviators whose works have acquired the status of classics and are an enduring mine of inspiration for others. Both of these writers are quoted in subsequent chapters.

The flow of mountaineering books has continued to swell and is now a flood, as many more men and women undertake serious climbing and more and more are making it a career, of which writing is an integral part. The character of the writing has changed enormously, particularly in the past two or three decades. The 'stiff upper lip' approach and understatement of the 19th century and even the 1950s and 1960s has been succeeded by an ever-increasing tendency to lay bare all the hardships mountaineers suffer on the great mountains. More and more of the unpleasantness of life in tented camps and snowholes at altitude are revealed to the armchair mountaineer. There is no longer any attempt to hide the practical problems presented by life and survival; the struggle to maintain health and energy by consuming enough food when it is unpalatable, if not positively repulsive, and of melting ice and snow to obtain enough fluid to avoid dehydration – and then to get rid of the waste products without minor disasters in the process! Indeed, these are not limited to minor disasters – several people have slipped and fallen to their death, especially at Himalayan altitudes, when leaving the relative security of a tent for just that necessity. Certainly the effect of such writing is to emphasise how maintaining normal routine and dignity becomes an increasing worry and source of unpleasantness to oneself and one's companions as height is gained. Yet the challenge is sought by ever-increasing numbers of people, in the course of which huge sums change hands.

Modern critical and investigative authors are finding that the realities of what happened on some of the mountaineering expeditions that were originally reported as great achievements in mental and spiritual experiences as well as in ultimate physical success are much more complicated and in some cases very different. The ascent of Annapurna, the first 8000–metre peak to be climbed, has been shown to have been carried out by individuals who were far from united in their perception of the difficulties and the actual events. At the time the sole account allowed was by the leader, Maurice Herzog, dictated from a hospital bed. (Herzog,1951,1952). An oath of absolute obedience to Herzog and an undertaking not to publish any account themselves for five years had been extracted from every member of the expedition. (Roberts, 2000, 25) Many telling passages were deleted from subsequent memoirs. This ascent inspired climbers of the 1950s and 1960s and continues to be regarded as one of the most impressive exploratory adventures of all time but the revelations of what really happened now need to be borne in mind in assessing individual contributions to the expedition.

There is comparatively little record in aviation of the utter weariness of the body and mind experienced by climbers in their battle with the mountain and often recounted at length. In pioneer flights tiredness presented an ever-present problem as fatigue induced sleep and sleep threatened disaster, so to that extent one can find some sort of parallel. The sufferings of bomber crews on long sorties to and over enemy territory during the Second World War occurred at a time when the stiff upper lip was still to be maintained – only in relatively recent recollections of survivors are there realistic and honest accounts of such experiences. Crashes in mountains and remote areas have given rise to other revelations by aviators and surviving passengers, one instance being a disaster in the Andes, infamous for cannibalism as a means of survival.

With the growth of the demand for rescue services from the air have come accounts of some of the difficulties, dangers and sometimes frustrations encountered by the rescuers on account of weather that rules out flying in the mountains, the occasional mechanical failures that interrupt missions, and the prolonged pain and suspense of those awaiting the arrival of the saviours from the skies. The technical limitations of even the 21st century restrict what is possible in the Himalaya and other high ranges and the airmen who carry out mercy missions at such altitudes among the glacial peaks do so at the most acute risks to their own lives. Their efforts are not always fully appreciated by those on whose behalf the flights are made, and this applies also to rescues that are only less spectacular in comparison with the extreme cases – almost all rescue work in the mountains (or at sea) is fraught with constant difficulty and danger. This, however, is part of the process in which aviation and life in the mountains has become inextricably intertwined.

CHAPTER 1

First Above the Alpine Peaks

Aircraft, now often the means of getting to the hills, and of rescue when an accident occurs, were seen by some alpine travellers as unwelcome intruders into the peaceful mountains, especially before air travel was available to the masses. Thus, Arnold Lunn in the Bernese Oberland in the early 1920s:

'. . . against the sky an arrogant aeroplane circled around and then swooped past the Jungfrau, a horrible reminder that the aerobuses of the future will doubtless invade these Alpine solitudes. The thought saddened us. We felt like the last survivors of a disappearing race, the race of men who climbed on foot.' (Lunn, 1925, 138)

Today, not only have most mountaineers (more numerous than ever) become used to such noisy disturbances, they have come to recognise the great value of aircraft in making life in the mountains more comfortable and safer, with helicopters especially now playing a vital role in the alpine economy and mountain rescue. Fixed-wing aircraft also have a large part to play, especially in tourist flights and communications, while gliding, paragliding and parachuting have become important sports. Ballooning has also found a new lease of life among a dedicated sporting fraternity.

It was, however, the silent lighter-than-air machine that first brought aviators to the Alps, which presented opportunities and challenges that aeronauts could not ignore. It was just three years before the first ascent of Mont Blanc that the first manned flight was made in a balloon, but the seeds for the flowering of

1

ballooning were already in gestation in the two preceding decades. Henry Cavendish, an English scientist, had, in 1766, discovered the properties of hydrogen (which he called 'inflammable air'). Dr. Joseph Priestley, who isolated oxygen in 1774, wrote *Experiments and Observations on Different Kinds of Air*, which was translated and published in French in 1776.

Priestley's book reached Joseph Montgolfier in Annonay, near the Rhone valley in France, and inspired him to make experiments, but the hydrogen leaked through the paper balloons he made (he was a manufacturer of paper). Observing that sparks rise above a burning fire he turned to hot air – 'rarefied air' as he called it. Montgolfier may not have fully understood what was happening – that the air molecules were expanding with warmth so they were occupying a greater space and rising through the ambient colder air. In 1782 he enjoyed his first success in getting a small balloon off the ground. His younger brother, Etienne, became enthused and they built bigger balloons and, on 5th June 1783, publicly demonstrated one of about 30m in circumference, which rose to a height estimated at about 2,000m. It flew for about ten minutes and landed about two kilometres away. In Paris, a physics professor, Jacques Charles, thought the Montgolfiers must have used hydrogen. He and the Robert brothers, Jean and Noël, set to work with the gas and managed to overcome leakage with a rubber-coated silk material sufficiently to get a balloon into the air in August.

The Montgolfiers, however, seized the great prize of being first to launch a man-carrying balloon. On 15th October 1783 at Paris, a tethered hot-air balloon carried Jean-François Pilâtre de Rozier into the air for 4 minutes and 25 seconds. He made several more ascents that day and began to acquire the knowledge needed to control the balloon. On 21st November, de Rozier and François Laurent, Marquis d'Arlandes, made the first manned flight – the first time man rose free into the air and returned safely to earth. They fed the fire with straw and extinguished several small fires that spread to the fabric and made a satisfactory landing after 25 minutes. (Rolt, 1966, 44–48, Acton, 2002, 30–44)

Within weeks Jacques Charles had ready a hydrogen balloon of much more sophisticated design and on 1st December 1783 he and Noël Robert soared away across the city and landed safely two hours later, 45km from the launch site. Charles then went up again on a solo flight and reached a height of some 3,000m, which provided him with some sensational new experiences. 'I passed in ten minutes from the temperature of spring to that of winter,' he reported. He also experienced acute earache but enjoyed a unique second view of a spectacular sunset. Again he landed safely. (Christopher, 2001, 6–12)

France became balloon-crazy and many adventurous persons in other countries joined in the new game. In the Alpine region, on 6th May 1784, 'Monsieur le Chevalier Dr. Chevelu' and an engineer named Brun climbed into the basket of their own 18m hot-air balloon at Chambéry and rose into the air to an altitude of 1,800m and landed safely 25 minutes later, much to the delight of the watching crowds. (Yves Borrel in Mure, 2002, 64)

The hydrogen balloon had a great advantage over the Montgolfière (as the hot-air balloon was now called) with the latter's vulnerability to fire and refuelling problems, until modern technology gave the hot-air balloon a new lease of life. It did, however, suffer from the long and expensive procedure then used to make hydrogen and the result was highly combustible. Unfortunately, Pilâtre de Rozier became a believer in the opportunities offered by combining the two types and in June 1785 he took off in such a lethal machine and paid the ultimate penalty when the balloon caught fire in mid-air – the world's first flying disaster had claimed the life of the first aeronaut. (Rolt, 1966, 92–3, Christopher, 2001, 19) The development of ballooning was set back by this tragedy, but in the early part of the 19th century it experienced a revival and became popular with professionals (who provided flights for others), showmen and sportsmen. Surprisingly, the idea of the combination of hydrogen and hot-air systems survived and finally late in the 20th century came into its own with modern technology. This became the favoured form for the challengers aiming to make the first round-the-world flight by a balloon. Helium, a safe alternative to hydrogen, provided the gas in the large envelope which provided the main source of lift, to be vented for descent, with propane gas providing the bursts of heat required to gain, hold or to regain altitude. This reduced the amount of ballast needing to be carried, mainly to be dropped to counter the loss of altitude when the helium contracted at night. In 1999 Bertrand Piccard and Brian Jones were finally successful with their epic circumnavigation in Breitling Orbiter 3, which also took the distance, duration and altitude records. (Piccard and Jones, 1999) Their experiences over the Burmese mountains are described in Chapter 13.

To return to the 18th century, the climbing of Mont Blanc had been achieved by Dr. Michel-Gabriel Paccard and Jacques Balmat on 8th August 1786. Horace Benedict de Saussure, the scholar and enthusiast who in 1760 had stimulated the exploration of Mont Blanc by the offer of a prize to reward the first ascent, thought about the possibilities of using a balloon on at least parts of mountain climbs. He studied the subject in a practical way, remaining, despite the great heat, eighteen minutes in the car of a Montgolfière while it was being inflated. He proposed alder wood as an alternative fuel to the straw generally used. He also made laboratory experiments and showed how the heating caused 'rarefaction' of the air, thereby providing lift. (Hildebrandt, 1908, 1973, 16–17).

The early balloonists had taken note, of course, of the proof provided by travellers and mountaineers that man could survive at the high altitudes that already had been reached, but many believed that the oxygen-rich strata might follow the earth's contours so it might not be safe to go so high over lower terrain. They had to discover for themselves whether this was so and how high they could safely go. They found in the mid-19th century that the Alps could be crossed without encountering serious altitude hazards, though there were plenty of other dangers. Even before the Alpine Club was formed, the first balloon flight over the Maritime Alps was made by a Frenchman, François Ardan, who flew from Marseille to near Turin in 1849. Ardan's description of his daring flight is worth quoting:

4

'I crossed Esterel forest at 4,000 metres. Already it was cold and my thermometer was reading four degrees below zero. The wind was blowing from the southwest and carrying me towards Nice. For more than two hours I was enveloped in thick cloud. My coat was insufficient to protect me from the cold and I suffered a lot, especially my feet. Nevertheless I resolved to continue my journey and decided to cross the Alps. Soon I reached the mountains; the wind became steady, the moon illuminated everything perfectly. The snows and the waterfalls glistened, the chasms and the rocks formed black masses providing shadows for this gigantic picture. From time to time I was forced to descend or to rise again to surmount the peaks that faced me without a break. At 11 o'clock in the evening I reached the highest point, the horizon became clear and I thought of supper. I found myself at 4,600 metres; I was forced to continue the journey and to gain Piémont, I saw only chaos before me; descent in these regions was impossible.

'At half-past one in the morning I was over Monte Viso. I recognised my position from my first trip in Piémont . . . the moon produced a mirage effect on the snows and clouds and I could have believed I was over the sea. But to my left and at my height, Mont Blanc dominated the clouds, resembling a huge block of crystal scintillating with a million fires. Then Monte Viso was behind me; I descended near a farm . . . it was half-past two in the morning. I was in the village of Pion-Porté, six kilometres from Turin. Distance: 270 kilometres as a bird flies. Duration of flight eight hours.' (Ardan, q. Dollfus, 1969, trans. LS)

Tragically, only a month later, Ardan was lost over the Mediterranean Sea on a flight from Barcelona. (Rolt, 1966, 104)

Balloonists intending to pursue mountain flying needed to learn the basic techniques of mountaineering and how to equip themselves appropriately, but not all did so, even half a century later. Such was the case with Captain Charbonnet of Lyon who was in business in Turin. On October 8th 1893 he decided that it would be appropriate to take his bride on a balloon journey over the Alps. In the evening after the wedding they made a flight of some sixteen kilometres. Next morning, with one of Charbonnet's regular crew and another man, they took off at 10.30, although it was stormy. After being carried in various directions they were soon lost in clouds and about 14.30 struck the ground, rebounded and crashed against the rocks several more times, then came to rest at about 3,000m on the flank of a mountain which turned out to be the Bessanese (3,632m, 11,917ft) in the Levanna area of the Graian Alps. All the occupants having survived the crash, they started down the mountain. They had no mountaineering experience and no alpine equipment. There was a small glacier to cross and Charbonnet, who had been injured in the crash, slipped and fell into a crevasse and did not answer their calls. Although they had cut up some of the balloon fabric for extra protection against the cold, they had not thought to take with them any of the balloon's rope. The others went on down to the valley and eventually, after another night in the open, found a shepherd, who guided them to a village. Charbonnet's body was recovered later from the crevasse at a depth of twenty metres. The *Alpine Journal* copied a report from *Rivista Mensile Italiana*, calling it 'as rash an expedition as was ever undertaken.' (*AJ*, Vol. 17, 1895, 41–2)

It was not only in the Alps that such risky flights took place. North America was the scene of many pioneering balloon flights. In 1881, the fate of two balloonists, John Bisley and Jonathan Wenslon, who had attempted to fly over the Rocky Mountains, had been discovered six years after their disappearance. Hunters looking for eagles found the remains of the balloon at about 3,700m on Mount Wasatch. A search party then found the skeletons of the unfortunate adventurers at the foot of a rockface, together with a record of the disastrous actions that had led to their deaths. Believing that the journey to the Pacific coast would not take more than thirty hours, they had jettisoned most of their food along with ballast when they had reached the Rockies. They had risen spectacularly but in the cold of the night, as the gas contracted, the balloon descended and crashed. With only one day's food, they set off on what would have been a march of several days, wearing only city shoes. Wenslon slipped and fell and suffered a broken leg. Bisley stayed stoically with him until death claimed them both. ('En planant . . .,' 1913, 299–300)

Given adequate experience and equipment, however, the balloonist who prepared adequately and waited for the right weather conditions could safely make impressive journeys. The Swiss aeronaut, Captain Eduard Spelterini, born Eduard Schweizer at Neuhaus in 1852, became famous in the 1880s for his aerial voyages, which included over a hundred Alpine balloon journeys as well as flights over Africa.

After a ballooning conference had taken place at Sitton (Sion) in the Valais, Spelterini made a determined effort at crossing the highest Alpine ranges. In the *Wega*, a 3,350m hydrogen balloon he took off at 10.45 on 3rd October 1898 with three companions, Professor A. Heim, Dr. J. Maurer and Dr. Biederman but was blown to the northwest across the Jura by Saint-Croix. He crossed the frontier at Les Verrières and landed at Rivières between Dijon and Langres near Besançon after a flight of over 200km but not in the intended direction, as can often happen in a balloon. (Dollfus, 1969, 10; Hürzeler, 1969)

On 8th May 1900, Dr Stolberg and Professor Hergesell flew from Friedrichshafen on the Bodensee (Lake Constance), later to become the home of Count Zeppelin's airships, over the Zugspitze (Germany's highest peak), to the Fernpass. Other flights took place in the following years, including several by Spelterini. From Zermatt he flew over the Simplon massif to Lake Maggiore (17/18 August 1903) and from the Eigergletscher station on the Jungfrau railway to the Blümlisalp near Adelboden. (20 September 1904) (Dollfus, 1969, 10–11). The Italians Usuelli and Crespi made a historic 300km flight from east to west over the Mont Blanc massif from Milan on 11th November 1906 via Monte Rosa, the Matterhorn, Grand Combin, Grand Saint Bernard Pass, and Annecy.

The alpine balloonists regarded as the 'last great problem', the crossing in one flight over the ranges from the Bernese Oberland to the Valais and on to Tessin or into Italy. After many weeks of waiting for the necessary north winds, Victor de Beauclair, an experienced alpinist as well as balloon pilot, having sent up meteorological balloons to find out what the winds high above had to offer and obtained telegraphed forecasts from Zurich meteorological office, launched his 2,300m balloon *Cognac* from the Eigergletscher station at 13.15 on 29th June 1908. Also aboard were the photographer, Conrad Falke, Gebhard Guyer and his wife, who became the first woman to fly over the Alps. They carried some 640kg of ballast and proper alpine equipment. The balloon flew over the southwest ridge of the Mönch, down the Aletsch glacier and over the Rhone near Brig. The high peaks around Zermatt were shrouded in threatening storm clouds but they were able to avoid these and crossed the Simplon Pass. It was a pitch-black night but behind them the sky was constantly lit up by lightning flashes, a heart-stopping display of fearsome illuminations. As dawn appeared in the east, Monte Rosa dominated the view and soon they could feel that they had crossed all the ranges to achieve their objective. They flew on, over Lake Maggiore at over 5,000m with the thermometer at –15 degrees C. It was a magnificent world of high mountains displayed in a glittering half-circle – Monte Viso, the Dauphiné, Mont Blanc, Monte Rosa, the central Alps, the Bernina massif and the mountains of Tirol. They came to a suitable landing place and Beauclair brought them safely to the ground. (Dollfus, 1969, 12–16) A series of fine illustrations appeared in Falke's book *Im ballon über die Jungfrau nach Italien.* (Falke, 1909)

On 9th August 1909, Spelterini, having made more successful flights over the Alps, including from Zermatt into the Ticino, from Murren to Turin and from Interlaken to Oberammergau, set off from Chamonix shortly after midday to attempt the first balloon flight over the summit of Mont Blanc. He was accompanied by three passengers, one being a journalist from *Le Figaro*. To 'cinematographe' the event, M. Gaumont was present, as well as a crowd of photographers. The balloon was borne away at first northward towards the Brévent but then swung towards the Dôme du Goûter. The flight looked likely to be successful. Then, however, a current of air from the south-west blew the balloon at 2,000m towards the Mer de Glace. It narrowly missed the Aiguille du Dru before disappearing into cloud over the Trient massif. Next day, M. Bossonet, mayor of Chamonix, received a telegram from Locarno. The balloon had crossed the mountains and had landed on a mountainside at about 1,800m. The voyagers had had to undertake a seven-hour walk down and another four hours of travel by carriage.

An English journalist described an alpine flight with Spelter-ini, illustrating the necessary precautions. They loaded adequate provisions for four days, along with two cameras, and 48 photographic plates, compasses, aneroid barometer and maps, warm coverings, nailed boots and ice axes. Also included in the equipment was a bugle, to alert the inhabitants when they landed. The balloon was launched from the Höhenmatte at Interlaken at 15.45 on a fine afternoon. It was necessary to throw out two bags of ballast to gain height to search for favourable air currents, which were found at some 3,000m, and which bore them towards the Lake of Brienz and the glaciers.

The villages looked like match boxes to the journalist-photo-grapher, who wrote:

> 'It seemed impossible to me that those black lines, thin as wisps of smoke, which streaked the glaciers, were impassable cre-vasses.'

The Englishman's enjoyment of the scene was interrupted by the pilot calling him to assist as they would strike the mountain if they did not rise some hundreds of metres within two or three minutes. Later, during the night they encountered many varying air conditions. Throwing out a bag of ballast would send them up a hundred metres only to be forced down again. Around 22.00 they entered a zone of calmer air and had their first meal; bread, cheese and chocolate accompanied by a glass of Bor-deaux. Soon, however, the journalist began to suffer the effects of altitude. Despite the entrancing sheen of the glaciers in the moonlight, he wanted only to sleep but was kept awake by the captain who knew the risks this entailed in the rarefied air and bitter cold. He did, however relent enough to bring the balloon down some 400m. At first light there was a crisis and frozen fingers struggled to eject more ballast and in the panic to avoid the threatening precipice five or six bottles of champagne went overboard. 'It was our last hope, we had only two sacks of ballast left,' explained the captain. 'A balloon without ballast is like a ship without a rudder.' Then, however, the sun rose and the gas expanded and the balloon shot up like an arrow.

Eventually they heard the welcome sound of cowbells and saw the brown and white spots of a grazing herd of cows, then huts, then a village. The pilot brought them skilfully and safely to the ground at 18.15. Spelterini sounded the bugle and peasants came hurrying to see the two strangers who had fallen from the sky. They began to dismantle the balloon to prepare it for transport to the nearest railway station, but there were still excitements to come. They had landed at Unter-Amergau in Bavaria and the local police arrested them, accusing them of being French spies. After a voluminous exchange of telegrams with the Munich authorities, the aeronauts were released. ('En planant . . .,' 302–306)

Meanwhile, dirigible balloons were being developed as 'airships' with much more control over flights, soon making them suitable for transport between selected points. The Alpine region was in the forefront of such developments in the earlier part of the 20th century, through the work of Count Zeppelin at Friedrichshafen. *Graf Zeppelin* was flown from Friedrichshafen to Luzern in 1908 and in 1910 *Parsefal* flew around the Zugspitze. (Pyatt, 1984, 208). In 1914, Hamel and Turner drew attention to the study of air currents by the airship pilots:

'The Zeppelin airship (No. 1) took advantage of the regular currents in the neighbourhood of the Rhine and the Swiss mountains, and by availing herself of these currents attained, on some occasions, a speed of seventy miles per hour. Thereupon

10

attention was given officially to the air currents of Germany and charts were drawn showing their seasonal variation.' (Hamel and Turner, 1914, 184)

Later the Zeppelins became famous for their long-distance commercial flights, but the mountains, with their uncertain air currents and lack of safe landing places, did not encourage routes over them or even through the lower passes. In the early years of the 20th century, however, far more important developments were taking place in the air. Reliance on lighter-than-air machines (aerostation) was giving way to dominance by aircraft that were heavier-than-air (aviation).

The coming of the aeroplane

The flight in Scotland referred to in the Introduction and those that followed there took place in September 1908. Just over two weeks later, on 16th October 1908, the first flight in a powered machine in Great Britain was made at Farnborough by Samuel Franklin Cody. Even after that, balloons and airships were still regarded by many as offering the best possibilities for aerial travel and the advocates of aeroplanes met considerable official apathy and discouragement.

When Cody achieved his breakthrough the experiments in the Highlands seemed to Colonel John Capper of the Royal Engineers (later Major-General Sir John Capper), Superintendent of the Balloon Factory at Farnborough, Hampshire, to be more promising than Cody's work. Capper's preferred designer, John William Dunne, while on leave from the army, had turned his attention to creating an aircraft that would be inherently stable. This was in contrast to those built by the Wright brothers, which required constant input of controlling adjustments on the part of the pilot. Dunne was not a trained engineer, but had great faith in his ideas, inspired by studying the wings of the seed of the Zanonia plant. So important was the work judged that it had been decided that it should be hidden away, far from Farnborough, in some remote part of the country.

11

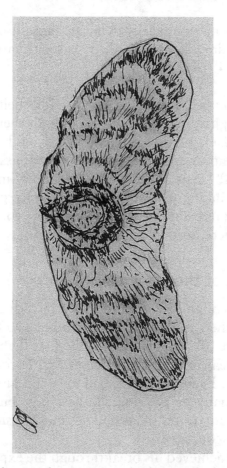

Seedpod of the Southeast Asian climber Zanonia macrocarpa
(syn. *Alsomitre macrocarpa*) which inspired the design of the
Dunne glider and other aircraft.

That it should have been thought appropriate to choose such a remote location for the development of Dunne's experimental aircraft is a little easier to understand if one appreciates that when the Wright brothers had tried to sell their design to the British War Office they were unwilling to reveal enough information about it for the negotiations to succeed. Their concern to maintain maximum secrecy about their designs was commercially motivated, that surrounding Dunne's aircraft reflected military attitudes.

Colonel Capper had written to the Duke of Atholl, with whose son he had been friendly when they were together in South Africa, to ask if they could base Dunne's work at his estate and had received an enthusiastic reply. The Blair Atholl estate is a few miles to the southeast of the Drumochter Pass, which carries the main road, the A9, from the central lowlands to Inverness. It is a road notorious for closures in winter due to snow. Today special 'snowgates' are closed to prevent motorists driving into danger when heavy snow is forecast, despite which vehicles already in the pass are frequently snowed in and rescue services required.

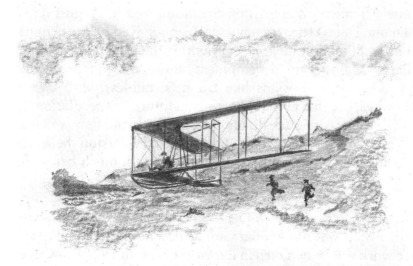

Artist's impression of the Dunne D.3 glider flown by
Launcelot Gibbs in the Scottish hills, 1908.

In 1907 the first Dunne glider, having been built in the south, was dismantled, taken north to Blair Atholl and reassembled, then carried up to an area in the hills, where the winds were thought to be favourable for the lift required. Newspaper reporters who had heard that something interesting was afoot in the hills tried to see what was going on but were kept away by guards provided by the estate. Attempts were, however, brought to a halt when Colonel Capper had the misfortune to crash on his take-off run. The first snow would soon be adding to the dignity and beauty of the mountains, but would make flying attempts in the hills impracticable, so the damaged machine was taken back down to the valley and later had engines fitted. The next year the experiments were continued with the powered machine and a new glider. It was the glider that made reasonably successful flights in the hills, the aeroplane's engine being inadequate for its purpose.

Government policy caused support for British work on aeroplanes to be seriously weakened by a decision in 1909 to favour airships and both Dunne and Cody were discharged from their Farnborough posts. Dunne was able to continue work in his privately-financed Blair Atholl Syndicate and in August 1912 the Dunne D8, its earlier engine problems solved by the acquisition of an 80hp Gnome, made a notable flight from Eastchurch to Paris. Mainstream development, however, had proceeded along other lines. Designs like Dunne's, tail-less, with swept-back wings, became favoured mainly in futuristic speculation. In 1926, however, one such design that was built and flew well was the Westland-Hill Pterodactyl. In the Mark IV version the wings had adjustable sweepback, another innovation much before its time.

The exact location of Dunne's experiments in the hills above Blair Atholl was not known until dedicated research and detective work was undertaken in the early 1970s. In 1971 Dr Walker visited the site and studied the ground in detail. The sketch of the glider and the hills here presented is based on his photographs and maps and diagrams appearing in his substantial work on the history of aviation at Farnborough (Walker, 1974) and in contemporary illustrations in Jane's All the World's Air-craft 1913. (Jane (ed), 1913, 1969)

It was unfortunate that, like so much more, Dunne's knowledge of the winds and their effects were virtually forgotten and whereas British climbers had dominated the mountaineering scene throughout the 19th century and were first to ascend most of the Alpine peaks, when it came to exploring the mountains from the air the British pilots were not among the foremost.

The 1910 Alpine aerial drama

After the first powered flight in the Alpine regions was made by the German, Paul Engelhardt, in a Wright biplane from the frozen St. Moritz lake on 10th March 1910 (Dollfus, 1969, 21), the new challenge was to prove that aircraft could fly on predetermined routes over mountainous terrain. This, at the time, required an aeroplane to climb almost to its operational ceiling merely to cross a col that had been frequented on foot for many centuries. In September 1910, machines little different from the Blériot monoplane in which its constructer had been first to fly across the English Channel the previous year, were gathered at Ried, above Brig, to attempt to win a handsome prize by flying over the Simplon Pass to Domodossola and Milan. The first prize offered was 70,000 Swiss gold francs with 30,000 to be split between runners-up. The aviation week had been organised by members of the Milan Aero Club who had put up the prize money, other funds being made available by hotel owners and the Wallis cantonal authorities, who also allocated 24 policemen to be stationed along the route from Brig to Iselle. The airfield was prepared at Brig-Ried and five hangars erected and a telephone line was rigged up along the route. Also provided were first-aid posts with signalling and smoke-signalling to assist the pilots. People flocked in for the event

Georges Chavez, Peruvian by descent but born in Paris, where his family were in banking, arrived in Brig on August 23[rd.] A wealthy young man, he had an adventurous spirit and had said 'Je n'aime pas vivre la vie bête des snobs à Paris,' and, having gained French pilot's licence number 32 on 15th February 1910, he proceeded to make good use of it. He reconnoitred the route over the Simplon Pass on foot and by car. He then returned to Paris and set a new altitude record for

15

aeroplanes of 2,587m (8,488ft) at Issy-le-Moulineux on 8th September in a Farman. He also made his mark by flying around the Eiffel Tower.

Chavez returned to Brig where he found himself with eight other pilots awaiting favourable weather. Most of the entrants decided to abandon the attempt. On the 18th September, when some 4,000 spectators turned up the weather was exceptionally bad and it continued so on successive days. However, despite winds still high and gusting on 23rd September, Georges Chavez prepared his Blériot XI for a final attempt.

'Je pars!' [I am going], he insisted. 'Wait until tomorrow' he was advised but at 13.29 he took off. 'The wind came from the icy peak of the Fletschorn and filled the valley' (Bierbaum 1910, 1985 edn. 82, 83) Chavez climbed in spirals over Ried forest to about 2,400m then turned towards the col, passing over it and the hospice with about a hundred metres clearance at 13.49. He continued over Simplon village and, failing to gain enough altitude to cross the Monscera pass, followed the Zwischbergen valley and dropped down by Gondo and Varzo. Church bells were rung as he flew over the villages and approached the marked landing ground at Domodossola.

Tragically, as the aeroplane came down to about 15m, the wings folded, probably weakened by the buffeting over the mountains and the machine crashed to the ground. Both his legs were broken but it was thought that his life was not in danger. The 23-year-old Peruvian, however, died five days later. His flying time for the 40km journey had been 42 minutes. A monument was erected to him in Brig. A recent multi-lingual presentation has gathered together a fine collection of photographs and maps of the event and the route, with its many peaks and glaciers. (Wenger, 2001)

Six months later Eugène Renaux, with a passenger aboard, landed a Maurice-Farman biplane on the rounded summit of the Puy-de-Dôme at 1,465m (4,807ft) in the French Massif Central, near Clermont Ferrand. Encapsulated in this flight was the first landing on an 'altisurface' – an unprepared landing area in the mountains and Renaux used the technique of landing upslope to reduce the landing run – which decades later was to become recognised as the most efficient procedure. (Mure, 2002, 12)

On a cold winter day, 25th January 1913, the Simplon Pass route was flown without mishap by Jean Bielovucic. In his Hanriot monoplane he flew from Brig-Ried at 3,000m over the Simplon and Monscera passes to land after 35 minutes at Domodossola.

Two days earlier, 23rd January, the Swiss pilot, 22-year old Oscar Bider, who was spending two weeks at the flying school at Pau, flew in a Blériot monoplane with a 70hp Gnome engine over the Pyrenees at 3,500m to cover 520km in five hours eleven minutes to Madrid. This flight established the reputation of the young Swiss pilot, who then gained more experience of alpine flying in his two-seater Blériot as he prepared for the major undertaking of flying over the central Alps. On 11th May he flew from Bern over the Bernese Oberland and landed in Sitten. After more exploratory flying, on the 13th July at 04.08 he took off from the military airfield at Bern, with minimal fuel to keep down the total weight of the aircraft, the motor of which was rated at 70hp but at altitude would develop only some 50hp. He flew over the Jungfraujoch (3,474m) and down the Aletsch glacier, over Valais by the Eggishorn and the 3,200m Helsenhorn and made a pre-planned landing at Domodossola. After taking on fuel, and fresh oil for the engine, he took off again at 08.00 and made for Milan where mist presented problems, but he landed safely at 08.44. He handed over letters from the Bern city mayor to his opposite number in Milan. His was the first flight at over 4,000m over the mountains; the temperature at -15 degrees C. His intention to return, making the first south-north transalpine flight, was thwarted by bad weather for almost two weeks but then he flew back by way of the Gotthard Pass. Mist and fog caused a diversion via Disentis, Luzern and Olten and an intermediate landing at Liestal because the engine oil was low. He then flew on to Basel, where he arrived at 08.15. That evening, with his brother, he flew on to Bern where he received a great and well-deserved ovation. (Dollfus, 1969, 26, and Vehrkehrshaus Luzern archives)

In the succeeding years steady progress was made with flying in the mountains. On the 11th February 1914, a Swiss pilot, Agénor Parmelin, working at the Deperdussin works and flying school at Rheims, succeeded in flying over the Mont Blanc massif. At 13.39 he took off from Collex-Bossy, near Geneva, in his Deperdussin monoplane powered by a 9–cylinder, 80hp, rotary engine. He flew up the Arve valley, past Bonneville, Cluses and Sallanches. He crossed the peaks between Mont Blanc and Mont Blanc de Courmayeur at 5,540m, his thermometer showing –32 degrees C, with a strong wind despite a brilliantly blue sky. After having passed over the summit of Mont Blanc he saw a sea of cloud on the Italian side, through which projected the 3,000m peaks. Then he turned down beside the Brenva glacier and glided down to 4,400m. Restarting the motor he cruised on over Aosta, then flying at only 50m above the ground he returned to land one kilometre from Aosta at Montfleuri. (Dollfus, 1969, 27) Next day he was able to fly to Turin, where he was met with an enthusiastic reception. (Borrel, 1983) The flight was reported in *The Alpine Journal* (Vol. 28, 1914, 95), possibly the first reference to an aeroplane in that distinguished publication, which had recorded so much of Mont Blanc's history.

The First World War stimulated an incredibly rapid development of aviation and soon aeroplanes were flying over the Alps and taking part in the fighting which raged in the mountain valleys and on the peaks that formed the front between the Italian and Austrian armies. After the war, it was not long before aircraft were put to use for both pleasure and commercial purposes and although, at first, most pilots considered it prudent to avoid mountains wherever possible, there were exceptions.

Thoret and the air currents of Mont Blanc

A French pilot, Joseph Thoret, became an apostle who preached the necessity to study the air currents that surrounded the mountains. He moved to the Arve valley and took over the little aerodrome that had been established in 1911 at Passy, close to Mont Blanc. Thoret opened a flying school there and continued a unique series of experiments in mountain flying which he had begun in 1922 in Algeria – then a French colony – and continued in 1924 at Saint Rémy-de-Provence, using a Hanriot HD14. (Mure, 2002, 9) He carried out wind-tunnel experiments and made a film, for which he was awarded the Prix Hirn by the Academy of Sciences. On one flight in 1922, having switched off his aeroplane's motor, he glided and soared upward and remained aloft for seven hours and three minutes. Many of his pupils were experienced flyers but they knew they had to learn new principles to avoid the fate of many of their fellows whose aircraft had been destroyed by the turbulent conditions in the mountains.

Much was achieved in the late 20s and 30s. Among the developments in different fields were the beginnings of air tourism in the Alps. In 1928, Thoret helped Air-Union to begin to exploit the possibilities of the Arve valley and the Mont Blanc range for tourist flights.

Thoret frightened many of his pupils and tourists by his practice of switching off his engines over the mountains. A graphic account of a sensational flight was given by Roger Frison-Roche, journalist, mountaineer and later member of the French Resistance, who became famous for his classic novel of the life of the Chamonix mountain guides, *Premier de Cordée (First on the Rope)*. Far above the normal ceiling of the Farman Goliath biplane over the Mont Blanc range, one of its twin engines caught fire, the passengers horrified as the flames streamed out over the wood and fabric wings. Thoret remained calm and switched off the engine and the air currents extinguished the flames. They had, Frison-Roche wrote, one remaining engine and the gliding ability of the aircraft to get them down safely to the valley. But Thoret switched off the other engine. Then, the wind whistling in the bracing wires, he brought them down over the mountains to the airfield. As they came to a standstill a kilometre from the hangar, Thoret shouted to his passengers 'Out you jump, you band of lazybones, and push on the wings!' (Frison-Roche, 1981, 142)

Such eccentricities did not amuse everyone, especially those on whom he relied for his continued operations at Passy. Frison-Roche was again Thoret's companion when one afternoon he took an unusual route and turned his aeroplane to swoop over the great ridges of the south side of Mont Blanc, the Innominata, Peuterey and Brenva – fascist Italy over which they were completely forbidden to fly. They flew back over the Col du Géant in a silence unusual for Thoret and landed at Passy. When they had taxied in, he took from his pocket a telegram – his dismissal. It had been his farewell flight over his beloved Mont Blanc. (Frison-Roche, 1981, 144) It should, however, be added that this was 1932, the middle of an economic depression, and wealthy tourists were few. Thoret did find other flying employment and continued to practise and teach his special skills and repeated the 1910 route over the Simplon Pass in a 20hp motor glider, saying 'I have an unlimited admiration for Chavez.' (Samivel/Norande, 1996, 204). In retirement, he became a sculptor, living as a hermit. (Mure, 2002, 35)

Alan Cobham, later to become one of the most famous of all long-distance flyers, and to be knighted for his achievements in developing British aviation, discovered in 1923 the fearsome dangers of mountain turbulence on a flight with a wealthy passenger who had hired him on a long-term arrangement with the De Havilland Company. They were flying back from the Middle East via North Africa and were making what Cobham thought was the first flight from Egypt to Morocco. Over the mountains they encountered the worst turbulence that Cobham had ever experienced. He descended lower – the aeroplane's ceiling would have severely limited the possibility of climbing out of trouble – and found himself in a downdraft in a cul-de-sac between rocky walls:

'I had to make the tightest vertical turn on record, with my undercarriage wheels practically spinning against the cliff face: I felt rather like one of those 'Wall of Death' motor-cyclists who drive round cylindrical surfaces at fairgrounds.' One of the bumps caused some of the luggage to go overboard. (Cobham, 1978, 79)

Extreme air currents endangered the largest aircraft of the 1920s and '30s. Even large four-engine aeroplanes, heavy for their day, had been thrown about by air currents like so many straws in the wind and dashed on to the peaks or glaciers. (Kossa, 1971, 14) In 1932 Sir Alan Cobham, having founded the largest and most successful touring air display company in Great Britain, took his show to South Africa and presented people all over the Union with unique opportunities to see the sensational flying of which his pilots were capable on a daily basis. There were many difficulties and hazards to be ovecome. The De Havilland DH66 'Hercules' airliner, employed in poviding joyrides, was nearly an example of the kind of disaster mentioned by Kossa. Hugh Johnson had a narrow escape when he encountered particularly severe air currents when flying in a valley bounded by four large hills. The 'Hercules' suddenly plummeted thousands of feet within a few seconds:

'Passenger seats were torn from the floor attachments throwing the occupants around and causing them to hit and puncture the fabric inner lining of the fuselage roof. Johnson himself suffered a nasty gash over his eye when the Verey light pistol flew out of its holster whilst he was struggling to maintain control. An equally strong upward movement then brought all the passengers hard down onto the floor and, the pilot's injury apart, it was miraculous that no serious harm was caused. Johnson however, was a little miffed when, back on the ground, Cobham casually enquired, "You are going to carry on, aren't you, old man?" as he dutifully applied perchloride of mercury antiseptic to the still bleeding wound!' (Cruddas, 2003, 68)

Already in the 1920s some airline pilots were meeting the dangers of the mountains on regular scheduled flights. Pierre-Georges Latécoère registered Lignes Aèriennes Latécoères at Toulouse, now the home of the giant Airbus company, in 1918, and founded a commercial airline, which became Aéropostale in 1927. Flights with ex-military aircraft took mail to North Africa in less than half the time of the surface transport.

21

Being based at Toulouse, the southbound flights faced the Pyrenées shortly after take-off. The dangers of the mountains drew special comment from Antoine de St. Exupéry who was to become famous as an author and has remained so, his best known work being *Le Petit Prince (The Little Prince}* , written ostensibly for children but beloved also by generations of adults. He was outstanding as a writer of books on the exploits of the legendary pilots of 'La Ligne' in the 1920s and 1930s, *Vol de Nuit (Night Flight)*, published in 1931,and *Terre des Hommes (Wind, Sand and Stars)*, which appeared in 1939, being classics of their genre. The latter won the Prix Goncourt of the Académie Française. The title adopted for the version in English was more descriptive but the French title emphasised the connections to the earth and their fellow men deeply sought by the pilots flying their missions in the solitary and dangerous skies. The book revealed a deep philosophy, hitherto totally unexplored by writers on aviation.

In 1926 St. Exupéry became one of the pilots who 'lived in fear of the mountains of Spain, over which we had to fly . . . In those days the motor would drop out without warning and with a great rattle like the crash of crockery . . . the important thing was to avoid a collision with the range . . . Navigating by compass in a sea of clouds over Spain was to be avoided if at all possible because 'below the clouds lies eternity.' (St. Exupéry. Trans. Galantière, 1939, 1943, 6).

Aéropostale and Sir Alan Cobham will feature further in the next chapter.

Aerial photography

Photography from aircraft, balloons at first, developed as a popular tool for military purposes, for geographers, geologists, meteorologists and, of course, for cartographers. Engineers concerned with transport links, hydrological and power developments, forestry and agriculture and many other sciences and enterprises took advantage of the new possibilities. Studies of the Alps were being pursued and published in such works as the successive volumes from Grenoble entitled *L'aviation de montagne; étude alpine*. The ability of the aerial observer and his photographic apparatus to record the detail of the mountains attracted enthusiastic comment from scientists and mountaineers. Professor Raoul Blanchard wrote in the foreword to the 1935 volume that never before had alpinists been able to distinguish with such certainty the details of their field of action:

> 'le gendarme sans pitié ou le couloir qui s'étrangle . . . la plus minuscule fissure, les bons et les mauvais passages' (Benoit, 1935, 8) ['The merciless 'gendarme' or the suffocating gully . . . the minute fissure, the good and the bad passages']

The combination of mountaineering on the ground and photography of the mountains from the air called for exceptional determination and skills, a leading exponent in the mid and late 1930s being the American, Bradford Washburn, who, in the early 1930s, was also using aerial drops to supply field parties in Alaska, thereby extending their range and the time they could stay in the mountains. (Washburn and Smith, 2002; Roberts, 2002, 67)

The subject of parachuting will be developed later and to Washburn's aerial photography and climbing exploits also there will be a return but attention will now be directed to the response of aviators to the challenge of flying over the highest mountains of the world.

CHAPTER 2

Over the Great Ranges

Flying over the great mountain ranges, with all the risks that this entailed, became an integral part of pioneer aviation, spurred on particularly by the pressure to transport the mails quickly over difficult terrain. The Americas provided forcing grounds for the opening up of regular routes over long distances and high mountains.

The American pioneer pilots

In the United States, after many trial flights and the linking together of shorter stages, the first regular day and night scheduled transcontinental mail flights began with a De Havilland DH4M leaving New York at 10.00 on 1st July 1924, carrying 455lbs of mail. Following transfers at Cleveland, Chicago, Omaha. Cheyenne, Rock Springs, Salt Lake City and Reno the final lap brought the mail to San Francisco at 17.45 local time on 2nd July, after the traverse of the Rocky Mountains, the Sierra Nevada and the Coast Range.

The mountains posed serious dangers for pilots flying between the eastern states of the USA and Canada and the west coast and many pilots were killed in crashes on these routes. At this time all flying was, of course, hazardous and many aircraft came to grief in all areas. Charles Augustus Lindbergh was a pilot for Robertson Air Transport who won the contract for the Chicago – St. Louis route when the carriage of airmail was handed over from the US Post Office to private firms in 1925. His subsequent solo flight across the Atlantic Ocean in the specially-built Ryan monoplane *Spirit of St. Louis* excited the world and suggested the possibilities of aviation in a way which the first direct non-stop Atlantic crossing on 14/15th June 1919 by Captain J. Alcock and Lieutenant A. Whitten-Brown in a twin-engine Vickers Vimy converted bomber, had failed to do. Lindbergh made his third parachute jump when he could not land owing to bad visibility on his regular run between St Louis and Springfield. The airlines also wanted to attract passengers as well. The airline for which Lindbergh flew experienced its first catastrophe with a passenger-carrying aeroplane in September 1929 in the mountains between New Mexico and Los Angeles. Although the peaks on this southerly route were not nearly as high as the Rockies further north, at around 10,000ft they were more than high enough to create problems. Lindbergh was about to set off with his wife on holiday when the aircraft was reported missing and they at once flew to the area in a fast, single-engine Lockheed Vega. The missing aircraft was found on the slopes of 9,264ft Mount Williams with no survivors. Lindbergh's rush to the search area, plus the fact that his attractive wife, Anne, was flying with him, helped to overcome potential passengers' fear of flying. (Berg, 1998, 207)

Even before the US government handed out its mail contracts in 1925, Lindbergh had been attracted to flying in the mountains during his barnstorming and flying circus days. He was based at Lambert Field, St. Louis and Richard Field, Missouri, where he instructed pilots on the Curtis Jenny, when he received an offer from Mil-Hi Airways and Flying Circus at Denver. 'I'd always wanted to fly around mountains' he later wrote, and Denver gave him 'the chance to explore the air currents around canyons, slopes, and ridges. I could study the effects of turbulence, about which aviators knew so little and speculated so much.' (Berg, 1998, 84–5) Despite the most sophisticated instrumentation both in the cockpit and around the airport, Denver is still treated with great respect by the pilots of modern aircraft, being one of the most notorious major airports for the sudden low-level turbulence and windshear often encountered

25

on take-off and landing. Turbulence and other aspects of wind conditions in and near mountains will crop up frequently in this book.

The Andes

In South America, the Andes provided even greater obstacles, including some of the highest mountains that had been climbed by the 1920s and frequent bad weather made hazardous all the passes that offered the only feasible routes for trans-Andean flight. However, the difficulties of surface travel stimulated the development of air services in South America and between 1919 and 1921 airmail services were established step by step over difficult terrain, notably in Colombia. (Mackay, 1971, 127–134)

The first aeroplane crossing of the Andes was made by Vicente Almondas de Almonacid, an Argentinian, who had flown for the French in the First World War. (Dunkerley, 2010) Then a 25-year-old woman, Adrienne Bolland, who was working as a test pilot for Caudron, the French aeroplane construction firm, caused a sensation on 1st April 1921 by piloting a Caudron G3, a frail-looking but relatively reliable biplane, from Mendoza to Santiago, accompanied by a mechanic. She was welcomed by huge crowds but the French consul was not present. He had thought the information he had received was 'un poisson [fish] d'Avril' – an April fool's joke. A commercial trans-Andean service, however, required extensive preparations. Again it was French élan that achieved this, as well illustrated by Angel (2004) and Dunkerley (2010)

As noted in the preceding chapter, Pierre-George Latécoère, using ex-military aircraft, established regular mail services across Spain and North Africa to Dakar. Then he turned to developing routes on the other side of the South Atlantic, beginning in 1925 in Brazil. The entrepreneur Marcel Bouilloux-Lafont, who took over the company in 1927, negotiated concessions for mail services in Argentina, Uruguay and Chile. All posed many difficulties, but overcoming the obstacles posed to the flights over the Andes was the biggest challenge. This would, however, be especially valuable when the railway over the pass was closed by snow or floods.

Jean Mermoz, whose flying exploits so captivated the French public that he became one of the most famous people in the country, approached the task facing Aéropostale, as it now was, in March 1929, flying a Latécoère 26. Unfortunately, the engine failed over the mountains but after a hazardous forced landing, his mechanic, Alexandre Collenot, who was accompanying him, managed repairs enough to take off and just get through to Chile. Four days later Mermoz tried to return by a more northerly route via Copiago. He succeeded in gaining enough altitude with the help of updrafts to gain the pass, only to be forced down by a downdraft. He made a landing but the aeroplane was seriously damaged. Collenot was extraordinarily resourceful in again making extemporary repairs. Despite suffering from severe frostbite and altitude sickness he worked for two days and two nights using metal cut from the machine itself, pieces torn from their own clothing and insulating tape. When at last he tested the engine the radiator burst and he used more cloth from their shirts to plug the leak. They laboriously pushed the machine to the top of an incline and Mermoz just managed to get it airborne. They got back to the airfield they had left three days earlier. Their return caused such astonishment that climbers went to find the debris at the repair site, so confirming their account. (Dunkerley, 2010, 70–72) Collenot and Mermoz survived many more crashes but both disappeared over the South Atlantic in different aircraft.

The transandean Aéropostale service was opened in 1929 with the same intention of maintaining a regular and reliable service as had been introduced against all the odds over Spain and the deserts of North Africa to Dakar, with the extension to South America always intended. The overriding principle was: *the mail must get through!* At Buenos Aires, a 'plane scheduled for the Atlantic crossing to Europe would await the arrival of the flights from Santiago, from Asunción in Paraguay and from the far south of Patagonia. Immediately the mails had been transferred from the other aircraft the flight to Europe would depart, unless the weather made it totally impossible. Even then the pilots might be penalised by the loss of their bonuses. In *Vol de Nuit*, St. Exupéry (1931) captured the tensions, the fears and the agonies of the pilots, their supervisors and their wives and of the resolute but caring flight director.

St. Exupéry has left us a truly remarkable account of the hazard that the winds presented to the pilots not only over but also in the lee of the great ranges. He was piloting his open-cockpit plane over the relatively narrow tract of Patagonia between the Andes and the Atlantic Ocean, where high winds and turbulence were always to be expected. On this day he became aware of the unusual colour of the sky – a hard blue sky that 'glittered like a new-honed knife.' Suddenly the aircraft was virtually stationary in the sky:

> 'I found myself imprisoned in a valley . . . Ahead of me a rocky prow swung to left and right, rose suddenly high in the sky for a second like a wave over my head, and then plunged down below my horizon. Vertical, oblique, horizontal, all of plane geometry was awhirl. A hundred transversal valleys were muddled in a jumble of perspectives.' (St. Exupéry, trans. Galantière, 1939, 1943, 36–7)

Thrown up and down, around and around again, he struggled to retain control. He understood how aircraft had been lost in the mountains when there was no loss of visibility. Exhausting himself in his battle with the elements, he saw a peak that he knew dominated the sea, where he might escape the destructive turbulence.

'But first I would have to wrestle with the wind of that peak . . . a giant . . . I was suddenly struck straight in the midriff by the gale off that peak and sent hurtling out to sea . . . The mountain range stood up like a crenellated fortress against the pure sky.'

Now he faced the risk of being forced down into the ocean, and, with the engines misfiring, of running out of fuel. Somehow he managed to climb, only to be thrown over and over 'and the sky became a slippery dome on which I could not find a footing.' In an hour and a half he had managed to climb to 900ft. It was still stormy but nothing like he had endured and he escaped and reached his destination. (St. Exupéry, trans. Galantière, 1939, 1943, 34–43)

Henri Guillaumet had already made 91 crossings of the Andes when he took off alone on Friday, 30th June 1930, in his single-engine, open-cockpit Potez 25 from Santiago in Chile to Mendoza in Argentina. He had turned back the day before because storm clouds blocked the passes but he was determined to get the mail through this time. The recognised ceiling of the aircraft was some 25,000ft but he exploited the air currents to climb above the clouds through which the highest summits protruded. The aircraft then violently lost height in the turbulent air and he was nearly thrown out of the machine, his leather harness cutting into his shoulders and seeming ready to snap. He saw below him Lake Diamante, which he knew was bordered by an 18,000ft volcano. Still blinded by the falling snow, he flew round and round the lake until his fuel was exhausted then he crash-landed.

When he climbed out of the cockpit, Guillaumet was twice blown off his feet. He dug a hole under the aeroplane and pulled his parachute and mail sacks around him and lay there for two days and two nights. He heard search aircraft but the crashed plane was not spotted. The storm had subsided so he started to walk, having scratched a message on the plane that his last thoughts would be with his wife. He took with him a compass, a torch, a bottle of rum, some condensed milk (later used mixed with snow), and some other tinned food, which, however, froze solid. In the absence of an ice axe, a tin-opener helped on the steep slopes that he soon encountered. His shoes were utterly inadequate for the trek and he had to keep cutting them down to accommodate his swollen and frozen feet. (Webster, 1993, 1994, 122–23) Clothing and matches were soaked and he abandoned one thing after another and one of his gloves was blown away. He fell many times and eventually thought he would give up and settle for death, then he thought again of his wife and how she would be unable to claim insurance because in France four years had to elapse before a claim would be met on a missing person. He struggled on and fortunately, on the sixth day after the crash, he encountered a peasant woman and her child. He collapsed and was taken to shelter and food.

St. Exupéry was one of the pilots who searched unsuccessfully for Guillaumet but met with refusals for help in a ground search because 'the Andes never gave up a lost person in winter.' He took off immediately on hearing that Guillaumet had been found. Spotting a car on the road, he landed beside it and found the near-dead pilot a passenger. He got him into the aeroplane and took him to hospital, where he sat by his bedside tending him for days. He quotes the words of Guillaumet:

"Ce que j'ai fait, je te le jure, jamais aucune bête ne l'aurait fait"–
"I swear that what I went through, no animal would have gone through." (St. Exupéry, 1939, 1943, 24)

Paul Webster, a biographer of St. Exupéry's, commented:

'That sentence . . . has become one of the most quoted in French literature, a summing up of the author's belief that man was born to surpass nature and himself . . . [though] . . . he (Guillaumet) was a modest and ordinary man at heart, and not predestined to be singled out in a crowd.' (Webster,1993, 1994, 119)

Eventually Guillaumet recovered but, like St. Exupéry, was shot down on wartime operations.

Opening up the British Empire

Meanwhile, British pioneers had also found themselves having to cope with the dangers posed by the mountains in their flights to explore routes to the eastern and southern parts of the British Empire. In 1924 Alan Cobham (knighted after his 1926 exploratory flight to Australia) piloted a De Havilland DH50 single-engine biplane with Sir William Sefton Brancker, Director of Civil Aviation, on board, investigating a route for an airship service to India. Between eastern Europe and Alexandretta (now Iskenderun) they crossed the Taurus Mountains of southern Turkey. These mountains rise to over 12,000ft and an account of the problems that they caused some thirty years later, leading to valiant work by the RAF Mountain Rescue Team, is given in a later chapter. Cobham found them covered in cloud and described his experiences as 'a real nightmare.'

'I threaded my way between them by way of a pass that would lead to the head of a river, and then I could follow its valley down to the coast. I was flying in effect through a tunnel, an extremely narrow one, which twisted and turned at every point; there were jagged mountainsides to left and right, disappearing overhead into a ceiling of low cloud, into which I could not climb without the near-certainty of hitting one of them. I could not turn back either. There was not enough lateral room for even the steepest turn, nor was there any possibility of landing among the crags and pinnacles below me. I had no alternative but to press on . . . Again and again, as I made my way down that winding ravine, I would find myself in an apparent cul-de-sac, heading straight for a vertical rock face with no possible way out. There always *was* a way out: it appeared at the very last minute, unexpectedly, perhaps on the left and perhaps on the right, and I then had to fling the aircraft into an immediate steep turn, squeezing through with just a few feet to spare, and then needing to repeat this hair-raising performance only seconds later.' (Cobham, 1978, 87–8)

Cobham's biographer and archivist, Colin Cruddas commented:

'The effect on Branckner and Elliott of such violent manoeuvres that went on for one and a half hours as an exhausted Cobham fought to miss the rocky outcrops can only be guessed at. The pilot later admitted this incident to be the most frightening he ever experienced.' (Cruddas, 2006, 112)

Airship endeavours

It is now perhaps hard to believe that at that time there were still many who believed that the future lay with airships. They could, for instance, carry more passengers than could aeroplanes over long distances and could even circumnavigate the globe.

The pilots of the German Zeppelins, successors to those that had raided England during the First World War, had been generally steering clear of mountains although they could fly at high altitude and had done so regularly to avoid gunfire and fighter aircraft when attacking Great Britain. The Zeppelin crews had suffered greatly from the bitter cold in operations at high altitude. Commanders reported that above 16,000ft crews suffered from severe headaches, abdominal pains and nausea. Physical labour quickly exhausted crews and Franz Stabbert reported that men carrying weights forward to stabilise the ship moved so slowly that it was endangered. He found that even not carrying anything it took him a quarter of an hour to walk from the rear to the forward gondola and that he arrived exhausted and gasping for air. (Collier 1974, 126, q. Jones, 1928–35, iii, 146, 171) The airship crews had not, of course, had the opportunity to acclimatise like mountain climbers with slow ascent on foot.

Sometimes the airships flew to almost 25,000ft and bottled oxygen equipment was essential. Even so they still frequently found their responses seriously affected. To add to the problems there was a belief that to resort to the oxygen bottles showed weakness and even Peter Strasser, commander of the Naval Airship Division, was no exception and a later report suggested that his judgement was sometimes impaired as a result. (Collier, 132, citing Robinson 1962, 129–30)

So, for preference, airship commanders chose to fly at much lower altitudes when no longer facing hostile aircraft and gunfire. They would try to negotiate routes through mountain passes rather than climb high over the ranges. Their designers and crews would have gained some early experience in what they could cope with, the factory being at Friedrichshafen on the

Bödensee (Lake Constance), just across the water from the Swiss ranges and with the mountains of Bavaria in their own back-yard. An obvious danger in the mountains was extra cloud cover and precipitation, which would lead to damage to the outer skin of the airship. At lower levels the dangerous downcurrents on the lea side of ridges could quickly bring down an airship. Also it was necessary to drop ballast in order to gain height and then to vent precious hydrogen to bring the ship back to preferred flight levels, so affecting the range that could be achieved.

Nevertheless, their successful transatlantic flights with fare-paying passengers led the Germans to decide to fly a Zeppelin round the world, commanded by Dr. Hugo Eckener, Count Zeppelin's indomitable chief pilot. The flight was financed by William Randolph Hearst, an American newspaper magnate, who stipulated that the circumnavigation must start and end in the United States. So the LZ127, *Graf Zeppelin*, made an extra flight to Lakehurst in the first week of August 1930. On the return flight, the first leg of the circumnavigation, Eckener's 61st birthday was celebrated over the middle of the Atlantic. The twenty passengers included representatives of the German, Russian and Japanese governments and additionally a young stowaway. A possibly coincidental illicit love affair was also present aboard because Hearst had engaged a female journalist, Lady Grace Drummond Hay to write on the trip from a woman's viewpoint, when he had also sent Karl von Wiegend who had had a recent affair with her, so there was scope for human as well as aeronautical dramas. The *Graf Zeppelin* paused at Friedrichshafen, then continued on over Russia, Eckener infuriating the Soviet authorities by turning away from Moscow, citing a depression forecast ahead but political over-tones were suspected.

The LZ127 crossed the Russian plain, the Ural Mountains west Siberia and Yakutia. Eckener had rejected the shorter route by Lake Baykal and Manchuria because of its very mountainous character in favour of a more northerly course but there were still the mountains of eastern Siberia to be crossed. Lady Drummond Hay, who as the only woman aboard, was destined

33

thereby to become the first woman to experience a flight around the world, admitted to some degree of nervousness as they approached the coastal ranges.

Soon after leaving Yakutsk, Eckener could look for the River Uchur which would lead from the Lena basin to the mountain passes. He chose the gap between the Stanovoy and Dzhugzhur ranges, the former rising to 2,412m and the latter to 1,906m, which Lady Drummond Hay described as 'a wall of mountains'. (Mensink, 2009) She reported how the airship went up in great jerks as ballast was released and they entered clouds. This exposed the airship to extra danger from unknown winds and possible navigational complexities, such as had been accepted in wartime operations, along with oxygen problems and increasing cold, in order to escape from interception by fighter aircraft, but were best avoided on an ultra long-distance passenger-carrying flight. Some, however, thought that Eckener cut it rather fine deliberately, so that it would not look too easy. (Collier, 1974) The sight of the lowlands bordering the Sea of Okhotsk enabled everyone to breathe a sigh of relief. In fact they were about to face a yet greater threat from a typhoon over the Pacific Ocean. Disaster was feared in America when radio contact was lost, but they landed safely at Los Angeles. Crossing America, Eckener was able to avoid the higher Rockies by taking a route between the Colorado Plateau and the Sierra Madre).

The British government decided in 1930 to demonstrate the capabilities of the airship R101, for the construction of which it had been responsible, with a flight from its home base, Cardington, to India. Sir Sefton Brancker, who was mentioned above as accompanying Alan Cobham on his reconnaissance of the air route to the east and had also provided vital help to enable Amy Johnson to make her great flight to Australia, was asked to accompany the then Air Minister, Lord Thomson, on the R101 to India. Branckner, after his pioneering flight with Cobham, had seen that the aeroplane would soon supplant the airship on such a service but agreed, against his better judgement, to go on the R101 flight. The airship faced its first high ground as it

34

approached a ridge near Beauvais in northern France. It never reached the ridge as it was unable to maintain a selected altitude of about 1,500ft and at 02.00 on 5th October 1930 it crashed into land less than 300ft high. Branckner and Lord Thomson were among the 47 crew and passengers who lost their lives. (Report of the R.101 Enquiry, 1930, 1999) The fault here lay with the design and construction of the airship and the stubbornness of the government in insisting on the ambitious flight when it was known to be suffering from serious defects.

Mount Everest

The 'twenties and 'thirties were times of great optimism among flyers who were seeking constantly to push the limits of their achievements further into the unknown, while imaginative explorers and climbers were dreaming of the possibilities that the conquest of the air might offer to mountaineers. The possibility of flying over high Himalayan passes had been discussed as early as 1917 by Dr. A.M. Kellas, one of the first explorers to get close to Mount Everest. (Kellas, 1917, 1918). The problem was that there was then no aero-engine powerful enough to lift an aeroplane to the required height.

In January 1925 Alan Cobham, on the journey with Sir Seton Branckner, and not intimidated by his flight through the Taurus Mountains described above, had time while they were at Calcutta to go and have a look at Mount Everest. Cobham flew to Jalpaiguri, where the crowd, who had never seen an aeroplane before, posed a serious threat to the fragile machine. This was a common problem but here the solution was, to say the least, unusual. A defensive circle of elephants was formed to protect it while a fence was built. On January 25 Cobham flew towards Kangchenjunga and Everest. The maximum altitude attainable by the DH50 was 16,000ft – about the height of Camp 2 on Everest climbs today – and the camera was in the hands of a passenger, the General's ADC. The lack of oxygen affected him and Cobham's attempts to shout instructions about the photography led to a high-altitude argument, then Cobham had to turn about as clouds enveloped the crags about them. Most of the photographs that were taken were seriously over-exposed (Cobham, 1978, 90) but an impressive picture of Kangchen-junga was among the successful ones.

Captain J.B.L. Noel, who had tried to approach Everest from the east in 1913 and had provided a substantial part of the finance for the 1924 expedition to the mountain, in return for the film rights, put forward an extraordinary scheme. From the failure of that expedition, which had culminated in the disap-pearance of George Mallory and Andrew Irvine while making a bid for the summit, Noel concluded correctly that the climbers of the time needed some extra help but then let his imagination run riot with the idea of an assault *from above*. He visualised an aeroplane flying over the summit (though it was to be almost another decade before there would be a combination of aircraft and engine capable, with the required load, of reaching the necessary altitude – over 29,000ft) from which a parachute descent might be made to the peak. Having seen for himself the banner of ice crystals that streamed regularly from the summit in winds that eventually were found to blow at around 100mph, he thought an aeroplane might be able, by flying into it, virtually to hover during the drop – apparently unaware of the likelihood that a machine of the period would probably be dashed to the ground or broken up by the turbulence. The mountaineer would have been prepared by prior acclimatisation and would carry oxygen equipment and, in theory, would be able to make the descent in two days to the East Rongbuk glacier, from which the 1924 attack had been launched, using food and equipment previously dropped from the air. (Ward, 2003, 107, from Noel, 1927) Unsworth (1981, 2000,) summarises this and other ideas put forward. In the end it was through air photography that aviation did assist at least in the planning stage of the ascent of Everest.

By 1933 the aeronautical opportunities had changed with technical evolution. The idea of practical flights over Everest was formulated by Lieutenant Colonel L.V. Stewart Blacker, a regular army officer serving in India. Blacker was descended from Valentine Blacker, first Surveyor-General of India, one of whose staff was George Everest, who later occupied the same post. When the Bristol Aeroplane Company produced the super-charged Pegasus engine and it enabled Britain to capture the international altitude record, he realised that it would make the projected flight practicable. Blacker, who had learned to fly in 1911 with the Bristol Company, took his plan to the Royal Geographical Society and, after refinement, it was submitted to the governments of India and Nepal. They accepted the scientific value of the proposed photographic survey and gave permission for the flights. (Fellowes et al, 1933). The expedition had been opposed by the Everest Committee on the grounds that it would upset the Tibetans and distract from the plans of the climbers but the Royal Geographical Society provided the organising committee and that and aviation interests prevailed. (Clydesdale and McIntyre, 1936) It was good preparation, though not then foreseen, for later wartime operations.

Squadron Leader Douglas ('Douglo') Douglas-Hamilton, Marquess of Douglas and Clydesdale, MP, was chosen as the leading pilot. Later he became Group Captain the Duke of Hamilton and Brandon, and to his many official honours was added the rather doubtful one of being the hoped-for contact of Rudolf Hess in his controversial flight from Germany to Scotland in 1941. Clydesdale described the Everest flight as 'the only one original flight worthwhile.' (Obituary, *The Times*, 2.4.73) It is true that by this time the public and therefore the media were no longer so interested in record-breaking long-distance flights but polar flyers would have hardly agreed.

Westland reconnaissance aircraft with single Bristol Pegasus engines were selected for the Mount Everest venture. One was the PV6 prototype Wallace army co-operation biplane, the other designated PV3, both being designed partly for photographic work and strongly built, so suited to the anticipated conditions. Finance was a problem and Clydesdale approached Lady Houston, a personal friend of his mother. Lady Houston had previously supported aviation projects. He persuaded her to contribute £10,000 to the enterprise and to guarantee an additional £5,000. The PV3 was named 'Houston-Westland' (and the expedition entitled 'The Houston Mount Everest Expedition'). The idea appealed to Lady Houston partly because it was thought that it would impress India and help consolidate the Empire. (Clydesdale and McIntyre, 1936, 9) Clydesdale's Unionist constituency initially opposed his proposed absence for three months on what was perceived as a dangerous undertaking but eventually agreed.

Blacker was to fly as observer with Clydesdale in the PV3 and Clydesdale's choice as pilot of the second machine was Flight Lieutenant David McIntyre, a member of 602 (City of Glasgow) RAF Auxiliary Squadron, which Clydesdale commanded. McIntyre took the job without pay but with a life insurance policy for £2,000 (McIntyre, 2004, 23), this being equivalent in 2010 to about £130,000, though more in terms of property values. Despite strong competition from full-time RAF pilots this choice was agreed and proved to be an excellent one. Sidney R. Bonnett of the Gaumont-British Corporation was appointed second photographer, the company having contracted to make a film of the enterprise.

Considerable attention was given to the photographic equipment, heated flying suits and the oxygen apparatus. High-altitude tests in pressure chambers for personnel and equipment took place at Farnborough and Clydesdale relates an amusing tale. Blacker wore a monocle, even on bathing parades and he entered the chamber with it. 'The diminishing pressure must have dislodged what nothing else seemed capable of disturbing.' The monocle fell into the oxygen mask and replacing it was a source of entertainment to his colleagues inside and outside the chamber. (Clydesdale and McIntyre, 1936, 15)

Three De Havilland Moth light aircraft were used in a support role – a Puss Moth high-wing monoplane loaned by Fry's, the chocolate manufacturers, a Fox Moth biplane which had a small passenger cabin, and Clydesdale's own Gipsy Moth open-cockpit biplane. These were used for the outward flight; the two Westland biplanes having been crated and sent by sea. (McIntyre, 2004, 26–27) The outward flights, which took eighteen days, were well sprinkled with problems and hazards, some natural, others the result of nationalistic cussedness, especially in Italy, where cameras were confiscated after photographs were taken of Vesuvius from the air. (McIntyre, 2004, 28) McIntyre, flying the Gipsy Moth across the North African desert, chose to fly at only 1,000ft as it was cold higher up. When challenged about this, he said he liked to see the expression on the camels' faces. His unerring navigation, despite a change of wind direction, elicited the equally apt explanation that he could see which way the 'the Arab gents' summer suitings were streaming out' (Clydesdale and McIntyre, 1936, 35). There were a few near-accidents and a forced landing in the Iraq desert because of a dust storm while following the normal procedure of those days of hugging the railway line. (Clydesdale and McIntyre, 1936, 42)

During the period of preparation in India many flights were undertaken in the Moths. Unfortunately, on March 12th a tropical storm blew the Fox Moth across the airfield at Alhallabad, where it had been carefully picketed for the night and it was wrecked. To return to Karachi, where the RAF had reassembled the Westland aircraft, the pilots had to travel by train and by hastily arranged and uncomfortable flights. There followed a flight of some 1,400 miles to the base at Purnea. There was a stormy period of twelve days, during which the Everest range was observed each morning from the Puss Moth, flown by Air Commodore Fellowes. Then, at last, the conditions were judged suitable for a summit flight, though a meteorological balloon showed the wind at 28,000ft to be 67mph, and they had been supposed not to go if it was more than 40mph. They calculated that their fuel would allow them to spend fifteen minutes at the mountain and just get back to base

The recently published book on David McIntyre's life by his son, Dougal, (McIntyre, 2004) gives a detailed account of the flight from his father's hand-written and unedited notes. They differ little from McIntyre's account in *The Pilot's Book of Everest* but both accounts make fascinating reading. A few summarised excerpts indicate the problems overcome and emphasise the narrowness of the operating margins. As they neared the mountain on the first flight to Everest, Clydesdale's machine was climbing better than McIntyre's, probably due to the heavier cine camera and film in the latter:

'We began to realise that we should have started to climb sooner but we reckoned we would clear the summit by perhaps a thousand feet. The wind was obviously much stronger than we had been told. The plume from Everest was streaking away over the twelve-mile range to Makalu at hurricane speed.' (McIntyre, 2004, 38)

Suddenly Makalu appeared to have risen a thousand feet above him – they were being carried downward in a rush of air and lost 3,000ft. Blacker, in the leading aircraft, was taking photographs through the hatchway in the floor when:

'. . . suddenly, with the door half-open I became aware . . . of a sensation of dropping through space . . . I grasped a fuselage strut and peered through my goggles at the altimeter needle. It crept, almost swung, visibly as I looked at it in astonishment, down through a couple of thousand feet . . . it seemed as though we should never clear the crags . . .' (Blacker's report in Fellowes et al, 1933, 188)

McIntyre explained the pilots' technique:

'Hemmed in on all sides . . . it was impossible to turn back. To turn to the left meant going back into the down current and the peaks below. To turn downwind to the right would have taken us instantaneously into Makalu at 200 mph. There was nothing we could do but climb straight ahead and hope to clear the lowest point in the barrier range . . . we crabbed sideways . . . A fortunate wind swirl arrived just at the edge of the ridge and we scraped over with just a few feet clearance.' (McIntyre, 2004, 38–9)

They had to turn and McIntyre swallowed hard as they faced the turbulence again to repeat the ridge crossing in order to gain height and they had to do it three times before they had enough height to venture over Everest.

Both aeroplanes passed over the summit just after 10.00, clearing it by about 500ft. But Bonnett had serious problems. McIntyre saw that his observer had sunk to the floor. He had crouched down to reload his camera and inadvertently placed his right foot on his oxygen pipe and fractured it as he straightened up. As he felt himself losing consciousness he sank down again, felt for the leakage and bound it with a handkerchief. He attempted to rise again with his heavy camera but collapsed into unconsciousness. McIntyre saw him slip to the floor and immediately took the Wallace lower and then found that his own facemask had lost its complete nosepiece carrying the microphone and oxygen feed. He had to hold it to his mouth with one hand while flying and operating all controls with the other. Fortunately Bonnett looked better when they got down to 8,000ft. 'He was a nasty dark green shade but obviously alive and that was enough for the moment.' (Clydesdale and McIntyre, 1936, 148) Bonnett had recovered by the time the aircraft reached the flying field and little was said about their trials at 30,000ft. McIntyre stripped off his complicated and uncomfortable flying suit, which he described as 'abominable' and dived into the swimming pool. Next day he flew to Calcutta to get the photographs developed and found, as they suspected, that they were of no use for survey purposes. (McIntyre, 2004, 39–40) However they had discovered much of technical and meteorological interest.

For the first time, the nature of the famous plume of cloud that streams from the summit of Everest had become clear:

'From the Moths we had seen what previous explorers had called 'the plume' of Everest . . . When, however, the machines went actually into it, we realised that it was something quite different to what we had conceived. Here was no drifting cloud wisp, but a prodigious jet of rushing winds flinging a veritable barrage of

41

ice fragments for several miles to leeward of the peak. The force of the rafale was indeed so great as to crack the celastroid windows of the Houston-Westland's rear cockpit . . . We realised that our passage though it, and through the complementary 'downfall' on the windward side . . . had been the great adventure of our flight.' (Clydesdale in Fellowes et al, 1933, 193–94)

This was the first experience by aeroplane pilots of the jet-stream, as it was later to be called, and which, we now know, blows over large parts of the world and has an immense effect on the world's weather. The significance of the Everest pilots' reports was completely overlooked and it was necessary for American bomber crews to meet these hurricane winds at 30,000ft over Japan during the Second World War before more was learned of them. Indeed, the reports by the bomber crews that the winds had prevented them from accurate bombing of selected targets were not believed by superior officers until the evidence became undeniable, special investigative flights having been made. As described later, the jetstream was used to good effect to make the first balloon flight over Everest.

In recent decades, the hundreds of mountaineers who have set out on the ascent of Everest have had to realise that the high altitude wind could spell the end of their attempt if they encountered its full force at the critical point of their climb. If it came and went as the climb progressed they just might be lucky. One of those who commented on it with insight and understanding was Matt Dickinson. In 1996 he was climbing with the IMAX filming expedition on the north side of Everest. The group that he was with, benefiting from the experience of their leaders, held back the launch of their final bid for the summit and thereby escaped being involved in the storm that led to the death of six people on the south face, followed by more deaths on the north side. Dickinson described graphically his climb with his leader, Alan Hinckes, and three Sherpas, as they battled against wind and extreme cold, sometimes wrapped in cloud. They reached the northeast ridge and looked down the fearsome Kanshung Face:

'. . . a billowing cloud of ice crystals was moving vertically up towards me. It was like looking down directly into the gaping mouth of a power station cooling tower. This is the tail of the massive 'rotor' that Everest spins out . . . As the ice crystals come up to the Ridge, they are blown to the south-east in a deadly plume which can be thirty miles long . . . Few people summit when Everest's plume is running' (Dickinson, 1997, 178–79)

Dickinson traversed the ridge, preceded by the Sherpas and followed by Alan Hinckes. On the summit he appears to have been as intrigued by the plume of ice crystals as he was impressed by the view. 'Seen this close, the plume has a hypnotic quality which is quite mesmerising.' The summit was calm and he realised that this was because the wind, blowing out of Tibet, was striking the North Face, then curling above their heads in the rotor before doubling back and hitting the Kanshung (East) Face. (Dickinson, 1997, 194)

To return to the 1933 flights, whose near destruction may be additionally appreciated from Matt Dickinson's remarks, a sortie to test the photographic equipment was made to Kang-chenjunga by Fellowes and the reserve pilot, Dick Ellison. While circling the mountain they experienced severe turbulence and almost collided in mid-air, then became separated. Fellowes ran out of fuel on the way back and had to make a forced landing. The Committee in London were so alarmed that they banned the second flight over Everest for which Nepal had given permission. In addition, a cable from 'a gentleman who was not even a member of the committee . . . read . . . "Machines uninsured. Nor will be."' (Clydesdale and McIntyre, 1936, 153) The Air Commodore felt he must abide by the ban and end the expedition. The official account of the expedition glosses over the situation but Clydesdale and McIntyre decided to use their own initiative and circumvent the ruling. It was an advantage that they were part-time members of the RAF rather than regular serving officers. As Ellison was just that, they did not involve him in their plans. Conveniently, the Air Commodore was suffering from a fever so they gained his consent for a local photographic flight and prepared for Everest in secret.

On 19th April at 07.50 they took off into a low cloud cover with a predicted wind speed of 110mph at 30,000ft as compared with their maximum speed of 120mph. McIntyre had decided to manage without the cumbersome headgear and heated goggles and flew with only a smaller oxygen mask and no goggles. He had nursed the survey cameras to the airfield, wrapped in silk and paper for protection and installed the equipment himself. They had planned a route to the west of Everest, then turning towards the mountain with the benefit of a tailwind. Oxygen was now in short supply so they did not switch it on until they reached 21,000ft – very high for pilots who did not have the acclimatisation gained by mountaineers. As they approached Everest, Clydesdale in the Houston-Westland experienced problems with his oxygen supply and, while struggling to fix this, lost his course and had to break off and head for base. McIntyre pressed on, though barely making headway against the air currents:

> 'There on my right front was the enormous pinnacle, the bright morning sun glinting on the frozen snow and throwing into strong relief the great rock faces . . . The next 15 minutes was a grim struggle . . . Petrol was getting low . . . We appeared to be stationary. I cast quick, anxious glances behind and below to see if we had passed over [the summit]. Then suddenly there was a terrific bump – just one terrific impact such as one might receive when flying low over an explosive factory as it blew up.' (Clydesdale and McIntyre, 1936, 160–67; McIntyre, 2004, 40–41)

Fortunately, the machine remained intact. He turned and as they came abreast of Makalu the survey film ran out. McIntyre's persistence had been rewarded by the observer securing an excellent series of survey photographs which, when they were developed, just overlapped those from the Houston-Westland.

In his introduction to *The Pilot's Book of Everest*, Lord

Tweedsmuir (John Buchan) wrote of the second flight that it might be described as 'a piece of conscientious insubordination.' (Clydesdale and McIntyre, 1936, x)

Sixty years later, when planning to fly over Everest in a hot-air balloon, Leo Dickinson learned that Dick Ellison was living in the south of England and Leo and his wife, Mandy, went to see him. Ellison recalled that after the first flight failed to pass over the top of Everest *The Times*, which had the newspaper rights, was asked not to publish anything, but an Indian working for Gaumont-British, which had the film rights, sent a telegram to the *Calcutta News* and a report appeared the next day, to the fury of *The Times*. (Dickinson, 1993, 51 – 57) Some of the photographs published as being of Everest were identified as not being so, but this error was subsequently corrected.

The immediate claims for the value of the photographs were relatively modest but the review in the *Geographical Journal* (Vol. 73, 51–3), reprinted in the *Alpine Journal* (Vol. 46), enthusiastically noted that:

'. . . the geographical features of Mt. Everest's S. face, now revealed, are startlingly different from those on the known faces. The thin overhanging buttressed southern wall of the western cwm, the magnificent truncated spurs separated by profound couloirs, are unsurpassed.'

These photographs were of little use to the climbing expeditions of the time as the only route open was on the northern side but later they were made good use of when assessing the approach to the mountain through Nepal.

A few months after the Everest flights, there was another full-scale expedition to try to climb the mountain and three climbers equalled the altitude previously reached by Edward Norton in 1924 (28,126ft) but the weather frustrated any additional progress. Meanwhile, however, the first attempt to use an aeroplane to assist in the ascent was launched by a man who had no knowledge of either flying or climbing. Maurice Wilson was a middle-aged man who, after prolonged health problems, had undergone a successful cure, involving prolonged fasting. He read about the Everest attempts and decided that to publicise his new healing method, he would make a solo ascent of Everest, and his achievement, where all the expeditions had failed, would convince the world. He actually considered asking the Houston expedition to take him with them, whereupon he would make a parachute jump on to the summit. This crazy and hopeless idea abandoned, he bought himself a three-year old De Havilland Gipsy Moth biplane and learned to fly at the London Aero Club. He bought a tent, a sleeping bag, an altimeter and a camera with a self-timer. He went to Snowdonia and the Lake District and did some hill walking and scrambling but sought no information on climbing techniques or safety procedures. The aircraft, on which he painted the name *Ever Wrest* was given an extra fuel tank and the undercarriage was strengthened.

The Air Ministry prohibited his flight to India but Wilson ignored the order and took off on 21st May 1933. Despite official obstructions en route, he reached India after two weeks, and, denied fuel by the British consul, bought petrol on the black market and flew on. Then, refused permission to fly over Nepal, he sold the Gipsy Moth and continued overland and, in disguise, into Tibet. The part of aviation in this extraordinary attempt was over. The whole endeavour was ill-conceived and doomed to failure, yet even to fly solo some 5,000 miles, with minimal flying experience, little preparation and no back-up, was a remarkable achievement. He perished in his tent on the Rongbuk Glacier, after having to retreat from the North Col. His three Sherpa guides had, apparently, and not without justification, refused to go on with the doomed adventure and he probably died alone.

The part played by flying in the planning processes for the eventual all-out assault that resulted in the successful ascent of 1953 was small but important. H.F.Milne, Chief Draughtsman of the Royal Geographical Society, and A.R.Hinks, the Society's Secretary, who was also secretary of the Everest Committee of the RGS and the Alpine Club, had made use of the air photographs in the files in constructing a 1:50,000 map of Everest

46

which mapped features on the south side for the first time. This map, along with the photographs, was used in planning the reconnaissance from Nepal. (Ward, 2003, 174–178) Also used were photographs discovered in the RGS archives by Michael Ward that had been taken by photographic reconnaissance aircraft. Mosquitoes and Spitfires had done magnificent work during the war, flying deep into hostile territory, unarmed to minimise weight and maximise speed. In 1945 a Mosquito XIX was flown covertly over Everest. A panorama made up of three photographs showed the Western Cwm, the north face of Lhotse and the South Col. Two other photographs from an unofficial flight of 1947 showed that the southwest ridge ended precipitately in the Western Cwm so attention was focused on a more practicable route avoiding this feature. These photographs and those of the 1933 flight were discussed in a paper read to the Society in 1999 by Michael Ward and P.K. Clarke. Ward had been instrumental in the launching of the 1953 reconnaissance, of which he was a member. This resulted in the exploration of the southern approach to Everest (Ward, 1999, 2003, 298–307 and 174–179) He was also a member of the victorious 1953 expedition.

Aviation experience also contributed to the success of the first ascent in 1953 through its experience with oxygen equipment. An RAF economising device was used to cut off flow of oxygen during expiration in the open circuit apparatus used for the successful ascent, so conserving the supply and minimising the weight of the equipment that the climber had to carry. (Ward, 2003, 236)

CHAPTER 3

'Aerodromes' of Snow and Ice from the Alps and the Arctic to Antarctica

The flying exploits described up to now have been entirely concerned with flying over mountains with any contact with the ground unintended, and serious if it occurred. Flyers knew that they would have to master the arts of taking off and landing on snow-covered terrain, virtually the only kind that could be exploited in the mountains for such a purpose. Such areas might be ready-made landing grounds if the techniques could be worked out.

The first steps were taken in Switzerland. In 1911 the Davos Tourist Office asked René Grandjean, who had begun building aeroplanes the previous year, to study the possibilities of adding to the tourist attractions in the area by providing flights for winter visitors. He made a pair of skis, sufficiently large and strong enough to support his self-built monoplane, powered by a 50hp Oerlikon engine, and move across the snow without sinking. In the winter of 1912 he took off from the frozen Davos lake at 1,600m over one hundred times, over forty times with passengers. One day a passenger who wished to remain anonymous was so enchanted by the experience that he forgot to pay for the trip. On making enquiries, Grandjean ascertained that his careless passenger was the crown prince, son of the German Emperor William I. (Biolaz. 1980, 165)

In 1919 a plan to exploit the potential of the Jungfrau Railway to help make the first landing and take off from a glacier was put forward by the Swiss balloonist, climber and ski-instructor

Victor de Beauclair (whose trans-alpine balloon flight in 1908 was described in Chapter 1) and the director of the Jungfrau Railway, Karl Liechtl. The Swiss army flying corps agreed with the plan and Major Arnold Isler and ten men stamped out a landing strip about 200m long and 15m wide about 150m below the 3,475m Jungfraujoch on the Valais side of the pass. The trodden-down ice and snow froze hard. On 17th August Lieutenant Robert Ackerman took off from Thun in a De Havilland DH3, with a 150hp motor, at 04.30, accompanied by Major Isler, and about an hour later was approaching the strip at about 70m above the ice. Unfortunately at that altitude even full power of the motor was insufficient, and the machine dropped to the surface short of the prepared area and sank into the snow of the Aletsch glacier. The aircraft nosed over and the propeller was broken. Fortunately the crew suffered no injuries and the machine was dragged to the strip, an arduous task. A replacement propeller having been obtained from Thun and the oil and fuel preheated because of the cold, Ackerman was able to take off, carrying no passenger this time, in the early morning of 19th August. The aeroplane rose just before the first crevasse that lay in its path, started to sink again, but then responded to the controls enough to fly out over the Aletsch glacier. Ackerman crossed over the Jungfraujoch and landed at Thun at 07.00.

Lieutenant Henri Pillichody, who on 19 July had been first to fly over the central Alps in a flying boat, landed nearby in another DH3 but was also forced down short of the prepared strip by some 20m. (Dollfus, 1969, 42) Unfortunately, this DH3 was seriously damaged and it was necessary to dismantle it and take it down by the railway. (Dollfus, 1969, 44,)

By 1921, only just over a decade after Chavez made his ill-fated flight over the Simplon Pass, François Durafour, another Swiss pilot, from Geneva, decided to attempt a landing near the summit of Mont Blanc. On July 20th he took off in the early morning from La Blécherette, near Lausanne, in a Caudron G3 biplane, with a 130hp nine-cylinder engine (a Le Rhone rotary in which the cylinders rotated around the crankshaft) and climbed steadily up over Thonon to 5,200m. He passed twice over the summit of Mont Blanc and then, after flying for forty minutes, put the machine down in the snow on the Dôme du Goûter (Dollfus, 1969, 44) on a hard and almost level area measuring 300m by 150m. This landing was at 4,331m (Biolaz, 1980, 165), about 500m below the summit, thereby making it the first on a high snowfield and, in fact, the first above 4,000m. The secretary of the French Alpine Club was awaiting him and took photographs and gave him a written confirmation of the landing. (Borrel, 1983)

Surprisingly, Durafour's machine was not fitted with skis. (Dollfus, also Bucher, 1961) The only alpine equipment was the pair of boots worn by the pilot. 'I was lucky,' he said, 'there was an ideal layer of wonderful snow over the ice.' (Dollfus, 1969, 44) The registration letters of the aircraft were F–ABDQ, which the mechanics expanded to *'Faut avoir beaucoup de culot'* – 'You need a lot of audacity.' (Geiger, 1956, 21)

Durafour needed not only audacity but also a great deal of skill and concentration, especially when he took off from the mountain. This was much more difficult and hazardous than the landing. The thinness of the air and violent gusts of wind prevented the plane from rising and several times he almost crashed. Finally he managed to pull the machine up just as he passed over the ridge with 'a 1,500m hole underneath his seat' (Dollfus, 1969, 44) and landed at Chamonix at 09.15. There he was the object of an enthusiastic reception. When asked if he might do it again he replied with a firm negative. (Geiger, 1956, 22)

On 19th March 1922 Franz Hailer flew with two passengers in a Rumpler C1 biplane, powered by a 150hp engine, from Munich to the Zugspitze and made the first landing on a glacier by a German, touching down at 2,700m. (Bucher, 1961, 23) Unfortunately his propeller suffered damage and the machine had to be dismantled. (Dollfus, 1969, 44) He continued flying his ski-plane into the mountains and made many deliveries of food and equipment to alpine huts. Bucher makes the point that Hailer should be regarded as the first glacier pilot. (Bucher, 1961, 23)

Six years later, on 24th July 1928, Hans Wirth from Bern landed his little Klemm monoplane, which had a motor of only 19hp (Dollfus, 1969, 44) on the Jungfrau plateau and took off again after he had fitted skis sent from Thun. On 6thAugust of the same year, Lasser, a German pilot from Stuttgart, followed suit with a Klemm-Salmson equipped with both wheels and skis. (Biolaz, 1980, 165) Also in 1928, for the making of the film 'The White Hell of Piz Palu', the German wartime flying ace, Ernst Udet, simulated a successful aerial search for a climbing party high up on the mountain. He made two landings in a Klemm aircraft, also fitted with skis as well as wheels, on the Trient glacier. (Geiger, 1956, 21–2, Bucher, 1961) On 21st May 1930, he again landed on the Trient glacier, carrying supplies to the actors, guides and film crew making the film 'Étoiles' [Stars] sur le Mont-Blanc.' On 28th March 1933, he landed his Klemm twice near the Diavolezza hut at 2,977m in the Engadin. A year later he made several more landings on the Trient glacier. (Biolaz, 1980, 165)

In 1935 Udet made an actual search flight to look for the first two climbers to attempt to climb the Eiger north face. Karl Mehringer and Max Sedlmayer had embarked on the climb in good weather on 25th August 1935.Their progress was followed through telescopes at Grindelwald and Kleine Scheidegg. At first the climb had seemed to be going well but after two bivouacs they were seen to be moving more slowly. Then a severe storm blew up and the clouds obscured the climbers. They were seen moving once more, climbing slowly toward the ridge feature called the Flatiron, below the Third Icefield. Then the mist came down again. On 19th September, when the weather was more settled, Udet flew to within twenty metres of the wall – so close that some considered it foolhardy. With him was Fritz Steuri, a Grindelwald mountain guide. (Harrer, 1958; 1989, 37–8) They both saw one of the two climbers buried up to his waist in snow (which of the pair could not be ascertained) and apparently frozen in the bivouac. It was known thereafter as Death Bivouac. Recovery of the bodies was not possible with the techniques then available but the following year Sedlmayer's remains were found at the bottom of the face by his own brother. Mehringer's remains were not found until twenty-seven years later, at the edge of the Second Icefield.

In the early 'thirties tourist flights and taxi flights were developing, notably in the Engadine with the wealthy visitors to St. Moritz an obvious stimulus. The Belgian King Albert and Queen Elizabeth were among the patrons. (Dollfus, 1969, 45)

Before moving on to the sensational developments in the techniques of glacier landings that were to be made in the Alps in the 1940s and 1950s, the exploratory flying that had been achieved in the polar regions many years earlier deserves attention.

The Arctic

Though glacier landings still appeared to many in more temperate regions to be foolish and pointless, the value of mastering landing and taking-off from snow and ice was essential for all operators in Arctic and near-Arctic conditions such as Russia, Scandinavia and Canada. By the late 1920s, in fact, techniques and equipment for landings on snow and ice, at least where the surfaces were reasonably flat, were well established. In 1929 a young Cambridge student, Henry George ('Gino') Watkins came up with an audacious plan to explore the possibility of a future air route between Europe and North America, which he submitted to the Royal Geographical Society. He planned to survey a route from the east coast of Greenland to Canada using aircraft and sledging parties. The result was the British Arctic Air-Route Expedition with fourteen members, mainly from Cambridge, and two de Havilland 60X Moth biplanes with 85hp Gipsy engines. The Air Ministry loaned two serving RAF pilots, Flight Lieutenant N.H. D'Aeth and Flying Officer W.E. Hampton but most of the finance came from the Courtauld family.

The expedition sailed in the *Quest*, a ship used by Sir Ernest Shackleton, and a base was established some thirty miles west of Angmagssalik, from where the terrain rose steeply to the ice-cap at around 6,000ft. The aerial survey programme, using both vertical and oblique photography, was started on August 3rd 1930, with one of the Moths equipped as a floatplane. Flights were carried out from several fjords and lakes, often hampered by the ice closing in, even while they were on short flights, and by storms. On 29th August, D'Aeth and Watkins saw a range of mountains away to the north, rising to some 12,000ft. The Danish administrators later named them the Watkins Mountains. Before the summer ended, 23 flights had been made, with photography on nine of them, covering the coast for over two degrees of latitude. Hampton built a hangar for both aircraft from packing cases. For the winter flying the Moths were fitted with skis. Unfortunately, on a flight to collect stores, one Moth had to be secured overnight in the open and was battered by a gale. It looked a write-off but Hampton and his team of helpers restored it in two and a half months of work, including the fabrication of a replacement tailplane and elevator spar from driftwood. The second Moth then hit a concealed ice hummock on landing but was also repaired by April 30th. Despite these setbacks and the limitations imposed by the weather, short days, bad light and the fact that it was never safe to leave the aircraft out on the ice because of the gales, more than half the total hours of flying were done during the winter period with the skis attached. (D'Aeth in Chapman, 1932, 265–268 and Grierson, 1964, 239–245)

The survey and research programmes were pursued with outstanding determination and many were the hazards and hardships cheerfully accepted by the sledging parties. Many times men and dogs fell into crevasses but the precautions taken permitted speedy rescues. A meteorological observation station was established on the ice-cap and, because conditions prevented adequate supplies for two men being got there, August Courtauld stayed there alone throughout the winter months, without radio contact. Fears for his safety were multiplied when relief flights failed because of the weather but Watkins, with John Rymil and Spencer Chapman, trekked in and located the station, buried by snow. Watkins found the ventilator pipe and shouted down it. A voice answered and, by excavating the imprisoning snow, they enabled Courtauld to struggle out. He had existed without light for weeks owing to fuel shortage and the Primus stove had just gone out with the last drop of fuel burnt when he heard Watkins.

With the return of more suitable weather, flying was resumed but an ambitious programme to fly across the ice-cap to Winnipeg was vetoed by the London Committee. In fact, the proposed flight with one of the Moths would have been very hazardous as it had neither the power to cope with the altitude nor adequate range for safety. The promise of a larger aircraft, a Saro Cloud flying boat, had come to nothing and, in any case, that also was not a suitable machine for such a long and risky journey involving mountainous terrain.

In his report, D'Aeth praised the Moth aircraft but thought that 'slightly more power would have been an advantage' (D'Aeth, 1932, 274) Today, it seems incredible that an 85hp engine should have been considered even nearly adequate for such an expedition but this emphasises the level of development of aircraft that was accepted for hazardous exploration at the time. For depot laying and support of a sledging party – essential for ground control of surveys – D'Aeth considered that a multi-engine aircraft with dual control and a navigator was desirable. 'Wireless would be necessary, and to aid navigation a direction-finding station at the Base would be an enormous help.' (D'Aeth 1932, 274) In the 21st century comment seems to be superfluous.

There followed other expeditions aimed at surveying the possibilities of this route between Europe and North America, which offered shorter distances and much less flying over water than the more southerly routes. Against these advantages were to be set the weather of the far north, the long polar winter and the mountains. Wolfgang von Gronau, after an unofficial reconnaissance in a Dornier Wal flying boat in 1929 – which took him to the Faroe Islands and Iceland – obtained the backing of Lufthansa and the German Department of Transport for a flight to New York via Greenland. This was carried out successfully in 1930 but von Gronau was not satisfied and decided the following year to follow a route that took him across the ice-cap. The heavily loaded Dornier Wal, though a later model with more powerful engines, had extreme difficulty in gaining enough height to cross the mountains and plateau of the ice-cap but eventually it reached 10,000ft.

Partly to support their claims to control Greenland, the Danish government set up a detailed photographic survey of the east coast, for which Heinkel HMII seaplanes were used. All the flights in this period illustrated well how even coastal operations in Greenland involved constantly flying in mountainous areas in weather that changed abruptly, and flights over the ice-cap needed more power and reserve range than was available in most contemporary aircraft. Von Gronau's considered view was that the Arctic route from Europe to North America would be practicable but not for the whole year and he favoured a route over south Greenland. (Grierson, 1969, 283) The German government and Lufthansa, however, dropped the idea and British government and airline circles were no more enthusiastic.

Pan American Airways showed more interest in the Greenland – Iceland route and the Lindberghs made a west to east flight over the Arctic in their Lockheed Sirius floatplane (previously used for a flight that had taken them into northern skies) to survey it. Anne, in the observer's seat, saw the Greenland peaks ahead:

> 'Below us glistened a few icebergs like small white snails. But the mountains towered up magnificently to meet us, a great wall against the sky.' (Grierson, 1969, 307)

Meanwhile, the Russians had been steadily consolidating their control over the eastern Arctic regions with bold and innovative use of aircraft. They had been well to the forefront in the development of long-distance air routes throughout the territories of the Soviet Union, which extended over 10,000km from east to west and thousands from north to south. Pioneer flights had been followed by airline development, first in their

European territories, then beyond the Ural Mountains across Siberia and Central Asia. They encountered the full range of difficult flying conditions from Arctic to hot desert temperatures and their pilots became adept at flying along narrow valleys in the mountains as they penetrated the ranges to the Transcaucasian, Uzbek, Kasakh, Kirgiz, Siberian and Far East regions. They also became among the most experienced aviators in the Arctic, in which they first flew in 1914, though it was not until the 1920s that they seriously developed their aerial exploration and services.

On 16 June 1933 *Chelyuskin* – a ship strengthened to face the ice on the northeast passage – sailed from Leningrad on the long journey to battle its way along the route. The aim was to link the settlements at the mouths of the rivers that flowed into the northern sea, with the hope of establishing a regular service of both commercial and strategic importance. It was under the command of Captain Otto Yuri Schmidt, who had previously explored the route. Eventually, however, in the Chukot Sea, on 13th February 1934, the thickness of the ice proved too much and the ship was brought to a halt. Like many of its predecessors in Arctic exploration including the vessels that had been pitted against the elements over the centuries to try to find the northwest passage round Canada, it was crushed by the pack-ice and the crew and passengers, including women and children, had to take to the ice, saving all they could to construct the best possible protection from the elements.

The ship carried a small seaplane to seek the best route through the icepack and the shipwrecked crew did not delay in starting to prepare a runway. The Russian seaplane did not have the capacity or fuel to get the survivors back to civilisation but they could hope for rescue from the Soviet air fleet, which was equipped with suitable transport aircraft and had experience in operations using skis. The castaways were, however, 2000km from the Soviet bases of Magadan on the Okhotsk coast and Petrapavlovsk in Kamchatka. Moreover almost all of the territory between them was seriously mountainous. Getting to 'Camp Schmidt' involved flying thousands of kilometres over hostile territory, where potentially disastrous icing of the wings of the aircraft was an even higher risk than on the Arctic coast itself, and the consequences of forced landings too frightening to contemplate.

The government's plan to carry out a rescue entirely by air was thought by many to be impossible and, in any case, involved some very dangerous operations. V. Lyapidevskiy was first to reach 'Camp Schmidt' in an ANT-4 and he was able to evacuate the women and children. Six other pilots, one of them military, flew in using Polikarpov P-5 and R-5 aircraft, amongst others, and all members of the expedition were eventually airlifted to safety. The pilots were honoured at a special ceremony in Moscow in April. It was the first time that the highest distinction of Hero of the Soviet Union was awarded to airmen in civil aviation and, specifically, in the polar aviation command. (Bugayev, (ed) 1983, 83–4, 340–1, 367) An American crew had also joined the rescue in a Consolidated Fleetster and were awarded the Order of Lenin. It was magnificent propaganda for Joseph Stalin. Stalin, of course, did not advertise the fact that at the same time prison ships were taking thousands of Soviet people who had displeased him in some way to the Gulag camps that had originated on the White Sea island of Solovki in what had been a monastic settlement from the Middle Ages. Many of the deportees died from hunger, disease and the cold before they even reached their destinations. Sara Wheeler has put the subject into perspective with other evils perpetrated by mankind throughout the Arctic regions, alongside incredible feats of endurance, bravery and sheer stupidity. (Wheeler, 2009)

The Antarctic

Flying across or in the Antarctic differed significantly from that in the Arctic in the greater height of its central landmass, the much more extensive and widely distributed mountain ranges and the greater distances involved. Any aviator seeking to reach the South Pole had to have at his disposal an aircraft capable of reaching the altitudes at least of the mountain passes on the approach and the polar plateau itself. First to fly into the Antarctic area was the Australian Hubert Wilkins, later knighted. Wilkins had already made history by being first, in 1928, to fly across the Arctic regions from Barrow in Alaska to Spitsbergen with Carl Ben Eielson as first pilot. They had previously survived a forced landing on the ice and a long and arduous trek back to civilisation. Undaunted, they returned the next year and made the successful flight. Descending through cloud, they almost flew straight into a mountain but Eielson banked sharply and Wilkins guided him down to a safe landing on the ice. After enduring four days of storm they eventually were able to complete the flight. Eielson went on to fly in Siberia but tragically was killed when his aeroplane hit a hillside.

In the Antarctic, as in the Arctic, Wilkins was interested mainly in exploration, especially the discovery of new land-masses. With Eielson as pilot, in November 1928, he made the first flight over the Antarctic continent in a Lockheed Vega monoplane from Deception Island down the Antarctic Penin-sula, which he thought was an archipelago – the 'channels' charted were later found to be glaciers. However, his 10–hour flight proved the value of aerial survey in the region and he also studied the characteristics and behaviour of the air masses. The aeroplane had introduced, Ronne later wrote, 'a new era of polar exploration' and Wilkins 'was the first man in history to use an airplane to discover new land.' (Ronne, 1979, 90)

It was, however, Richard Byrd who seized the opportunity of further fame by aiming to be first to fly over the South Pole. With elaborate preparations and back-up, including two ships, three aircraft, 50 men and 95 dogs (Trewby, ed., 2002, 45) he started the flying programme in January 1929. During the flights, Byrd carried out the first air rescue operation made in the Antarctic. Sledging parties had gone out, laying depots to support flying operations planned for the following spring, and other tasks. One of the aircraft, a Fokker Universal, was used in support and the pilot, Balchen, landed at the foot of Chips

Gould Mountain and was then trapped by violent storms, which totally wrecked the machine. With no radio contact, Byrd became alarmed and set off in the Fairchild, piloted by Smith. They were fortunate in locating the stranded party and landed on the ice. Byrd sent the Fokker crew back in the Fairchild and he was then stranded with two companions by storms that made flying impossible for several days. When at last Smith was able to fly back with a radio operator, he was not deterred by having to pick up three men and cheerfully shouted 'Hop in: room for everyone on board; next train leaves in six months.' (Grierson, 1964, 191–2)

After overwintering at the base they called Little America, Byrd and his team began preparations for the flight of 2,600km to the Pole and back. With emergency and photographic equipment on board, the range of their Ford Trimotor – meeting the requirement for the attempt that it should be an American-built machine – was inadequate without an intermediate refuelling point. Dog teams were sent out with the necessary supplies to establish a base at the Axel Heiberg glacier, 550km from the Pole. The machine had originally been fitted with three engines of 220hp but the one in the nose had been replaced by one of 550hp to boost the performance. If any one of the engines failed the aeroplane would be unable to climb to the required height. In fact, it was found that the performance was in any case inadequate and some rather risky modifications were made to the fuel jets, which fortunately had the desired effects.

On 18th November a flight was made with provisions for the advanced base. On the way back they discovered a fuel leak and, despite weakening the mixture, Smith had to make a forced landing. The oil was drained from the engine to prevent it freezing, a tent was pitched and the emergency radio transmitter put to use. They could get no acknowledgement but after three and a half hours the Fairchild appeared with spare fuel, the failure of the transmissions from the air having been rightly surmised as possibly indicating a problem. The Fairchild flew back to base but the engines of the Ford refused to start and more repairs were undertaken. Next day, however, the Fairchild returned and provided a boost, which got the Ford's engines started and both aircraft returned to base.

A report of good weather having been received from the camp at the Queen Maud mountains the Ford took off on 26th November with Balchen as pilot, Byrd acting as navigator, June as radio-operator and second pilot and McKinley responsible for photography. The machine, with this crew and extra fuel, was overloaded and problems were expected in the climb to the pass over the 'Hump' – the rise to the polar plateau – which had been estimated by Amundsen to be about 3,200m. Byrd decided to follow Liv's Glacier as there appeared to be cloud over the Axel Heiberg glacier. They flew over a spectacular and menacing sea of crevasses, séracs and icefalls with mountains towering above the aeroplane, which bucked around in the turbulence. The pass narrowed and there was no room to turn as the summit neared. Weight reduction became imperative. The emergency rations were thrown out and the machine gained just enough height to clear the pass. Now at over 3,200m, the flight continued until at last from dead reckoning and astro-plots they thought they should be over the South Pole. They circled and dropped the US flag then turned for home. They landed at the fuel dump after 13 hours and 5 minutes in the air. After hurried refuelling they took off before an approaching storm arrived and got back to Little America after being airborne for 17 hours 26 minutes, to which was added 1 hour 13 minutes for refuelling. (Grierson, 1964, 200–203)

Ronne recorded that, when it came to the official record, Lt. Cdr. Robert A English, the officer compiling the account referred to the flight as 'to the polar plateau.' Byrd asked for the words 'and on to the South Pole' to be added but English refused to do this without supporting data. Byrd became angry and threatened him with court martial, to which English replied 'Admiral . . . I would welcome the opportunity for a court-martial to clarify some points.' Byrd became ashen-white and walked out. (Ronne, 1979, 122–3) In *Antarctica, an Encyclopedia*, it is noted that research has convincingly shown that

Byrd could not actually have flown over the Pole. (Trewby, ed. 2002, 15),

However, Byrd and his team also carried out valuable scientific work and this was followed up in a second expedition in 1933–35. He again had two ships and three aircraft, plus 56 men, 154 dogs, tractors and snowmobiles. Fresh milk was provided by three cows, which were housed in a heated barn. Byrd spent four and a half months alone in a hut to study the weather. Unlike Courtauld in Greenland, he did not run out of fuel but the radio operator at base suspected he was ill and a flight was made to rescue him. He claimed that he was suffering from poisoning from the kerosene stove but some thought he had just not been able to cope with the solitude on what was basically an ill-chosen publicity stunt. (Ronne 1979, 36)

A most ambitious and daring flight was carried out in 1935. Lincoln Ellsworth, who had flown into the Arctic with Roald Amundsen in 1925, aimed to fly over more than 3,000km of the Antarctic ice-cap, mountains and glaciers, to clarify the geography of the continent. For this purpose he chose a new Northrop Gamma all-metal monoplane, with a 600hp Pratt and Whitney Wasp engine. He named the aeroplane the *Polar Star*. Its low-wing layout would enable the wing to be lowered to rest on the surface of the snow relatively easily if trenches were dug for the skis, so that the risk of the gales destroying the machine would be minimised. The first attempt in the Antarctic summer of 1933–34 ended abruptly when the break-up of the ice caused the aircraft to sink into the water and to be nearly lost altogether. It was eventually rescued but so badly damaged that it needed a factory rebuild.

The Ellsworth family finances permitted another attempt, which was nearly terminated when a mechanic failed to follow the starting procedure of turning over the engine by hand. A connecting rod was fractured. The expedition ship went a thousand miles back to the nearest port to which replacements could be flown. At last on the tongue of a glacier the plane was prepared for flight. With little time left before the ice closed in, the pilot, Balchen, who had been Byrd's pilot, decided that the weather was still not good enough and turned back without even consulting Ellsworth. Ellsworth, still determined, realised that he would have to find another pilot.

Sir Hubert Wilkins, who was acting as manager of Ellsworth's expeditions, found a pilot with adequate experience of flying in the Arctic who was confident that he would not require the extra man on board to help with preparing take-off strips at intermediate landings as demanded by Balchen, with all that meant for the loads to be carried on the flight. This was Herbert Hollick Kenyon, born in London but flying for a Canadian company. The choice of Dundee Island, near the northern tip of Graham Land, as base, revealed a fine, hard snow surface. The distance to the Little America base in the Bay of Whales was some 3,500km. Though flying time might be only some fourteen hours, the *Polar Star* carried emergency rations for two men for five weeks, a collapsible sledge, a silk tent, a coil of rope for dealing with crevasses – Ellsworth had nearly lost his life in one – and numerous other items, including a pistol for a reason unknown.

A bumpy take-off then damaged the fuel gauge and after an hour and a half, Kenyon turned about and flew back to Dundee Island for a repair. Two days later the next attempt was made and all went well until stormy clouds forced them to climb above hitherto undiscovered mountains and Kenyon decided that too much fuel had been consumed in the turbulent air and again he returned to base. Ellsworth was furious but Wilkins pointed out that to return was good sense. On 22nd November, another start was made and this time the weather was better. With prior knowledge now of the mountains Kenyon climbed beforehand to a sufficient altitude. After thirteen hours the weather deteriorated and a decision was taken to land to check fully their position. The conditions made the landing difficult and the fuselage suffered damage. Sextant readings revealed that they were only about half-way, ground speed having been much less than hoped. Now worried about the fuel consumption, they refrained from using the aircraft's radio and worked hard on a hand-driven emergency set but failed to establish communications. They took off successfully but after only thirty minutes were forced down again by the weather, still high on the plateau.

They were pinned down for three days by storms and still Ellsworth could not get a satisfactory position check and when they took off again it was more in hope than conviction that they were on the right track. Again they were forced to land and this time were barely able to erect their tent before a horrific storm broke and such was the wind that it threatened to carry away the tent with them inside. During a lull the two went outside and tried to build a windbreak with blocks of snow. The temperature was down to –23 degrees C. During the enforced stay of seven days at Camp III, Kenyon found that the bubble adjustment screw on the sextant had worked loose, hence the erratic readings. New readings indicated that they were still 800km from Little America. After two days work to uncover the 'plane and empty the fuselage of snow – with the aid of a bucket and a pemmican mug – they hoped to move on but after a long battle to unfreeze the engine with a blow lamp, yet another storm drove them to unload and stay put.

Next day, 4th December, despite a threatening horizon, they were desperate to escape from their icy prison and a flight of four hours took them down off the plateau, which Ellsworth appreciatively named the Hollick Kenyon Plateau. When the surface permitted, another landing was made. The fuel tanks were almost empty. Next day, the *Polar Star* was able to fly only long enough for the Ross Sea to appear before the petrol was exhausted. Kenyon was prepared and landed safely. They were disappointed to see no signs of the Little America base but thought it should not be far away. In fact it was only 25km away (after they had flown 3,360km) but their sufferings were far from over. They dug the skis of the aeroplane into the snow and prepared to trek on. The first target turned out to be only an empty oil drum left as a beacon by the Byrd expedition and Ellsworth and Kenyon struggled back exhausted. Another disappointment next day caused them to return and fix up the sledge, which took a day and a half. They had more frustrating struggles before, on 14th December, nine days after their last landing, they finally reached the sea. After one more night in the tent they reached Little America. The base was deserted but they dug down to get into a hut. They were able to light the stove, enjoy hot pemmican and sleep in comfort. Their erratic trek had involved them in a distance about six times greater than a straight line from the landing.

They still had to await their ship and the wait was tedious. Ellsworth was suffering from a frostbitten foot and leg and gangrene was developing. Fortunately, the *Polar Star* was spotted from a naval Gipsy Moth seaplane and a note was dropped to which Kenyon was able to respond and go out and meet a rescue party. Ellsworth was helped to *Discovery II* and was taken to Australia for treatment. When Ellsworth's own ship, *Wyatt Earp*, arrived the *Polar Star* was dismantled and shipped back to the United States.

Ellsworth and Kenyon had made a most remarkable journey, with numerous landings far from the possibility of rescue if they had been unable to take off from the intermediate and hastily chosen landing areas on the ice, but proving the practicality of such bold endeavours. (Grierson, 1964, 350–374) Among their other achievements was the discovery of the mountain range that was named the Ellsworth Mountains, culminating in Mount Vinson at 4,897m. (16,062ft). This peak has become the principal target for mountaineers in the Antarctic and a 'must' for those who seek to climb the highest mountain in each continent.

This was the aim of Frank Wells and Dick Bass in 1983 with Chris Bonington and Rick Ridgeway as climbing experts and Steve Marts as climbing cameraman. This is of special aviation interest as to overcome the logistical problems they hired a Douglas DC3 – the wartime Dakota transport – to be flown by Giles Kershaw, a British pilot with extensive Antarctic experience. Modern turbines replaced the old piston radial engines, a third one being added in the nose, and skis were fitted. They flew from Punta Arenas to the British/Chilean base at Rothera and on to land on the ice-cap about five miles from Mount Vinson. Then they sledged to the head of the glacier and climbed the

64

head wall and ridge, following the route of Nick Clinch in 1966. Bonington reached the summit on 23rd November and the others on a week later. Bonington commented:

> 'There had been another ascent by some American geologists surveying the area but they had cheated, using a helicopter to get them quite close to the summit.' (Bonington, 1984)

The need for regular flights in Arctic conditions was entirely appreciated in the 1930s by Canadian and American bush pilots and industrial companies, and by Soviet developers and suppliers of remote communities in the Arctic regions. As more suitable aircraft became available they were routinely used for transporting surveyors, miners, doctors and others for necessary purposes. Mountaineers were already being transported into the back country, saving days or even weeks of trekking through arduous forests or negotiating hazardous rivers by canoe, a theme which will be taken up in a later chapter.

CHAPTER 4

Mountain Rescue Takes to the Air

The use of air ambulances for the rescue of wounded personnel lying on battlefields had been suggested, even before the First World War. Colonel S.F. Cody, who, at Farnborough, had built and flown the first aeroplane to fly in England, made such a suggestion but it was not followed up, though during the fighting many individual pilots landed and rescued comrades who had been forced down behind enemy lines. In 1917 a courageous French doctor made a number of mercy flights at Amiens to carry out seriously wounded men. (Bucher, 1961, 139)

When flyers came to grief in the mountains, their colleagues could do little to help except search for a missing aircraft and then send out ground rescue teams that were, in most areas, organised on an *ad hoc* basis until well into the Second World War. The RAF built up a long history of arduous operations on rescue missions in the British hills and mountains, modest though their height might be, as many airmen had the misfortune to crash into high land owing to the rudimentary nature of navigation equipment, engine failure or other causes. At first it was up to individual RAF stations to organise searches for missing aircraft. One such mission in 1938 was led by Squadron Leader D.F. McIntyre, who, in 1933, had been one of the pilots on the photographic flight over Mount Everest. He was in command of the RAF station that had taken over from the flying school he had established before the war at Prestwick in Scotland. (McIntyre, 2004) Learning of a crash in the hills, he hastily assembled a stretcher party of 40 men. Ill-equipped and without proper protective clothing, they had to wade through deep icy streams and get what sleep they could in a barn until daylight came. On that Ayrshire hillside he was probably reminded of the Everest downdraft, because, at the site of the crash, they found a civilian Tiger Moth, which had encountered an air pocket when the pilot had gone down to inspect the previous crash and had ended up nose-down in a bog. Fortunately, whereas the occupants of the crashed Avro Anson had been killed, this pilot and his passenger were uninjured. (Card, 1993, 1–2) This was one of many accidents that have occurred as a result of the air currents to be found among the mountains, a subject already mentioned and which will be returned to in later chapters.

During the war years the necessity of dealing with the growing number of crashes in the mountains became evident and groups of volunteers were formed at RAF stations near the hills and mountains. In the conditions of flying before modern navigational aids, hills did not have to be very high to feature as death traps to flyers. The North Yorkshire Moors rise in only a few places above 1,600ft (487m) but it was believed that between 1935 and 1959 over 170 crashes occurred on this high ground. (Earl, 1995, 26) In wartime, even not taking into account damaged aircraft returning to Britain after operations, many pilots became lost over the hills in bad weather and at night – when all lights on the ground had to be masked so that enemy raiders should gain no help from them.

The immense efforts that the RAF rescue teams put in with minimal official support and equipment in the early days have been described in detail by, among others, Moffat (1964), Card (1993) and Earl (1995, 1999a, 1999b). Eventually, in 1944, the RAF Mountain Rescue Service came into being. Many were the problems to be met and overcome in the succeeding years and the RAF became deeply involved in civilian rescue work. Its nine mountain rescue teams were permitted to become involved in any rescue and the post-war boom in hill walking and climbing resulted in their being called out with increasing frequency. All searches and rescues were done the hard way, by teams that struggled up the mountain on foot, thankful for any help that could be got from trucks and jeeps merely to get into position to set out on the hill. Rescue by other aircraft had to await the coming of the helicopter and it is worth taking a step back and dwelling for a few paragraphs on what those wartime and post-war search operations involved.

In his investigations into aircraft crashes, David Earl discovered that one of the members of the first official RAF mountain teams had kept a detailed diary of his activities among the mountains of North Wales. John Campion Barrows, known as 'Campy', attended some 24 air crashes as well as rescuing stranded and injured civilians. His accounts convey many of the human aspects of the work as well as the procedures involved in the days when all depended on the ground searches. Often with inadequate clothing and equipment, especially unsuitable boots, and with no food available for hours on end, the volunteers struggled through all kinds of weather, often in darkness, to reach the wrecks and offer whatever help they could, but usually finding only dead bodies to recover.

As just one example of this work, the task on November 2nd 1944 was to go to see what could be done in the case of a Mosquito that had crashed while on a night navigation exercise. 'Campy' recorded that the Tannoy awoke him at 02.00 and soon thirteen members of the team were on their way from Llandwrog to the scene of the accident. At 04.15 they started up the hillside with two sledge-type stretchers and climbed a steep shoulder, a very strenuous climb when hauling heavy stretchers, and found the wrecked aircraft just below the 698 metre (2,290ft) summit. The crew, a French pilot and a Belgian navigator, had been thrown clear and lay some way below, all dead. The team wrapped the bodies in parachutes and tied them to stretchers with climbing ropes. It began to drizzle as they began the descent at 06.30:

'Just then a couple in the party slipped! . . . for safety's sake we let our stretcher go . . . and it went down at a terrific speed for about 150 yards before grinding to a halt in the thick heather . . .

once off that nasty ridge, we waited for the other party . . . arriving at the farm at 9am. Famished and tired, we soon polished off some cheese sandwiches and tea, before packing up for a return trip to camp.' (Earl, 1999b, 56–7)

Between crashes they climbed hills to service the 'Squeekers' that were installed on summits to warn low-flying pilots and on one of these jobs they found above Llyn Dulyn a US C-47 Skytrain (Dakota) of an American Transport Squadron, which had been returning to the USA and had been diverted to RAF Valley, Anglesey, because of weather conditions, only to crash into a cliff face. It had lain undiscovered for nine days. (Earl, 1999b, 57)

Alpine mercy flights

In the Alpine regions, much thought had been given to the use of aircraft to help in rescue missions. On 31st July 1929 the *Neue Zurcher Zeitung* carried an article by Lieutenant Fritz Morgenthaler, a pilot in the Swiss Air Force and a member of the Swiss Alpine Club, drawing attention to the possibilities of using aircraft in rescue work. This was reproduced in *Alpen*, the SAC bulletin. There followed an account of the first coordinated air and ground rescue in the Swiss Alps in which four missing skiers were located by a military pilot and observer in a Potez reconnaissance aircraft from Dübendorf. Food, drink and other items were successfully parachuted down, then the aircraft flew back and forth to guide a 14–strong rescue column to the spot and then to guide the party to the best descent route. (Bucher, 1961, 24)

Although the creation of an integrated and effective air-rescue service did not then come to pass as Morgenthaler hoped, in the ensuing years there were some dramatic operations in which, often in appalling weather conditions, food and medical supplies were dropped to meet emergency situations, such as when the residents of mountain villages were cut off by avalanches or deep snow drifts. Careful attention to techniques and persistence, despite the risks involved, ensured the safe arrival of the parachuted supplies. Many drops were made in the eastern Alps by Franz Hailer, and in 1926 Thoret dropped 1,100kg of materials for the Vallot observatory on Mont Blanc. (Dollfus, 1969, 45)

In 1931 the Swiss Alpine Club and the air force collaborated in a series of exercises to determine the capabilities of aircraft in high mountain country. A group 'lost' in the Weisshorn massif was found fairly quickly but the observer had difficulty in fixing the position on the map needed by the rescue column. The need to have aircraft with sufficient ceiling and rate of climb to meet the dangerous geographical conditions was noted. A second exercise was mounted three months later. The target group was more difficult to locate owing to weather and topographical conditions but was eventually found and supplies were dropped. A third exercise in August was also successful but the need for a recognised signal code was stressed. In the same month a party became stranded on the Aiguilles Rouges above the Val d'Hérens. No less than seven rescue teams failed to reach it because of the bad conditions but supplies were successfully dropped from a military biplane. In 1934 a seriously ill patient was transported by air from Montana to Envers, probably the first alpine air-ambulance mission. (Biolaz, 1980, 166–9)

In March 1943, two German Fieseler Storch high-wing reconnaissance aircraft made forced landings on Swiss territory, an event that was to have far-reaching significance for alpine aviation. Major Pista Hitz and Captain Victor Hug at Meiringen fitted aluminium skis to the aircraft (the prototype had been tried out with skis in the winter of 1936) and obtained permission to use it to transport supplies and personnel to the firing range at Axalp at 1800m (Dollfus, 1969, 46), which normally took two and a half hours to reach from the main base. This was followed by accepting responsibility for aerial surveillance of hydro-electric barrages and delivering supplies to them in bad weather and, above all, for high-mountain rescue support and the formation of one or two rescue teams on each important military aerodrome. (Biolaz, 1980)

The value of these measures was proven the following year, 1944, when a military patrol was caught by an avalanche above the Tschingel glacier. Rescue teams, with search dogs, were transported to the scene by the Storch aircraft in forty minutes, whereas on foot it would have taken seven hours. (Biolaz, 1980, 169) In 1948, the Swiss, now experts in the field, gave instruction on take-off and landing the Storch in the high mountains to French military pilots. (Biolaz, 1980, 168)

Worldwide attention was attracted in 1946 to search and rescue in the mountains. A Douglas DC3 Dakota of the USAF military occupation force disappeared on 19th November on a flight from Vienna to Marseille, following a route via Munich and Basel. The weather forecast was for cloud at 1,700m with high and gusty winds. Aboard the aircraft were twelve persons, including three women and a child. After two hours of flight, as excessive turbulence led to the captain taking control back from the autopilot, the Dakota crashed on a cloud-covered glacier. SOS messages contained the information that the accident site was at over 3,000m altitude, but where was not known. Tracking the signals gave a location between Grenoble and Mont Blanc. American and British aircraft from Germany, Austria and Italy were deployed but failed to locate the crashed machine, hidden by cloud and a metre of snow, which fell in the first night.

Though largely covered by snow the wreck was finally sighted from a Swiss aircraft 72 hours after the crash. The location on the Gauli glacier in the Bernese Oberland was relayed to Meiringen. Captain Victor Hug then took off and surveyed the scene and assessed the problems – such as distance, fresh snow and crevasses. As soon as he returned to Meiringen, a rescue party of 29 men set out. Further parties followed; eight guides, two doctors and about sixty mountain troops and others, fully equipped for the task with ice axes, crampons and a dozen Canadian sledges. Despite the darkness, falling snow and bitter cold, the Rosenlaui refuge was reached that night. Captain Hug dropped supplies over the Dakota and was lucky to escape being hit by items dropped from an American aircraft flying above him. He then decided to land near the crash, despite the fact that it was on a deeply crevassed glacier. He had a Storch prepared and on Sunday 24th November, with great concentration, at 10.25 he put the machine down on the snow at 2,850m, 500m below the Dakota. (Itin and Rutschmann with Odermatt, 2002, 12) He had by that time made more than two hundred landings in the high mountains, but his arrival caused astonishment among the Dakota crew (Biolaz, 1980, 171–3) and they lavishly praised his courage and skill.

Major Pista Hitz followed in support of Captain Hug in another Storch and landed ten metres from him. They immediately evacuated a member of the crew who was seriously injured and two less seriously injured passengers. In nine further flights they completed the transport of all the occupants from the wreck and all survived their ordeal, which had lasted almost five days.

After this remarkable rescue – the first by air from a high glacier – instruction in landing and take-off from mountain sites was given to more officers to build up the cadre of experienced pilots. The rescue organisations at military aerodromes were improved and containers, filled with necessities, were held ready for parachuting from the bomb racks of C-36 aircraft to settlements isolated by heavy falls of snow. (Biolaz, 1980, 174) In May 1947 a Messerschmidt fighter disappeared in the Bernese Alps. A massive aerial search led to the discovery of the wreck in the Lötschenlücke and ground teams were directed to it. The Storch aircraft again provided valuable assistance by transporting tools and a Canadian sledge to the site. (Biolaz, 1980, 174) In April 1949, aerial supply and readiness for glacier landings contributed to a large-scale search embracing all the Haute Route from Zermatt to Verbier. In December 1950 and January 1951, containers were parachuted to people caught up in avalanches in the Valais and Grisons. (Biolaz, 1980, 175)

Aerial contributions to rescue in the mountains of New Zealand

In 1948 Ruth Adams suffered a fall descending an ice slope on La Perouse, a peak in the Mount Cook range, which at that time had only been climbed twelve times. She was roped to a guide,

Mick Sullivan, but suffered severe injuries to her back, a broken wrist and concussion. Fortunately close by were another guide, Harry Ayres, and Edmund Hillary, who five years later made, with Tenzing Norgay, the first ascent of Everest, for which he was knighted. Sullivan and Ayres went down and Sullivan brought up a sleeping bag and other items from the Gardiner hut, arriving after dark, while Harry Ayres rushed on down to the Hermitage Hotel at Mount Cook to report to the chief guide, Mick Bowie. Hillary remained with the casualty and built a shelter. Mick Bowie called on three trainee guides and telephoned for more help from Christchurch, 170 miles away. Norman Hardie, an engineer at a hydro-electric construction party, was also able to join in and was taken to the Hermitage in a car by his boss, together with a local policeman, because the police had been given responsibility for rescues, though he was relieved when he found out that it was out of his area that the accident had occurred.

Meanwhile Harry Wigley, a leading mountain pilot, had been got out of bed at Timaru and asked to make an airdrop of equipment, including a stretcher, a tent, food, fuel, medical supplies and another sleeping bag. There were no aircraft in New Zealand equipped with skis or pilots who had the experience to land on snowfields so there was no possibility of landing on the glacier to offload. However, Wigley set off before daylight in his war-surplus Tiger Moth, with which modest biplane he was building an air service. The first load was roped under the fuselage and the second seat was taken by Harry Ayres, whose job was to guide the pilot to the scene of the accident and then to cut the rope to release the load. The Gipsy piston engine of the Tiger Moth was hardly capable of lifting the load to 11,000ft but Wigley circled round seeking updrafts and slowly gained height until at 11,000ft he could turn in to the ridge. Such was the turbulence that he nearly abandoned the task but after several runs Ayres succeeded in cutting the rope and Wigley shot off down the valley, dropping violently in the air currents, almost striking the glacier. Four more trips were made. Some things were lost in crevasses or damaged but valuable items were retrieved at the accident scene. When Wigley checked his aircraft he found the fabric of the fuselage was gashed in dozens of places where his passengers had struggled in the turbulence to cut the rope. 'It did let in an awful lot of cold air on the way home' was his restrained comment. (Wigley, 1965, 110)

Additional rescuers followed a line of steps cut by Mick Bowie directly up to the ridge to save time and continued until midnight with only one torch between them and despite rocks falling around them. After then bivouacking until morning, they joined the others forty-eight hours after the accident. There were two possible routes off the mountain – the one by which the party had ascended, where the risk of further accidents was very great, and the other to the west coast by a long but technically easier route. It was decided to take the latter though it involved a long trek through trackless gorges and forest – 'bush' as the New Zealanders call it – and the party would be seriously short of food.

The first task was to make the 500ft climb to the ridge of La Perouse. This was extremely trying and involved constantly climbing back down for packs and equipment. For the descent on the other side Mick Bowie tied 400ft of rope, which had been dropped by Harry Wigley, to the stretcher and the carriers lowered it to the full extent, then Bowie established a new anchor and the process was repeated. After descending the steepest slopes and negotiating a crevassed area they bivouacked on an exposed and wet rocky terrace. Only the injured Ruth had a tent which sheltered her from several showers. There was very little food, and no hot drink. The next morning there was an awkward descent of a loose rock gully and it took all day to reach the Gulch Creek Rock where there was shelter and fuel to make tea and dry clothes. Ruth, who had been heavily sedated, was temporarily released from her tight bindings. Four climbers came up from the coast but owing to a misunderstanding about the airdrop had brought only a little extra food. Earl Riddiford was one of the four and he now met Ed Hillary for the first time. Later they were together on three Himalayan expeditions and helped to pave the way for the first ascent of Everest.

The next morning the sixteen men carried Ruth over the ice and sharp rocks of the moraine of the lower glacier. In mid-morning a small aircraft came up the valley, dropped a note requesting news of Ruth and returned to drop a huge cake from her father whose Ernest Adams cakes were staple diet throughout New Zealand. Thus fortified the rescuers went on, toiling through a steep-sided gorge over boulders washed by the torrent. Then came mile upon mile of close bush, through which a track had been cut but which was not wide enough for the whole stretcher party so frequently the stretcher had to be passed from one set of hands to another. Mossy boulders, steep bluffs and the raging river all added to the difficulties. More helpers came up the valley, including Ruth's three brothers.

On the seventh day Ruth was carried to a car. Flown to Christchurch she eventually made a full recovery and became a doctor herself. Norman Hardie, on whose full account this summary is partly based, walked back over the ranges to return to work while the guides accepted a lift to Christchurch from where they could continue their journey back. (Hardie in MacInnes, 1980, 132–145)

Glacier flying developments in the Alps

By 1951 it had become apparent in the European Alps that although there was no possibility of a rescue being carried out at high altitude unless there was a suitable area of relatively smooth snow-covered surface available for a landing and take-off, it was desirable for expertise in glacier operations to be extended to civil pilots. One of the first to learn the techniques from Captain Hug was Freddy Wissel, the enterprising hotelier at St. Moritz who, with skis fitted to his Piper Cub, proceeded to gain experience relevant to collaboration with the Engadine rescue services, with which he had worked for some years. He landed the Piper at about 2,300m near the upper station of the Corviglia funicular railway on 23rd February 1951, and this success led him to aim next for a landing at 3,000m. Selecting the Diavolezza, he made a successful landing up-slope on 2nd March and came to a halt after only twenty metres. Take-off in the opposite direction necessitated a run of 150m. (Biolaz, 1980, 179) On 23rd April he landed and took off from the 3,400m Pic Corvatsch. (Dollfus, 1969, 47) Wissel considered that the slightest element of tailwind would have endangered the operations and that, although the Cub was an excellent machine for the purpose, more power was needed. (Biolaz (1980, 179) Fortunately, at this time, the Piper company had just developed the Super Cub with almost twice as much rated horse-power.

Hermann Geiger, a native of Sion, who had learned to fly in a homemade glider, was another pilot who benefited from Captain Hug's instruction in 1951. In 1948 the flying club raised the money to buy a Cessna 170, a high-wing 4–seat monoplane suitable for tourist flights and which had a ceiling of about 5,500m (18,000ft). Geiger decided to move into Alpine transport flying and designed a simple supply-dropping mechanism, which was attached to the Cessna. Rejecting the use of parachutes as too inaccurate a means of delivery because of wind currents, as well as expensive in parachutes, he found that if he made the drop at a normal speed from a low level the tangential landing of the package on snow saved it from damage. (Geiger, 1956, 25–6) He began serious dropping with supplies for a dam under construction in the Val des Dix. One day he was entrusted with the weekly wages for the workmen but difficulty with the opening of the container resulted in the packet being dropped a long way from the intended site. Fortunately, after a night search on skis and on foot the package was found. (Geiger, 1956, 28–9) In 1951, when avalanches blocked in workmen at the Mauvoisin site at the head of the Val de Bagnes, he was given the task of dropping food to the men and in doing so noticed the plight of a snowbound herd of chamois. On the next trip he dropped them hay, commenting, 'It certainly would not do to drop the hay to the workmen and the meat to the chamois' (Geiger, 1956, 30). After that there were other supply drops to chamois and sheep and then he was commissioned to take the post to Zermatt while the railway was cut by avalanches.

Servicing the mountain huts became a frequent task and his loads ranged from cheese to dynamite.

On 5th October 1951, André Zehr made an attempt to repeat Durafour's exploit of 1921 by landing a Piper high on Mont Blanc but it fell foul of two climbers who stood in the way of the landing run, waving a welcome. Zehr took avoiding action, which resulted in a crash-landing and a broken propeller. (Biolaz, 1980, 180) The Swiss Federal Air Department asked Geiger to take a replacement propeller, together with another – just in case it was needed – and drop them, along with tools, near the crashed machine. It was a difficult task and the first approaches were spoiled by rising air currents. Geiger then flew in at about 300m below the dropping point and allowed the current to lift the machine. He released the first propeller some six metres above the snow and about thirty metres from the crash site. Seeing that the propeller was apparently undamaged he dropped the tools and the second propeller only about ten metres from the stranded machine.

It was not until ten days later, after repair, that the Piper was launched into the air, with the aid of catapult gear, carried up on foot. As the Piper climbed away, its skis were released and plunged into a crevasse at the end of the 70m run which was all that was available for take-off. (Biolaz, 1980, 181)

The Swiss Federal authorities gave a concession for air transport to the Valaisan section of the Aero-Club and it was decided that a new aircraft was needed to supplement the Cessna 170. The committee chose the Piper Super Cub with a 135hp motor. Various modifications were made to the aircraft to suit it for its very demanding tasks. Most important was the fitting of metal skis of a type that had been proven by American and Canadian pilots. The position of the skis could be changed while in flight so that the aircraft could take off from an aerodrome with its wheels and then land on skis on the glacier, a system that had been vital to operations in Alaska and the Arctic regions. The entrepreneur Ulrich Imboden offered to pay for the skis if the aircraft were used to transport materials to the Kander glacier for the enlargement of the Mutthorn hut.

On 10th May 1952, Geiger set off at daybreak to make his first landing on a glacier, accompanied by André Burdet, a former military pilot who had made ski landings on snow-covered aerodromes. Geiger had previously reconnoitred his chosen spot on the Kander glacier on foot, and he made a perfect landing and subsequent take-off. Both pilots then made several landings. They made regular flights to the site with the required timber, sand and other supplies, Burdet flying in the mornings and Geiger in the afternoons. As a result of their efforts the new hut was opened on 7th September, three months earlier than the original date set. They had transported twenty tonnes of materials, landing 220 times on the glacier. In the process, on 13th July, Burdet had made the first rescue with the Super Cub. Two Belgian tourists had been making for the Mutthorn when a snowbridge had collapsed, precipitating one of them into a crevasse. After the guide had, with difficulty, rescued him, they decided to return to the hut, but the rescued man's wife then fell and struck a rock. Fearing a serious back injury, the guide went for help. The injured woman was moved to the hut and from there Burdet flew her in ten minutes to the hospital at Sion. (Biolaz, 1980, 184–5)

In the following years, Geiger and other pilots, many of the them trained by him, made thousands of landings on glaciers and snowfields, frequently on small and steeply sloping areas, which made possible tasks such as deliveries to the Rossier hut on the Dent Blanche and the Cabane du Mountet at 2,866m in the Val d'Anniviers. Demands from skiers for lifts into the mountains were accompanied by rescue work. On one occasion Geiger was flying over a glacier and noticed someone sitting by a crevasse with a rope going down into it. He made a landing and helped the grateful guide to rescue his astonished clients from the crevasse and transport them to Sion hospital. (Geiger, 1956, 63)

Inevitably not all such rescue work ended so happily. One accident on Mont Calme in 1954 necessitated six successive flights to collect the victims of an avalanche that had overwhelmed local men whose knowledge had been not quite good enough when they thought that conditions would be safe on the chosen route. (Geiger, 1956, 71–5)

Sion became a centre for training pilots in the art of glacier landings. Two more Super Cubs were added to the fleet. On one course in September 1955, 246 landings were made on the first day. On the third day, after it had become routine to land on the Théodule and Trient glaciers, the course moved on to the Plan glacier below the Dent du Midi. There the trainees learnt to fly towards a 600m precipice at 140km/hr and touch down on the hanging glacier. Nine hundred glacier landings were made during the whole course, with individuals exceeding one hundred, with no mishaps. (Spahr et al, 1967)

In 1959 a Pilatus P6 Porter, capable of carrying a useful load of 800kg was purchased. A castoring tail-ski facilitated manoeuvrability on snow and ice. This was an excellent aircraft for parachute and ambulance operations because of the wide door that was one of its features. For skiing purposes, it could carry seven skiers with their equipment. With an 800–litre tank fitted in the fuselage it was also used for fighting forest and other fires. (Biolaz, 1980, 187)

In 1963 Geiger and Fernand Magnoni gave instruction in glacier and mountain flying to Bruno Bagnoud. In 1965 these three and Louis Dallèves founded Air-Glaciers. From September 1965 to the end of 1966 they did 2,265 hours flying with aeroplanes and 1,278 with helicopters. Of 23 authorised landing sites in the mountains, 19 were in Valais and to these Air-Glaciers made 553 flights out of a total of 778, carrying 3,117 passengers. Air-Glaciers fought a long campaign with the Swiss authorities to increase the number of altiports – landing places above 1,100m – such as were already common in the other alpine countries. (Bagnoud, 1967, 99) Tragically Geiger died on 26th August 1966 after a collision with a sailplane over his own base. Bagnoud himself took Geiger to Sion hospital while the two other casualties were conveyed by ambulance. Geiger had already become a legend in his time and Rudolf Bucher in his history of the Swiss Air-Rescue service described his contribution as beyond assessment and indispensable. Apart from all his other work, he had carried out over 2,000 rescue missions.

The development of Air-Glaciers and the other leading forces in Swiss air rescue, Swiss Air-Rescue (Rega) and Air Zermatt, is treated in Chapter 6.

Innovation in search and rescue in the Alps

Even after landings by aircraft on glaciers became common-place, it was often not practicable to set down fixed-wing aircraft – or even helicopters when they first became available – near to the scene of a search for avalanche victims. Swiss Air-Rescue (Rega) was formed in 1952 as a specialist section of the Swiss Rescue Society (founded 1933) on the initiative of its president, Rudolf Bucher. (Itin and Rutschmann with Odermatt, 2002, 7, 10) It was decided to extend the use of parachutes, already in use for dropping supplies and equipment to rescue teams, to dropping men and search dogs and the Swiss took advantage of the experience of the Royal Air Force, which they credited as being by far the most advanced in parachuting techniques at that time.

Selected Swiss mountain rescue experts were given a course in parachuting at RAF Abingdon and on 22 Dec 1953, Freddy Wissel flew over an avalanche exercise area near Davos and Hans Walti made the first parachute drop from 1,800m to show the newly acquired techniques of the rescuers (Bucher, 1961, 29) More trainees were sent for training at Abingdon, and their value was shown when, on 12th January 1954 a terrible avalanche struck in the Vorarlberg. The Swiss sent in fourteen men, six avalanche dogs, two helicopters and a hired DC3 with five rescue parachutists. (Itin and Rutschberg with Odermatt, 2002, 23)

Another contingent was sent to Abingdon, then the Swiss set up their own parachuting school. Instructor Friedrich Kauffun-gen recalled a disturbing incident at the first course in August 1956. Many of the trainees were accompanied by their wives and sweethearts, some of whom expressed anxiety at the train-ing. To reassure them, Kauffungen fixed up an 80kg dummy and had it launched from an aircraft with an automatic release line, having assured the womenfolk that this would open automatically in any circumstances. The parachute – which was an old one, used for economy reasons – failed to open. Kauffman wrote 'The dummy crashed to the ground 50 metres in front of the women and exploded in every direction.' After that, most of the women went home but all the trainees qualified the next week. (Itin and Rutschmann with Odermatt, 2002, 30, 32)

The Swiss parachute rescue teams used a number of different kinds of aircraft. They included the Helio-Courier, a versatile single-engine American high-wing monoplane that could carry either four parachutists, two parachutists with two dogs, or four casualties, two on stretchers and two seated. They also made use of the twin-engine Douglas DC3 Dakota, the aircraft most used by Allied air forces during the war for transport and dropping parachutists. This machine could carry ten or more parachutists and supplies, so could deal with major avalanche situations. This capability was invaluable in assistance sent to the Netherlands to deal with the catastrophic flooding of February 1953 and the avalanches in the Vorarlberg in January 1954, when a DC-3 took five parachutists to the scene and six avalanche-search dogs were deployed, two helicopters also being used. (Itin and Rutschmann with Odermatt, 2002, 22–23)

Parachutes used included the 32–foot-canopy Irvine with a sinking speed of three metres per second and some with a lower descent speed, in either case with a reserve 'chute. RAF techniques for dropping men with a 40kg assault kit were adapted to the rescuer carrying his search dog in the drop.

Search and rescue dogs

The training of search and rescue dogs as organised and dedicated helpers, always on stand-by, probably had its origins in the work of the monks of the hospice on the Grand St Bernard Pass. The need for rapid deployment of rescue teams had become increasingly apparent in the alpine regions after the Second World War as the number of skiers rose rapidly and the toll of avalanche victims caused increasing concern.

The experience of the Red Cross in the use of dogs to trace survivors on the battlefields in the First World War and among the rubble of bomb sites in the Second World War led to their widespread introduction by the Swiss in searching for avalanche victims.

When the use of a search dog was combined with parachuting, following RAF techniques with military equipment, the dog would be on a line to touch down first and await the arrival of his handler, ready to start work. Rudolf Bucher developed a method of dropping a dog on a parachute automatically from a container carried under the aircraft. (Bucher, 1961, 260–1) For this purpose the Fairchild 24 was found particularly suitable, having a high undercarriage, between the legs of which the container was mounted. It was divided into two compartments, one containing the parachute and the other the dog, which was fitted with dark goggles to protect it from sudden exposure to the brilliance of the glacier, which would cause snow blindness. The pilot controlled the release mechanism from the cockpit. (Bucher, 1961, 258–60) This method had been developed because the doors of the then-available aircraft were too small to drop man and dog together. Later, the container method was no longer needed.

Throughout the 1950s parachuting was further refined to improve the rescue possibilities offered by the use of fixed-wing aircraft and the first useful helicopters. Inevitably there were many casualties among the rescue personnel who willingly took so many risks. Some of the fatalities occurred on exercises. On 3rd October 1957 the Pilatus P4 high-wing monoplane, which could carry two stretchers, (Pilatus Fugzeuge, 17), piloted by the experienced Otto Weber, was caught by a violent gust of wind above the Stein glacier near the Susten Pass and thrown down to the ice. Günther Erzinger, a gymnastics teacher at a Basel college and one of the most experienced rescuers, was seated by the open door ready to jump. He later died in hospital, but his dog, held in his arms, was uninjured, as was the dog of the other parachutist, who, like the pilot and a guide, was seriously injured. Earlier in the year, the director of the Air-Rescue

Service, Ernest Pichler, a Zurich veterinary surgeon, had been killed in a similar crash in a Fairchild at Birrfeld aerodrome. (Itin and Rutschmann with Odermatt, 2002, 49–51, Bucher, 1961) Despite such disasters, parachutists were responsible for many successful drops to bring rapid help to the victims of accidents and the method was practised alongside landings on glaciers by ski-equipped aircraft.

Similar efforts to perfect the emergency services occurred in other parts of the Alps. In Bavaria, the German air force and army collaborated with the Red Cross and local mountain rescue services, Garmisch-Partenkirchen in particular being a base for concentrated effort in the nearby mountains. German and Austrian rescue services were helped by Swiss experience. The Americans gladly accepted Swiss help in 1956 when a Douglas DC6 and a Lockheed Constellation collided over the Grand Canyon. A team of fourteen guides and parachutists went to Colorado and deployed their abseiling and other skills for two weeks helping with the recovery of the victims. (Itin and Rutschmann with Odermatt, 2002, 43) Helicopters were now available to undertake many such tasks but were not yet at the stage required for some tasks and there were few of them available.

In 1958, help with a helicopter could not be obtained for a farmer who had been seriously injured when he fell into an Alpine gorge while looking for a cow. The accident was reported by two tourists and possible sources of helicopter help came to nothing owing to work elsewhere, or, in one case, the high costs of flying one from Sion to Canton Glarus for what the pilot thought was 'a mere bagatelle.' Three parachutists volunteered to attempt the rescue and were flown to the scene in a Dornier 27, which was in the area on other work. The parachutists landed successfully despite extremely difficult terrain and very bad weather and carried the injured man in pouring rain to the nearest cable car, where a Swiss Alpine Club team took over. Nothing was charged by the Dornier company for the use of the 'plane and the rescuers suggested that no other charges should be made for this mission. (Itin and Rutschmann with Odermatt, 2002)

Helicopter development had, however, reached the stage where landings on glaciers and snow-covered peaks could be considered practical even in restricted and difficult areas where it had not been previously possible to land an aircraft. It is thus time to turn to the history of helicopter use in the mountains – to the trials and tribulations of the early days and the remarkable achievements that have now been built into the everyday work of mountain rescue services.

CHAPTER 5

Helicopters Enter the Mountain Rescue Scene

By the mid-1940s, helicopter development was at last reaching the stage of practical use. A flying machine with rotating wings had been envisaged, drawn and probably successfully modelled by Leonardo da Vinci around 1486–90. The term is derived from the Greek *helix* – spiral and *pteron* – wing. In the 19th century, Sir George Cayley, whose gliders pioneered heavier-than-air flight from 1796 onward, and aeronautical engineers in many countries made important contributions to the development of rotary-winged aircraft but their complexity compared with fixed-wing aircraft posed immense problems. Juan de la Cierva, in the 1920s, solved many of the problems of rotor engineering with his 'Autogiros' but these were gyroplanes, which depended on forward flight for their lift and could not hover, the rotors not being powered.

A German helicopter, the Focke-Wulf Fw 61, with twin three-bladed rotors, mounted on inclined pylons each side of the conventional fuselage, was demonstrated to senior Luftwaffe officers in 1937 by the famous woman test pilot, Hanna Reitsch. She was then persuaded to fly it inside the Deutschlandhalle exhibition stadium in Berlin in 1938, which drew the attention of the aeronautical world to the technical achievement. It proved itself on longer flights and a development, the Focke-Achgelis Fa 223, which first flew in 1940, had two large rotors powered by a Bramo BMW engine of nearly 1,000hp. Its all-up weight was 3,900kg and it could lift a useful load of 800kg. (*Jane's all the*

World's Aircraft 1945–6, 112c) Used to carry supplies to mountain troops during the latter years of the Second World War, (Bradbrooke, 1972, 1) it made a sudden and unscheduled landing at Passy airfield in the shadow of Mont Blanc in 1940. It appears to have been the first helicopter to see service in the mountains.

Igor Ivanovich Sikorsky, who had emigrated from the Soviet Union to the USA, had by then produced the first of his designs to be adopted by the US military. The Sikorsky R4 first flew in 1942. Early examples were sent for testing in extreme conditions in Alaska and Burma. The US Navy and Coastguard, the RAF and the Royal Navy were also equipped with the type. By 1945 at least five other American firms had prototype helicopters on test, including the Bell and Hiller companies, whose products became among the most successful designs. The American national helicopter fleet expanded rapidly and led to an American lead in the post-war years, despite impressive designs in Britain and other European countries. Driven by military requirements, the US developed a wide-ranging and effective military helicopter rescue system alongside its adoption of attack and transport helicopters, so that its deployment of helicopters in all fields and on widely varying terrain far exceeded those of other countries.

The Royal Air Force set out in 1947 to determine the value of a helicopter for their mountain rescue needs. The exercise was held in May at Llandovery in South Wales. The objectives were:

'To test the organisation and training of mountain rescue units in large scale and small scale searching, and at the same time to investigate the practical use of a helicopter in mountain search and rescue' (Card, 1993, 69)

An aircraft was postulated as having crashed in the hills in the Llandovery area and three ground teams were to carry out the search. The available helicopter, the Sikorsky R6, developed from the R4, was a type that had been used by the Americans and RAF in support operations in Burma in 1944. This machine received the name Hoverfly in RAF service. Two of these helicopters, from RAF Thorney Island, were moved to RAF St. Athan in South Wales for the operation. Unfortunately there were various problems with radio communications and some of the ground teams got lost. Also they lacked training, while equipment and support in terms of food, vehicles and fuel were quite inadequate and the exercise was aborted. Nevertheless the report was enthusiastic, noting that the helicopter could work in confined valleys and could search terrain that would defeat fixed-wing aircraft, as well as delivering men and supplies and evacuating casualties. However, the two-seater R6 was considered unsuitable for the job. (Card, 1993, 71–2) Later, one Sikorsky design after another would become standard RAF equipment and the mainstay of the RAF and naval rescue units. The successor to the R6, the Sikorsky S51 was built under licence in the UK by Westland, called the Dragonfly and used in 1950 for casualty evacuation in the campaign in Malaya. Though able to lift only one stretcher patient at a time it confirmed the potential for helicopter rescue.

The Times of 9th September 1947 showed a photograph of a Bell 47B helicopter landing on the Teidemann glacier in British Columbia, carrying part of a rescue party to the scene of the accident. It was claimed to be the first time that a helicopter was actually used in a mountain rescue operation, though at the time when the Swiss succeeded in rescuing the crew and passengers from the Dakota that crashed on the Rosenlaui glacier in Switzerland, described earlier, a dismantled helicopter was being flown across the Atlantic by US Transport Command. (BMC *Mountaineering*, vol. 1 no. 1, June 1947.13, based on an article in *The American Helicopter*) The Americans were now ready to use helicopters anywhere in the world, having taken four on their Antarctic Development Project, generally known as *Operation Highjump* in 1946–47, followed in 1947–48 with more survey work in *Operation Windmill*, so called because of the use of rotorcraft. (Trewby, ed. 2002, 136) They had yet, however, to be developed for specialised mountain rescue and other mountain flying purposes. In 1948 the International

Commission for Alpine Rescue was formed with 28 member-organisations worldwide, indicating the growing awareness of the need for sharing information and coordinating international action, and the use of helicopters was an important discussion point

American designs provided most of the helicopters that were tried out in the Alps and other mountain ranges during the ensuing years. On 12th December 1952 a Hiller 360, piloted by Sepp Bauer, landed at 1,600m in the mountains near Davos, with a dog and its handler, W. Scherrer, this being believed to be the first alpine avalanche rescue operation with a helicopter. Bauer went on to become one of the most famous of rescue pilots and instructed Hermann Geiger in his helicopter training. The problems of landing and taking off again at high altitude led to many debates and tests to evaluate the merits of helicopters compared with parachute descents, the more proven method. Another practice was for the helicopter to hover as close as possible above the ground and for rescuers to jump out directly from two or three metres off the ground. The British Bristol Sycamore was found to have the right qualities for this hazardous operation. From greater heights, the rescuers abseiled on double ropes from the hovering helicopter.

The first small helicopters, such as some of the Sikorsky models, the Hiller and the Bell G2, were adapted for evacuating casualties, when landings were practicable, by mounting a stretcher along the outside of the fuselage, sometimes one on each side. The Swiss rescue teams were delighted when in 1957 the Swiss Co-operative Society presented them with a Bell 47J, capable of carrying two stretchers in its cabin. Hermann Geiger was one of the pilots who used this machine.

The limitations of these early helicopters can be illustrated with reference to a major exercise carried out by the Swiss rescue services in August 1953. Aircraft were employed to parachute personnel and supplies to teams on the glacier below the Jungfrau and to bring 'casualties' to a point from which they could more easily be transported to the mountain railway at the Jungfraujoch. Only after being brought down on the railway to

Wengen was it considered practicable to use a helicopter for the last lap to hospitals at Interlaken and Meiringen. (Itin and Rutschmann with Odermatt, 2002, 24–29)

Meanwhile the RAF had moved on to use much larger and more powerful helicopters that met their needs for search and rescue operations as well as other military purposes. The Sikorsky S55, with a 608hp engine, made its appearance in 1952. Built under licence in Britain by Westland Aircraft at Yeovil and named the Whirlwind, it could carry ten passengers. Two years later, the S58, also built by Westland, was available. As the Wessex, this became the workhorse of the British mountain rescue services as well as of air-sea rescue for many years. With a 1,525hp engine, it could carry up to 16 personnel in addition to two pilots. Both types were used in alpine regions as probably the best all-round transport helicopters at that time but the service ceilings were only about 3,000m and they could not hover much above 1,500m, far short of what was needed in the Alps.

As the era of the helicopter in Alpine rescue work was clearly still in its infancy, it is appropriate to remember the progress that had been made with the use of the light aeroplane, equipped with skis, for operations to glaciers and huts high in the mountains and also in rescue work, described in the previous chapter. Such aeroplanes continued to be used by Hermann Geiger and other alpine pilots alongside the early helicopters. The Swiss Air-Rescue Service devised a plan to cover the whole of Switzerland from five bases at which light aircraft, including those fitted for high glacier work, parachutists and helicopters, were available in readiness for rapid deployment. Contracts with private firms assured the service but the service itself owned two aeroplanes, one being equipped with skis for high mountain work, one helicopter and a Volkswagen bus. They had 13 rescue dogs, 22 parachutists and a variety of doctors and other specialists available. (Itin and Rutschmann with Odermatt, 2002, 49) The number of rescues they carried out grew steadily; 1953 –6; 1954 – 11; 1955 – 26; 1956–15; 1957–63; 1958–70. (Itin and Rutschmann with Odermatt, 2002, 38)

Although at this time helicopters were severely limited in the tasks they could undertake because of their restricted performance, especially as regards altitude and weight-carrying capacity, those responsible for rescue operations could see that there was great potential value in the helicopter for rescue work at altitude. In July 1954, for example, a Bell helicopter was brought to Chamonix and it was shown that it was possible to take-off with a passenger at around 2,800m from several glaciers. (Ministère des Travaux Publics, 1954, 30–31)

On 6th June 1955, Jean Moine set off for Mont Blanc in his Bell 47 with every item on board carefully weighed. His equipment prudently included a pair of skis, snowshoes, ropes, ice axes, crampons and survival necessities. His aim was to try a landing on the summit at 4,807m. He was accompanied by a mountain guide, André Contamine, whose tasks were to assess the state of the snow and to lead down the pilot if the take-off from the summit failed. They landed first on the Dôme du Goûter. The weather was poor, which delayed the party coming up on foot to mark out and assist with the operations, but the pilot decided to go ahead without them as cloud threatened to envelop the summit. As it was, the wind was blowing at 25 knots and whipping up snow in the well-known summit plume. Winter conditions still prevailed with the summit ridge sharp, which threatened to make it impossible to land. However, an area just large enough for the skids was spotted and Moine put the helicopter down on it, the first landing on the summit of Mont Blanc. The temperature was –10 degrees C. Photographs were taken but the engine was not stopped and ten minutes after landing the pilot sent the instrument needles briefly into the red as he used maximum power for take-off and a brief vertical ascent before he plunged the Bell towards the valley. At 06.15, an hour after setting out, he landed at Chamonix. (Potelle, 1990)

The lift capabilities of helicopters with piston engines were, however, very limited. Assessing the performance of those that could be hired by the Swiss air rescuers before they acquired their own Bell 47G2, Richard Haller commented that:

'The few helicopters available in Switzerland were like aged dragonflies . . . taking off again around 2,000 metres was, for the pilot, a struggle, with a patient on a stretcher strapped to one of the skids and wrapped in a bearskin to afford protection on the flight to hospital . . . several times I had to return on foot or on my short skis . . . our first aid chest had the quality of a travel pack.' (Itin and Rutschmann with Odermatt, 2002, 35, 37)

The tragedy of Vincendon and Henry

Together with the limited altitude capability of the helicopters, a lack of experienced pilots trained in alpine flying contributed to the problems encountered. In the winter of 1956–57, there occurred on Mont Blanc one of the great tragedies of Alpine history in which the deployment of helicopters only worsened the situation. The gallantry of the pilot, untrained in mountain operations, though prepared to sacrifice his own life – he did, in fact suffer permanent disabilities – was of no avail. Claude Deck, who analysed the events in *L'helicoptère et la montagne* (Romet, 1990) ranked the disaster along with that of the accident that followed the first ascent of the Matterhorn, in terms of the public reactions and emotions that it produced. Perhaps one should add that it has not been equally remembered throughout the world.

On 22nd December 1956, Jean Vincendon, a 23-year-old student, who held an aspirant-guide's certificate, and François Henry, a 22-year-old Belgian student, set off from Chamonix to make a winter ascent of the Brenva Spur, first made in February of that year. At the time, difficult winter ascents were not common and the view of many in Chamonix was that those who undertook them must rely only on themselves if something went wrong. All went well at first, but on Christmas Day a storm attacked suddenly in the afternoon and they had to bivouac in a hurry, a hundred metres below the Col de la Brenva. Close by were the famous Italian climber, Walter Bonatti, and his friend, Silvano Gheser, a lieutenant in the Italian mountain corps, who had turned aside from another route when the weather had looked uncertain. They all suffered a frightful night and in the morning Bonatti climbed down to the others and they agreed to rope-up all together. They gained the upper slopes around 4,300m and decided to aim for the Vallot hut, although this meant gaining more height and crossing the summit of Mont Blanc. On the easier slopes they separated into two ropes but later, in darkness, Vincendon and Henry fell behind without the knowledge of the Italians. Bonatti's companion was suffering from frostbitten feet and Bonatti concentrated on getting him to the refuge.

Bonatti could only expect Vincendon and Henry to follow them in, but to his amazement he realised eventually that they must have decided to bivouac again. The following morning, after a bitter night in the Vallot hut, Bonatti knew they could not go back to search. Gheser's feet were so swollen that he could not even get his boots on. Bonatti contrived some foot coverings to enable them to start out and the conditions caused him to decide to descend by the normal route of the Italian side. That descent was an epic in itself, with Bonatti falling into crevasses, followed by another bivouac before they eventually were able to attract the attention of rescuers.

Meanwhile, in Chamonix, friends of Vincendon and Henry alerted the rescue services. At this time responsibility for rescue at Chamonix was divided between three bodies – the Guides Company, the military École de Haute Montagne (now the EMHM) and the École Nationale de Ski et d'Alpinisme (now ENSA) operating alternately. (Sauvy, 2005, 133) It was ruled that the mountain was too dangerous for the rescue teams to do anything. An appeal to St. Gervais was no more successful. However, the weather was fine and the friends set out for the Aiguille du Goûter. The Chamonix authorities then requested help from the military, who could provide a helicopter from the base at Bourget-du-Lac. A Sikorsky S55 took off at 12.30 and reconnoitred Mont Blanc, including the Italian side, where it was seen by Bonatti and Gheser, unfortunately without them being spotted. Another flight was made in the late afternoon but again without success. Vincendon and Henry had started to descend to the Grand Plateau, and on Friday 28th December they were seen from Chamonix to be moving down slowly, one of them falling every ten metres or so. Their friends returned, having found their route impracticable.

Another helicopter reconnaissance was requested but low cloud delayed departure from its base at around 575m (Chamonix is at 1,050m). When a helicopter did arrive, an Auster high-wing monoplane from Passy aerodrome, piloted by Firmin Guiron, was setting off and this enabled the position of the two men to be confirmed. On returning to base the observer transferred to the helicopter, which took off at 14.00. It was now found that unfortunately the two men had descended into an area of séracs which had brought them to a halt and now prevented the helicopter from landing. The helicopter returned and was loaded with supplies, which were dropped from another flight with a message to the two men to climb back up 600m towards the Grand Plateau. They made a final effort and got back up 150m to what turned out to be their final resting place, around 4,000m, where they were to suffer for another week.

The following day was fine at Chamonix but again the cloud ceiling was low at Le Fayet and not until 15.30 was a helicopter able to take-off. It dropped a tent designed for Himalayan conditions, a butane stove, a thermos of hot tea and more warm clothing, which fell close to the bivouac. On the next day, Sunday, the weather was bad with an abnormally high wind and much of the day was spent trying to extend the insurance cover for the participants of a planned ground rescue team which, eventually, at 17.00, as darkness fell, reached Plan de l'Aiguille (Dittert, 1959, 200), the upper station of the old Glaciers téléphérique.

It was not until Monday, 31st December, that the aerial rescue, on which much reliance had been placed, eventually got to the stage of two helicopters and the Auster arriving at the bivouac site. Disastrously, the pilot of the S58, trying to land 'in a cloud of snow' (Dittert, 1959, 200) with no experience of such conditions, crashed, and he and his co-pilot were injured.

The crew of a supporting S55 helicopter saw the accident and returned to base, as did the pilot of the Auster. On the way back to base the Auster passed over the rescue column led by Lionel Terray making for the Grands Mulets. The pilot cut the engine and the guide with him shouted down a message. Tragically, this was misunderstood and the rescuers turned back. When they met others coming up and learned of the mistake they turned again, and Terray and four companions reached the Grands Mulets refuge at 20.00.

Second and third Sikorsky helicopter missions set down rescuers with duvets, food and medical supplies on the Dôme du Goûter. Ice on the rotor blades endangered these flights and the batteries of the radio equipment at the Vallot hut froze up. At last, however, rescuers reached the wrecked helicopter, in which the two pilots injured in the crash and the two mountaineers had survived another dreadful night. The rescuers could move only two persons initially and made the hard decision to take the injured pilots and leave the climbers to the next day. Vincendon seemed to be already in a coma. Henry bravely wished the rescuers good luck. It took all night to get the rescued pilots to the Vallot hut.

The help of the air force Alouettes was officially requested and another Sikorsky S58 was brought in. The appalling weather continued to defeat the flyers. Hermann Geiger arrived in Chamonix with his Piper Super Cub ski-plane, with which he proposed to land near the wrecked helicopter. Geiger had had to wait for permission to land at high altitude, which at that time was contrary to French regulations. He thought he could have done so on the Grand Plateau in the first days of the drama. (Poulet and Raylat, 2001, 43) At last the weather improved and the Alouettes, which had now arrived in the area, were able to operate. It was too late for Vincendon and Henry. Not until March did a combined ground and helicopter effort retrieve their bodies. Meanwhile the pilot of the crashed Sikorsky had lost five fingers and three toes as a result of frostbite.

French mountain rescue reforms

At Passy, Guiron turned his attention to developing his skills with his ski-plane, following Thoret's studies of the mountain flying conditions described in Chapter 1. Such was the national outcry at the failure of the rescue services that the government accepted that it must act and the Minister of the Interior took over responsibility. Eventually the tasks of actual rescue work were divided between the gendarmerie, under the control of the Ministry of Defence, and the Civil Security (Compagnies Républicaines de Sécurité (CRS)).

This system was introduced in the department of the Isère in 1958 and then extended throughout the Alps and Pyrenees. In the three departments of the Isère, Savoie and Haute Savoie, there was to be synchronisation of the duties – when the CRS was responsible in one department it would also be on alert in the others, so facilitating coordination. Chamonix had separate and different arrangements because of the high number of interventions necessary and the specialist local organisations wishing to participate. From 1958 to 1972 five bodies, in rotation for fifteen days at a time, shared responsibility – the gendarmerie, the CRS, the Guides Company, ENSA (The National School of Ski and Alpinism) and EHM (the Military School of the High Mountains). Any one or all could be called out for an emergency. In 1958 almost all rescue missions were still carried out by ground teams so large numbers of personnel were needed though the potential of helicopters for rescue services was increasingly recognised.

The Chamonix rescue system was, despite the reforms, again found wanting in August 1966 when the EHM, on call at the time, failed to reach two German climbers stuck on the face of the Dru. The EHM had no less than forty climbers strung out across the mountain trying to solve the problem. A helicopter crew undertook to set down a winch on the summit but failed in its attempt. The Chamonix guide, René Desmaison, volunteered to join the rescue bid but was told he was not wanted. He went anyway and joined amateur climbers, including Gary Hemming, who had been one of the pioneers of the West Face route. They took that route and were first to reach the two men. They took them down by the same route, believing that it was better than the route preferred by the EHM team. On the way down they survived a formidable electrical storm. Hemming was treated as a hero but Desmaison was dismissed from the Guides Company. (Desmaison, 1982, 3–20) He was later involved in an even bigger controversy, as described in Chapter 7.

Further reforms led to the emergence of the Peloton de Gendarmerie de Haute Montagne (PGHM) as the main rescue service at Chamonix. The CRS was confirmed in its alternation with the gendarmerie and the availability of helicopters with improved performance facilitated the emergence of highly qualified teams. The role of the fire service, the sapeurs-pompiers, who like the CRS, come under the Ministry of the Interior, should be remembered. Added to their role in fire-fighting, they have a major responsibility for rescue work, including on all 'montagnes moyennes' (middle mountains). They have special groups, including mountain guides and volunteers in some areas and may be called on to help in the high mountains. (Poulet and Raylat, 2001, 36–39) Determining responsibility remains the task of the gendarmerie, in the mountains usually the PGHM.

As part of the improvements made after the reorganisation, new bases were set up for helicopter teams throughout France. While the first, in 1956, was at Paris, the second, in 1957, was at Grenoble. That at Annecy was established in 1964. (Frison, 1985, 12)

Getting more out of the helicopter

An example of the spectacular progress made by this time in the art of rescue by helicopter was later given prominence in a special publication, *La 'chamoniarde,'* celebrating in 1998 the history of the rescue services in Chamonix. Among the incidents recounted is one in which an Alouette crew from Grenoble achieved a remarkable rescue in the Mont Blanc massif. This was carried out by their most experienced pilot, Alfred ('Freddy') LePlus, who had piloted P47 Thunderbolt fighters, and had been among the first to demonstrate the scope for helicopter rescue work in the Alps. (Lumpert, 1973, 28) He used his skills to the full when an aspirant-guide suffered a fall on the Grandes Jorasses. He flew in with the wind and ragged clouds, which rebounded in turbulence against the barrier of the Jorasses, seeming to cling for a moment before tumbling at full speed down the Italian side. It seemed impossible to land but he saw that there was a little col between the Pointes Walker and Whymper that was almost always clear. On the southern side, the clouds were like an enormous cataract, plunging down at great speed into Italy. He used the full power of the Alouette to hold the machine stationary facing into the blast of the wind, the tail turned towards the immense wall. Then, slowly, guided by his co-pilot, who was catching only occasional glimpses of their goal, he closed the machine up against the vertical cliffs and managed to get the its tail between the steep walls of the narrow col to touch down where no one had ever before put down a helicopter. The astonished guides on the ridge moved quickly to embark their seriously injured colleague who was soon in hospital. (*La 'chamoniarde'* 1998, 38, based on an account by Lumpert, 1973)

Although a rescue could now often be made within 15–20 minutes of the call-out, the need for a landing place near the hospital at Chamonix was not easy to satisfy. Several places were used – golf course, station yard, by the ice rink and the central square, the Place du Mont Blanc – but it was evident that a permanent, specially-designed and constructed base was desperately needed. This was eventually found and established in 1965 at the present site near Les Praz and Les Bois, not far from where the first excursions were made to the Mer de Glace (then known as the Glacier des Bois) more than two hundred years earlier. (*La 'chamoniarde'* 1998, 37–39) The base became known as the 'DZ' – the dropping zone.

The Alouette III turned out to be the dream machine for the Alpine rescue services and quickly became the helicopter most in demand. With more powerful turbine engines – Turbomeca Artousta (Alouette II SA316B) or Astazou (319B) – and a bigger rotor than its predecessor, it provided significantly higher performance. It could carry six people to the top of Mont Blanc and was better adapted to the needs of the medical staff and carriage of stretchers. The rescue helicopters still, however, had to try to make a landing, often hazardous and sometimes impossible, so for a time the parachuting of rescuers from aeroplanes, roping down or simply jumping from a hovering helicopter, had to continue. Winching up a casualty to a hovering helicopter had, however, been developed for air-sea rescue and other purposes. In February 1953 during the floods in the Netherlands, Royal Navy S51 Dragonflies rescued 800 people, including 64 by winch, about 40 of them in one day. Not all the helicopters were equipped with a winch and those picked up that way normally had to secure themselves to the cable. (Winton, 1992, 44, 49) In the next chapter the application of winching techniques to mountain rescue will be described.

RAF mountain rescue teams in the Turkish Mountains

While helicopters were still of little help in difficult rescue jobs, fixed-wing aircraft continued to give substantial assistance. In April 1959 the RAF Mountain Rescue Service, a section of which had been formed in Cyprus some five years earlier, was called out to search for an Avro Tudor four-engine transport aeroplane which was carrying secret military equipment, and twelve men to deal with it, from Britain to the Woomera rocket range in Australia. It had disappeared over the Turkish mountains not far from the Soviet border en route to Bahrein. Search aircraft were deployed and six days after the crash, the wreckage was spotted from a Handley Page Hastings, the Tudor having flown into the snow-capped massif of Sûphan Dal (Mount Suphan), a peak of 4,434m (14,547ft), north of Lake Van.

It was decided to send the Mountain Rescue Team and two Land Rovers to an airfield 160 miles from Mount Suphan. Flight Lieutenant Robertson, put in charge of the operation, had the foresight to request that crampons, for which no need had been previously foreseen in Cyprus, should be sent from Britain and these were hastily obtained from Robert Lawrie, supplier of equipment to Everest expeditions, and flown out by Canberra jet. A Turkish helicopter flew over the members of the team when they were on the ascent of the mountain and dropped photographs of the wreck but these were of no help in finding the route and the only map they had was an aeronautical chart on a scale of 1:1 million – not much help in mountain ascents.

Unfortunately, the Hastings observers had thought that the best route lay over the western summit from where there appeared to be only a slight drop and rise to the eastern summit where the wreckage lay. The gap turned out to be a great rift of perhaps one thousand feet depth. Lashed by the wind, the team crossed the gap and ascended the final slopes. They then saw four other climbers behind them, these having been taken to 11,000ft by a helicopter. Unfortunately the eight men now on the mountain had only one tent and little food. They dug a shelter in the snow, a job they had been trained to do only a few weeks earlier. They were also suffering from the altitude and fatigue. More tents had been dropped by a Hastings higher on the mountain but they could not be found that night. Next day all the men were unwell but four of them struggled up a steep slope in deep snow to the wreck on the summit plateau. As expected, there were no survivors. On May 3rd a second party joined the first on the plateau. A simple burial service was held and the team destroyed as much as they could of the secret equipment with their ice axes. When they got back down to 9,000ft they sent up a green Very light, which was spotted by a villager and, as it was correctly interpreted, a helicopter picked them up.

There remained the task of demolishing the remaining secret equipment. Four men were taken by helicopter to 10,500ft on the opposite side of the mountain, as it was thought this might be a better prospect, but they had to retreat and, being on the wrong side of the mountain, it took them two days to get back to their base camp. Another six men were put down on another ridge at 12,000ft by a helicopter, one at a time because the machine could only take one passenger to this altitude. Hovering was also a problem, so the first man jumped from a greater height than usual and fortunately was not injured but it was thought that this procedure was too risky so the others were set down a thousand feet lower. The following day the Hastings emerged from the clouds and dropped three containers, thereby setting up a record for the highest altitude parachute drop at that time. The explosives that were dropped were detonated, not without difficulty and danger, because the explosives expert had failed to get to the site so there were only written instructions to help the team. Well-deserved decorations and special leave were later awarded to the group. The whole job had demonstrated the need to improve the high-altitude skills of the rescue team and this was later undertaken, including training on the Turkish mountains. (Moffat, 1964, 58–68; Card, 1993, 242–50) It also clarified the limited capabilities of the available helicopters and pilots on high mountain work.

Nine months later the need for the team's services arose again in Turkey, following the disappearance in the Taurus Mountains on 19th January 1960 of an American Martin P4M Mercator naval aircraft, carrying sixteen men. This type of aircraft was used for spy flights along hostile frontiers, so again secret equipment was on board. Nineteen RAF men, two Land Rovers and a trailer were flown to the American base at Adana, near the Mediterranean coast. Again it was one of the Hastings which located the aircraft at 9,000ft on the northern side of Karanfil Dal (Mount Karanfil), a peak of 3,059m (10,037ft). The journey from the American base was itself arduous, particularly after the team crossed the pass known as the Cilician Gate, used by the armies of Alexander the Great. Eventually they reached the remains of the Mercator, which had crashed straight into a 60–degree precipice above steep snow slopes.

Conditions were appalling with low temperatures, cloud and near-whiteout conditions. American support at this stage was limited and only the RAF team with one American enlisted man succeeded in reaching the crash site. Later, a Turkish Sikorsky helicopter transported more American troops close to the wreckage and twenty Turkish soldiers from a nearby military mountaineering school arrived. Joined by over fifty villagers, a total of eighty people were now at work. Even so, the six RAF men were asked to stay on because of their expertise and the way they coped with the conditions. They left only after the arrival of two American officers with experience in the Rocky Mountains. (Card, 1993, 251–58)

CHAPTER 6

Helicopter Rescue Comes of Age

Following the successful application of winching techniques in helicopter rescues over the sea and lowlands, the technique was soon being used in mountain situations, but at first it was practicable at only relatively low levels. In 1961 a winch was used on a Sikorsky helicopter on the east face of the Watzmann, a peak near Berchtesgaden. (MacInnes, 1980, 72) The early winches were ineffective at high altitude because of low air pressure. (Poulet & Raylat, 2001, 43) The turning point came with the development of an electric winch with a 40m reach, as compared with the 25m of the pneumatic winch. (Frison, 1985)

New technique on the Grépon

In 1967, the Chamonix rescuers were ready to try the new methods on a high and difficult peak. On 7th August a climber fell on the Grépon (3,482m) and suffered a broken leg and head injuries. A rescue team reached the accident site but realised that it would be difficult and dangerous to get the casualty down from the peak to the glacier, which in any case was extremely crevassed. The leader of the team had worked with the Sécurité Civile pilots on the development of winching methods and radio contact led to the decision to try out the new technique. A helicopter was despatched and hovered 20m above the casualty. The pilot lowered the cable and the casualty, prepared by the rescuers on the mountain, was made secure for the lift. In the streets of Chamonix, watchers who had been surprised to see the Alouette hovering above the Grépon, were now astonished seeing an object rising towards the helicopter. There were anxious moments while the casualty was got into the cabin but minutes later the rescued climber was in hospital. Henceforth, providing weather permitted, long, dangerous and painful manual carries could be avoided, even from peaks where the helicopter could not land. (Poulet and Raylat, 2001, 60)

The experience of being rescued by winch from an extreme situation has been graphically described by Joe Simpson in *This Game of Ghosts*. He and Ian Whitaker were attempting to follow Walter Bonatti's solo pioneering route on the Dru when the part of the pillar on which they were preparing to bivouac broke away. They were left hanging on to a rope that they had fixed as a handrail, their two climbing ropes cut to pieces by falling rocks and their boots and other equipment lost in the collapse of the ledge. They could climb neither up nor down and had too little rope to abseil. They were twelve hours hanging on to the handrail, feeling a shock of fear whenever it moved and suffering agonising cramps as their harnesses cut into their thighs and waists. Fortunately the flashing of their torches in the night led to a helicopter setting out. On the way, however, the team rescued two other climbers, a guide and his client, both partly paralysed after rocks had fallen on them while they were retrieving abseil ropes. This rescue had taken nearly seven hours. At last the two British climbers saw a helicopter hovering in front of them and a man was lowered on a 'silk thin wire.' Four more followed, the team being deposited on the summit.

The team fixed up a hand-operated Troyes winch which enabled one of the rescuers, Yves, to descend over the overhanging granite roof to where Simpson and Whitaker were clinging on, fearfully watching the peg on which they depended gradually working looser. Simpson described how first Yves took the injured Whitaker on his back up over the overhangs, secured him on a ledge, then returned for Simpson. (Simpson, 1993, 160–166) Once both men were on the ledge, Yves called in the helicopter. He attached Whitaker to the cable and, wrote Simpson:

'As soon as he felt the cable tighten and begin to lift he twisted round and, with a violent swinging movement, hurled Ian out into space . . . With Whitaker safely aboard the helicopter, he turned to Simpson: "Salut!" he yelled, as he hurled the protesting climber off the ledge and grinned as a stream of obscenities came back to him.'

Simpson tried to climb up the wire to the metal ring intended as a handgrip to stop a lifted person from falling backwards, but had to give up:

'The Nant Blanc glacier spun giddily below my feet. There was a fall of some four thousand feet beneath me. I stared up the wire . . . I shut my eyes and didn't open them until I was sprawled on the floor of the helicopter.' (Simpson, 1993, 166–7)

Winching is now routinely employed by all specialist helicopter rescue operators in mountainous terrain as well as maritime and sea-cliff situations, when a landing is judged to be not practicable and there is no other way of getting quickly to the casualty. It remains, however, a potentially hazardous technique like others that will enter into the description of operations in the following chapters.

The Chamonix system today

Visitors to Chamonix today will note that some of the helicopters seen frequently over the valley and the mountains are blue and others red. These are the machines of the two rescue services referred to above – respectively, the Air Section of the Gendarmes, carrying the letters PGHM, and the Sécurité Civile. The two alternate the helicopter service, week by week, covering every day of the year throughout the 24 hours. Haute Savoie is divided into two areas – the Mont Blanc massif and the rest – mainly comprising the mountain areas to the west. When the blue helicopters are covering the massif, the red ones are working over the other areas from their base at Annecy.

In the late 1960s, rescues by the French services in the Mont Blanc area fluctuated around 100 per year. By 1975 the number had jumped to over 200, by the late 1980s it had surpassed 400. From 1994 the figures for the whole of the Department of Haute Savoie were grouped together and exceeded 800. In 1997 the unit's rescue missions rose above 1,000 and 1,281 persons were rescued. After following the usual pattern of slight declines, the total rose again to 1,140 in 2000. After little change in 2001 (1138) and 2002 (1182), the number shot up in 2003 to 1,497.

In 1997 there were 80 fatalities, 6% of the individuals involved, but there would have been many times that number had it not been for the helicopter rescue service. Indeed, in an analysis when there were about 600 rescues per year, earlier in the 'helicopter era,' Dr. Bernard Marsigny of Chamonix hospital had found deaths prior to the arrival of the rescue missions amounted to 9% of those brought in. Moderate injuries, such as fractures and dislocations, were found on 71% of the victims, with 8% unharmed. (Poulet & Raylat, 2001, 93)

'The most remarkable helicopter rescue in the Alps'

Few people have been more involved in mountain rescue or written more widely about it than Hamish MacInnes. In 1999 there occurred the accident leading to the rescue by the PGHM, helped by a private helicopter operator, that led to what MacInnes judged to be 'possibly the most remarkable helicopter rescue ever conducted in the Alps.' (MacInnes, 2003, 7) Organised by Blaise Agresti, the PGHM rescue co-ordinator, members of the gendarmerie risked their own lives repeatedly and also sought help from Chamonix Mont-Blanc Helicopters, operators of a powerful Lama helicopter. This company is constantly involved in transport and supply work, tourist flights and other operations and joins in rescue work when required, including the all-important intervention in avalanche situations.

On Monday, 24 January 1999, two experienced British climbers, Jamie Andrew and Jamie Fisher, set off to climb the North Face of Les Droites, overlooking the Argentières glacier.

After good progress they continued confidently the next day, though a snowstorm arrived as forecast about 14.00. This turned out to be an unexpectedly severe storm with winds that soon rose to over 130km/hr and temperatures far below zero. Desperately, the two climbers fought their way to the *brèche*, only the narrowest of resting places, a mere notch in the ridge with precipitous drops on either side but there they had to stay, descent in the heavy snow being out of the question. The PGHM was alerted and seized the first chance to send up an Alouette III. They located the pair and immediately tried to winch down a rescuer but the wind of almost 150km/hr prevented him from reaching the climbers, though he got to within some five metres of them. After several attempts, with the helicopter thrown around by the vicious updraft, they had to abandon the attempt. They turned to CMBH whose Lama, which was not only more powerful but, with a lighter body and a framework-type rear fuselage, was able to cope better with the wind, and Pascal Brun, a civilian pilot, took aboard the PGHM rescuer to try again. Unfortunately the result was the same and then the clouds swept in again and nothing more could be done until there was another clearing. (Andrew, 2003, 86–7, Agresti and Andrew, 2003, 8)

As soon as the clearance came, Corrado Trucher, Brun's colleague, brought back specially from a trip in Italy, took the Lama up again and, making no attempt to hover at the *brèche*, deposited the rescuer on the ridge from where he abseiled into the gap. A quick examination revealed, unfortunately, that Fisher had died so he turned to Andrew and gave him hot tea then secured him to the rescue harness. The helicopter came in and again did not hover but swept by trailing the line. Andrew's saviour deftly caught the karabiner as it swung past and clipped it to the harness. Andrew had only about two seconds to brace himself before a 'stomach-lurching jerk' whisked him into the air and away to hospital. (Andrew, 2003, 97–99) After months of pain and rehabilitation he was eventually able to return to Chamonix, to be taken by Truchet in the same Lama (inside this time) to see the scene of his imprisonment and eventual rescue. (Andrew, 2003, 258–9)

Amazingly, despite the amputation of frost-bitten limbs, Andrew learned to climb again and participated in other demanding activities, including running the full 26–mile London Marathon.

In 1999 about 40% of those rescued by the PGHM were skiers, 26% were from mountaineering parties, 19% were walkers, and 7% parachutists. The remainder (938) included canyonists and mountain cyclists, and victims of avalanches, such as the disaster at Montroc in February 1999. In his earlier work, Dr. Marsigny had found that mountaineers had accounted for the much higher proportion of 45%, balanced by the lower figure of 15% walkers and 35% skiers and 5% parachutists. One-third of the victims were from abroad. The rescues tend to be at peak levels in July (there were 167 in July 1999) or August, but with secondary peaks in January and March, reflecting the large number of skiers at those times. (PGHM leaflet, 2000) Dr. Marsigny found a peak late morning when parties were returning from excursions, and another late in the afternoon, as skiing was ending for the day. He also found that most of the fatal accidents were caused by stonefall and avalanches, occurring especially in long couloirs. (Poulet & Raylat, 2001, 93) The one on the Aiguille du Goûter on the normal Mont Blanc route is notorious.

A PGHM officer told the author in 2004 that it was considered that the advent of the mobile telephone had led to an increase in the number of missions. He believed that many climbers and walkers were now able to call for helicopter help in circumstances from which they would otherwise have had to try to extricate themselves, depend on others for assistance, or simply wait much longer for help. Knowing that they can so easily call on the rescuers means also that many will venture on expeditions and take risks that they probably would not previously have done and for which they are not adequately prepared.

Despite all this, the main French mountain rescue service remains basically free, including to off-piste skiers. The PGHM are frequently called out to skiers in the Vallée Blanche on Mont Blanc which is a zone in which many problems occur because downhill skiers take the cable car to the top station at the Aiguille du Midi from where they can enjoy a long and exciting run down. This is, however, a high mountain environment and many who undertake the descent lack adequate skill and training and the gendarmerie and civil security helicopters are often involved.

In 2002 new legislation was passed, making it the responsibility of the prefects of departments and communes to decide whether charges should be imposed for their services in rescuing people engaged in sporting and leisure pursuits. Jean Faure, Senator-Maire of Autrans (Isère) who initiated the legislation, argued that small communes should not have to bear the rising costs of rescue work. The argument in favour of charges was that most mountaineers and virtually all skiers had insurance cover and it was therefore unreasonable that the costs should fall on the public purse. This measure was strongly resisted by organisations such as the French Alpine Club although the Club did, in fact, have an excellent and inexpensive cover in place for its members. Bernard Mudry, president of the club, spoke out fiercely against the new law in *Alpinisme et Randonée* in the autumn of 2003 (No. 24, Sept/Oct). He was supported by Bruno Pelicier, president of the national syndicate of mountain guides, and many others. Chamonix insisted that it would adhere to the principle of free rescue, including off-piste skiing, whereas at Val d'Isère the new law was welcomed.

In 2004 the Alouettes of the Gendarmerie were replaced by Eurocopter EC145s and a similar changeover followed for the Sécurité Civile. The EC145 is a much larger machine and has two engines and therefore meets new regulations restricting the flight of single-engine machines over built-up areas. The new helicopter is also faster, so enabling casualties to be got to hospital more quickly. The higher power available means that full loads can be taken to greater heights. Its larger fuselage permits eight people to be carried, hence more casualties can be taken inside. Less juggling is needed as to which personnel (rescuers, doctor, casualties) can be carried on any one flight in addition to the pilot and winch operator. Ideally on each mission there are two gendarmes qualified in mountain-rescue who must be registered high mountain guides and a specialist doctor from either the rescue service or the École Militaire de Haute Montagne. Some of the doctors are also certificated mountain guides and expert skiers. The greater load capability almost completely avoids the need, previously encountered, to leave a rescuer behind on the mountain to enable seriously injured persons to be taken without delay to hospital. It is also practicable for two persons to descend together on the winch cable, which is 90m long – more than twice the length of the cable used on the Alouette and nearly four times the length of the original 25m cables.

Over 90% of rescues in the French Alps are now carried out by helicopter. The long and wearisome caravan of the overland rescue team still has to be resorted to when weather conditions make helicopter operations impractical. The final decision on whether a flight can be undertaken rests always with the pilot.

Recent developments in Switzerland

Rega, the Swiss Air-Rescue Service, the formation and early days of which have been described earlier, plays a central role in the organisation and control of mountain rescue and other rescue work in Switzerland as well as operating abroad. The name is made up from the initials of the German and French words for aerial rescue organisations – Rettungsflugwacht and Guard Aerienne. It was transformed into an independent foundation in 1979, adhering to the principles of the Red Cross with which it has always been closely linked, assisting in saving life and health of anyone in need of its services, without discrimination. It is non-profit-making, but it relies on income from payment for its services (mainly met from insurances), subscriptions and donations. The head office and operations centre is at Zurich-Kloten Airport. There are 41 radio stations in a country-wide radio network for the control of rescue work and anyone can request assistance by telephoning an emergency number – 1414 – at any time.

Rega has twelve helicopter bases distributed through Switzerland with another operated by a partner organisation. Of Rega's own bases, eight are classed as mountain bases with those at Wilderswil, near Interlaken in the Bernese Alps, and Samedan, near St. Moritz, the two most involved in mountain rescue operations. In Canton Valais (Wallis) special arrangements have been made, authorising the private firms, Air-Glaciers and Air Zermatt to be permanently responsible for rescue work. They have helicopters dedicated to this purpose always on standby, matching Rega's provisions elsewhere.

Rega has made a point of keeping up with the latest technical developments. By 2004 Rega helicopters were equipped with an electronic anti-collision device called FLARM. This gave optical and acoustic warning of other aircraft in flight, provided they were similarly equipped. It also warns of cables and other obstacles. Because it is small and light it can be fitted to gliders. Together with GPWS (Ground Proximity Warning System) it greatly increased safety in flight. (Rega, *1414* No. 64, June 2005) Rega has also utilised night vision goggles (NVG) for many years. Recent versions amplify light sources 20,000 times, so although the images are in green monochrome, the pilot can see around him almost as if it were daylight. (Engesser and Kurz, 2002, 15)

In 2010 Rega's fleet comprised six Eurocopter EC145 and eleven AgustaWestland Da Vinci machines (replacing the Agusta A109K2 helicopters selected in 1989) together with three Canadair CL-604 Challenger jet ambulances. The DaVinci was specially developed to meet Rega's requirement for a rescue helicopter capable of high-altitude missions with specialised medical treatment in flight. It has state-of-the-art avionics, including a dual duplex four-axis digital Automatic Flight Control System (AFCS) with Flight Management System, 3D Synthetic Vision and Terrain Awareness Warning System (TAWS). It is also equipped for the use of NVG and for single pilot Visual Flight Rules (VFR) operations. (Rega and Agusta-Westland communications)

The number of rescues carried out has risen year by year.

From 526 in 2000 the number of mountain rescues of climbers and walkers increased to 807 in 2009. Callouts to winter sports accidents rose from 1,226 in 2000 to 1,714 in 2008 and were 1,424 in 2009. In addition Rega sent out helicopters to mountain farms 1,056 times in 2000, and 1,116 times in 2009. To appreciate the scale of Rega operations as a whole, there were in 2009 14,013 interventions of all kinds, including ambulance flights, as compared with 11,895 in 2000. (Rega statistical report)

The work of a Rega rescue pilot was described by Giorgio Wedtgrube. He joined their staff in 1964 and went to Rega's newly formed Locarno base in 1980, where by 1993 he had carried out more than 3,000 rescue missions. He began his book with a tribute to his colleagues and his family for their acceptance of his turbulent way of life and his many sudden departures in the middle of the night with no knowledge of where his flying would take him or when he would return. His recognition of the stresses faced by the families of all mountain rescue pilots, crews and doctors is pleasing to see expressed specifically. (Wedtgrube, 1997)

Rega has produced its own lavishly illustrated account of its operations, describing examples of the range of work it undertakes. (Engesser and Kurz, 2002)

Air-Glaciers and Air Zermatt are responsible for Canton Valais (Wallis), covering Mont Blanc, the Matterhorn and other frontier ranges. Air-Glaciers was founded on 1st August 1965 by Bruno Bagnoud, Jacqueline Panchard and Herman Geiger. Geiger, whose mountain rescue and other exploits with fixed-wing aircraft have been described in the previous chapter, had quickly come to recognise the advantages of the rotary-winged machines and to become proficient as a helicopter pilot. The creation of Air-Glaciers followed an incident in 1963 when an aspirant-guide fell and broke a leg while on a course in the Aiguilles Dorés area. Geiger was called out and arrived over the accident site but, after overflying the prepared area twice, flew away. The injured man had to be carried down with considerable difficulty, and pain for the casualty, on an improvised

111

stretcher, to the Orny refuge where Geiger was waiting with his Bell 47, and at once flew the injured man to hospital in Sion. Bruno Bagnoud was on the course and could not understand why Geiger had not landed at the prepared place on the glacier. Geiger explained that it was because of the gusty föhn conditions which made neither a hover nor a landing feasible. When Bagnoud pointed out that a helicopter had been put down over a thousand metres higher on Mont Blanc, Geiger replied "Ah, but that was a helicopter of the Alouette III type, with a turbine engine and a much higher performance." For that machine there was no money immediately available at Sion but Bagnoud persevered and eighteen months later Air-Glaciers was formed. (Air-Glaciers, 2002) Year by year the number of rescues carried out by Air-Glaciers increased and exceeded 1,200 in 2000, and 1,800 in 2008. (Air-Glaciers website 2011)

Air Zermatt was founded on 1st April 1968 with just one helicopter, entirely devoted to rescue work. The Jet Ranger flew its first rescue mission fourteen days later. In the same year an Alouette III was acquired. The Alouette was the first helicopter in Switzerland to be equipped with a winch for rescue purposes. Three years later an epoch-making winch-rescue was carried out on the north face of the Eiger. (Air Zermatt 2001, 26) Two German climbers, Peter Siegert and Martin Biock, ran into increasing problems. The climb was delayed while Siegert descended to replace crampons lost when a rucksack was dropped hauling it up at the Difficult Crack. (MacInnes, 1980, 73–4) Then, when they bivouacked, the climbers discovered that their stove had been damaged when the rucksack had been dropped. Despite this they carried on but at Death Bivouac they were pinned down by bad weather. It snowed all day on Saturday, 11th September and the temperature fell to –5 degrees C. Shouts and signals for help alerted the rescue services. A weather forecast caused a planned air rescue attempt on the Sunday to be postponed but, in a mist-free patch of 50–100m, Gunter Amann flew a Lama to within two metres of the wall and, despite the two men having descended two rope-lengths towards the Second Icefield to a place which was actually more difficult

112

for the rescue, a guide was lowered to a minute stance. They lifted out the two climbers, one at a time. (MacInnes, 1980, 74; Stangier, 1981, 1982 (Fr.) edn. 170–7; Anker, 2000, 220)

This was the first winching operation to make a rescue directly from the Eiger North Face. The technique had been demonstrated the previous year during the Second International Helicopter Symposium at Grindelwald. With Siegfried Stangier as pilot and Beat Perren as winchman, the guide Hans Kaufmann had been lowered to five different places on the wall.

Six months later another rescue was carried out on the Eiger, also from near the top of the Second Icefield. Four Czech climbers, including Sylvia Kysilkova, who hoped to be the first woman to make the climb in winter, had been six days on the face. After four days, with clothing and equipment wet through after the first bivouac, they were still only in the middle of the wall and two of the climbers gave up and descended. Sylvia and Jiri Smid continued, but on the sixth day, exhausted and lacking food, they were unable to continue, despite better weather. Fritz von Allmen was watching the situation and alerted the rescue forces.

The only pilot stationed at Interlaken was on leave so Siegfried Stangier flew the Lama in from Zermatt. Üli Roth, a young Grindelwald guide, undertook the descent. Hans, the winchman, equipped him with a new radio that would transmit on voice-activation and so left both hands free, a marked advantage in the Eigerwand conditions. Stangier wrote that the rescuer, as he descended, looked like a combination of extreme climber and Second World War bomber pilot. His helmet was high on his head because the earphones prevented it being positioned properly, the mouthpiece around his neck like a dog-collar, the antenna projecting from the left side of his head and numerous wires, plus, of course, all his climbing equipment, because it was impossible to know when he could be picked up. (Stangier, 1981, 1982 [Fr. edn. 172–3]) It was the second rescue from the Nordwand and the first in winter conditions. In 1975, two aspirant–guides were rescued direct from the northeast wall of the Piz Badille (3,307m) in the Bernina Alps, in exceptionally difficult conditions. (Air Zermatt, 2001, 27)

113

In the same year, Gunter Amann flew the first night winch rescue mission to the Engelhörner in extremely bad weather with heavy snowfall. In the winter of 1972, another 'first' in worldwide helicopter rescue was the evacuation of 72 passengers from a stranded cable car on the Schilthorn, 240m above the mountainside. In 1973 the practice of carrying medical staff on rescues was introduced. (Air Zermatt, 2001, 26)

By 2003 the Air Zermatt fleet numbered eight helicopters, with ten pilots, undertaking a variety of work. In addition to three AS315 Alouettes and three AS350 Ecureuils (Squirrels) there were three SA315B Lamas. The eighth machine was an EC135T2 which could carry seven passengers on taxi flights. (Air Zermatt, 2003) Their first heliport was built in 1968 on a prominent rock outcrop on the north side of Zermatt. Three or four helicopters were based there, one being always reserved for rescue work. In 1980, a new maintenance base and head offices were opened at Raron. Small bases are also maintained at Sion and Gampel.

In 2001 the firm opened an Alpine Rescue Centre to provide training courses for both professionals and amateurs in the fields of emergency medical treatment and rescue operations. Courses were also offered in other fields related to skiing and snowboarding, such as avalanche dangers. In 2004 Air Zermatt flew a record number of rescue flights – 1,496. In February 2004 the firm reached 25,000 rescue missions since its beginnings in 1968. (*Walliser Bote*, 21 June 2005) Techniques are continually refined and winching operations include long-line work with up to 220m of rope to deal with particularly difficult locations.

The success of modern developments in helicopter rescue can be illustrated by the decreased rate of deaths from mountain accidents despite immense increases in the number of participants in climbing and other mountain sports. Thus, in the case of the Matterhorn, with hundreds of people now setting out on the ascent on many summer days, the statistics showed in 2006 that there had been 427 fatalities since Edward Whymper and his party were the first to reach the summit in 1865, when five fell to their deaths in the descent. Ninety-eight years passed before the death toll among those who undertook the climb had risen to one hundred, but the second one hundred deaths occurred in only 15 years as the boom in climbing in the 1960s and 70s brought ever-increasing numbers of climbers to the mountain. The third one hundred to pay with their lives did so within another ten years. By then, however, vast strides had been made in mountain rescue with the aid of the helicopter and thirteen years – to 2001 – passed before fatalities topped the 400 mark.

Other operators cover other areas, in collaboration with Rega; for example Air Bohag, based at Wilderswil near Interlaken, is primarily responsible for rescue operations in the Bernese Oberland. The firm has frequently provided its powerful Lama helicopter for work elsewhere.

Avalanches and rockfalls

In any winter a substantial number of missions are flown throughout the Alpine regions to rescue and evacuate victims of avalanches and to provide food, medical aid and reconstruction supplies. In the winter of 1999 there were exceptionally heavy falls of snow across the Alps from Savoy to the Tirol. In addition to many communities being cut off and deprived of electricity, many lives were lost. More than 10,000 people were evacuated by helicopters. From Galtur in the Tirol alone, 1,800 people were evacuated and helicopters were sent by German, French, Swiss and American military and civil operators to supplement the Austrian rescue teams. Throughout the Alps avalanches continued to fall and there were times when the helicopters could not operate, not only because of low cloud but also because all rescuers were themselves at risk from the avalanches that could be set off by the rotors and noise from the turbines. Numerous reconnaissances were carried out and in the course of one of these, tragically, on 28th February, a Lama collided with a cable and the three persons on board were killed. On one day sixteen civil and four military helicopters were deployed in the Bernese Oberland alone. Throughout

115

Switzerland, nine military Super Pumas and a similar number of Alouettes rescued around 4,500 civilians. (*Helico Review*, No 42, May 1999)

Winter and spring are the seasons when avalanches are most to be expected, with snow the main threat. Summer and autumn often have rockfalls brought on by severe storms and particularly heavy rainfall. Mid-October 2000 was particularly bad. Numerous villages suffered damage, some road communications also being temporarily blocked. An immense rock avalanche struck Gondo in the Simplon Pass at about 10.30 on the morning of Saturday, 14th October. The scale of the disaster was enormous. Villagers themselves did what they could to help the injured and within the hour a helicopter had flown to the village from Zermatt with the first rescue team. They would never forget the scene of destruction amid the mountain of debris, rocks, mud and snow, with torrents of water pouring down the cliffs. At midday, it was practically dark. The scene prompted the thought that this must be what the end of the world might be like. All available resources were mobilised. In sodden clothing the rescuers toiled until they were utterly exhausted.

Next day they started again at 04.30. Two Army Super Pumas joined the Lama in bringing in heavy equipment. A civil helicopter pilot from Italy disregarded attempts to keep the skies free for the emergency work and landed with a reporter and camera team. The rescuer in charge, Bruno Jelk, pointed out forcibly that they were endangering the essential helicopter traffic. The searchers did not give up hope of finding more survivors until 18th October. Casualties were evacuated to hospital, while rescue, medical, engineering and other staff were flown in along with food and other requirements. The emergency work lasted a full week, restoration and rebuilding many months. Unfortunately there were fifteen deaths, thirteen of them in Gondo. (Gauderon, 2006, 114–21) In all, eight helicopter companies and the Swiss Air Force deployed 18 helicopters.

Other countries have tended to follow the Swiss or French approach to the provision of aerial rescue services. The Italians realised that they had lagged behind during the 1960s, although their military helicopters carried out a substantial number of rescues. Their base at Linate was too far from the main area of activity and the helicopter crews lacked specific training in air rescue techniques, though there was close collaboration with the Chamonix gendarmerie and the Swiss organisations. The French and Swiss Alouettes provided the necessary help with the most difficult and high-level rescues. Following the opening in 1970 of a new heliport at Pollein, which was provided with appropriate hangars and offices and six Agusta Bell 205 helicopters, intensive training was introduced. The Italian service accordingly improved, but, while its military helicopters had ample power and plenty of interior capacity, they lacked the advantages of the Alouette III, which, with its low-diameter rotors and short fuselage, could get into extremely difficult and restricted places. (*Il Soccorso Alpino Valdostano/Le Secours Alpin Valdotain*, 2002, 40–41)

In 1975, the Unione Valdostana Guide di Alta Montagna (UVGAM: Union Valdôtaine des Guides de Haute Montagne) was made responsible for the 'Soccorso Alpino Valdostano' (SAV: Secours Alpin Valdotain). The first director of the SAV, Franco Garda, enthusiastically recorded the development of a 'mountain rescue triangle' of French, Swiss and Italian services, cooperating in the study and comparison of rescue techniques and equipment. He also spoke of his great satisfaction in finding acceptance by the mountain guides of the pilot's place as 'premier de cordée' in helicopter operations. The authorities decided that the military helicopters should be withdrawn from the service in 1984 and the regional administration engaged the civil firm 'Elialpi' to carry out the tasks. (*Il Soccorso . . .*, 2002, 48–49)

Sometimes complicated frontier situations arose. On one occasion an Italian climber fell on the Kuffner arête on the Italian face of Mont Blanc. A French Alouette lifted out the casualty. Sadly, he died on the way to Chamonix. His body was repatriated through the Mont Blanc tunnel. At the Italian frontier post an inspector, newly arrived from Rome, was confronted by the problem of dealing with a deceased Italian,

117

injured in Italy, picked up from Italian territory by a French aircraft, which deposited him in France from where the corpse was returned by road. The officer in charge of the carabiniers at Courmayeur was, however, equal to the intricacies of the task to secure the release of the sad cargo from customs. (Sabittoni and Halet, 1982)

Complications also arise owing to the different methods of charging for rescue work since some countries and some organisations charge for rescue and others do not. Excellent insurance schemes do exist at moderate premiums. However, a person starting out from a country with free rescue services may not have arranged insurance cover, yet may cross a border or in some other way require rescue from a service which expects payment. The rescue teams and helicopters will in any case go out immediately, taking the chance that payment may or may not be forthcoming. Relying on state-provided services may also cause problems if it happens that a private operator answers an emergency call, and this can arise particularly when the rescue services are under pressure, but again the code is positive – the rescue takes first priority, finance is sorted out later.

CHAPTER 7

Will the Helicopter Come?

It is not surprising that even in relation to areas where helicopter rescue is fully organised, the *International Mountain Rescue Handbook* contains cautionary notes: 'The helicopter has come to stay, but its advent should be accepted with caution.' There are certain conditions when helicopters cannot operate or the aircraft's capabilities are restricted, such as dense clouds, fog, icing, severe winds and turbulence. In Britain, deployment of RAF and RN helicopters on non-military incidents is necessarily dependent on availability. Hence, local rescue units 'must not be run down . . .' (MacInnes, IMRH, 1998; 159) Even when a helicopter is expected, a rescue team must continue to make preparations in case it fails to arrive.

British Columbia, where one of the first helicopter-assisted rescues took place, as referred to in Chapter 5, has vast areas of mountain ranges and wilderness areas where the helicopter has made possible rescues on a scale formerly impracticable. In the 1990s over 6,000 air rescues were carried out annually. (Ward et al, 1995, 535) Fixed-wing aircraft continue to provide many evacuations, often taking advantages of the possibilities for alighting on lakes or glaciers. The floatplane has never lost its role in the back areas throughout Canada since the craft of the bush pilot first became a growth industry between the two world wars.

Combined forces in the American Cascades

Inevitably there are sometimes delays in any area when there are too many calls for the available services to handle simultaneously, exacerbated when aircraft become unserviceable. After a fall in the Cascade Mountains 38-year old Peter Potterfield, had all too much time to wonder whether help would come in time to save his life. Potterfield's companion had gone for help, leaving him in great pain on a tiny ledge below an overhang, with a wonderful view but little else to recommend it. He had a disappointment when a light helicopter flew up, executed some manoeuvres and flew away. He was not to know that this, the county helicopter, had then become unserviceable, but from what followed it would seem clear that the task of rescuing him was far beyond that crew and their limited resources. As he longed for dawn he saw a glow in the sky, but it was in the south, not the east, and later he learned that it was a forest fire burning out of control.

With the dawn, Potterfield became terrified of the coming of the sun, which had roasted him the day before and he was already in desperate need of water. He could not understand the delay, but perhaps it was as well that he did not know that there was a major rescue operation out beyond the logging road, involving 25 climbers and professional rescuers including the Red Cross, the US Forest Service and two military teams. After more hours of suffering and despair had been added to those of the previous day and night, he saw movement on the glacier, some 1,500ft below and a mile or two away. He distinguished three figures slowly trudging up the slope. He could see that they were climbers but calculated that it would be no earlier than 14.00, twenty-four hours after his last drink, before anybody would get to him – always assuming they were rescuers and not just heading for another climb.

Then suddenly came the 'heavy, percussive sound of a big helicopter.' (Potterfield, 1998, in Miller, 2001, 349) Out of a burgeoning cloud of dust climbed a large helicopter, heading directly for him. 'The whop and slap of its rotors grew rapidly to a deafening racket as it flew towards me at an impressive speed.' He recognised it as a 'Huey' [Bell UH-1B], the standard rescue helicopter used in the war in Vietnam. As it closed in he could see a red cross on a white background but otherwise it was a drab green. As it hovered close to him, he could see the pilots, visors down against the sun. They acknowledged his wave then climbed higher to examine the face above, then higher yet, then away to one side out of sight. Reverberating off the cirque walls, the noise 'became Wagnerian, loud and spooky.' After ten minutes or more it flew back down the valley, landed, then took off again and flew out of sight into the cirque. Then it returned to the valley, landed and again took-off, but this time flew away to the south, leaving Potterfield puzzled and very worried. He slumped back against the rock. Then rocks fell around him and eventually voices came from above.

The description of the procedure of rope engineering by which, eventually, climbers came down to him takes up several pages as related by Potterfield though there is hardly a wasted word. As one by one they reached him, he greedily drank the contents of their water bottles until he had consumed a gallon of the precious liquid. A paramedic began to administer what were to become, in the hours ahead, frequent injections of morphine. A metal litter was lowered close enough to him for the rescuers to ease him into it as they hung in their harnesses and then he was lowered bit by bit until – hours later – he was on a level with the top of the glacier. He overheard his rescuers saying that another helicopter had been requested but that there was growing concern that the darkness would beat them. A new group of people appeared and suggested that the stretcher be dragged over to a place where the rock met the ice to give the helicopter a better chance to reach him. The litter with its human cargo – which is what Potterfield had long felt he was – scraped on rock at the edge of the glacier. The helicopter pilot undertook to do his best but was not optimistic.

The helicopter came in – and went away yet again. Clearly it was not easy to get a big helicopter close in to that steep and difficult slope on the glacier, the light was failing and a dangerous wind blowing. Back again, however, came the Huey and as before, his carriers knelt around him to protect him from the flying bits of ice:

'The chopper sounded even louder this time, kicking up ice like crazy, the noise growing until it sounded as if it were right on top of us. The rotor wash blew like a hurricane, flapping the clothes of those around me. Over the din someone shouted, "Now!" The stretcher was jerked off the ice, and I looked up to see the open door of the helicopter, two green-helmeted crew members reaching out to take the litter. I was fairly tossed on board, sliding across the floor. The door slammed shut. Immediately we lifted off. But rather than climb upward, I felt the helicopter fall away down the valley . . . It was warm inside the Huey. I lay sideways, head toward one door, feet toward the other. . . . A minute or two before, I had been lying on a glacier not sure I'd survive. Now I lay there in the vibrating machine, on the wings of an angel, flying full speed towards salvation.' (Potterfield in Miller, 2001, 368)

As the effect of the morphine wore off the pain came back. Potterfield asked if he could sit up and look out. This was turned down. A little later they arrived at the Seattle trauma centre and the long road to recovery began. It had been no straightforward lift out to a hovering helicopter, but an almost incredible combination of technical rescue work by a dedicated team of climbers and the crew of the military helicopter.

Multiple air and ground cooperation in a classic New Zealand rescue

One of the most dramatic rescues was carried out in the Southern Alps in the early summer of 1982. Two experienced mountaineers, both rescuers themselves, were deposited on 15th November by ski-plane at Plateau Hut on the eastern flanks of Mount Cook. Mark Inglis and Phil Doole intended to make a rapid ascent of the East Ridge and took no bivouac sac, sleeping bags or cooking stove. They reached the summit ridge about 18.00 but found they could make no progress against the fierce wind from which they had been sheltered on the East Ridge. They decided to spend the night in a small crevasse. The

122

following days, however, produced no let-up in storm conditions and each attempt they made to move on ended in retreat to their shelter. By the fourth day rescue teams were waiting to move up the mountain but waiting was all they could do in the appalling conditions. On Sunday 22nd November, in a brief clearing a reconnaissance flight was made but the cloud closed in and a quick escape was necessary. The following day, the same pilot, Ron Small, managed to fly four mountaineers up to the Hooker hut in a Squirrel helicopter. As he put them down the wind was blowing at eighty knots. In the evening he flew again and a red figure was seen waving from the col. Drops were made and later there came a contact from the crevasse. 'This is Hotel Middle Peak. Mark lost feeling all toes, no food since Wednesday. Phil, two big toes frozen.' At least they were still alive and dredging up some humour.

More bags were dropped and some were lost over the edge but others landed on target and one actually hit Phil Doole. The stranded climbers now had food and sleeping bags. The winds continued unabated day after day. On Friday 27th November the RNZAF sent in an Iroquois helicopter to help ferrying in strong ground teams to attempt the climb, as it looked increasingly unlikely that Inglis and Doole could be lifted out by helicopter. As the Iroquois hovered above the ice the rotors raised a cloud of snow and the pilot lost his horizon in the whiteout. The helicopter overturned, its rear rotor hanging over a precipice. Amazingly none of the occupants was seriously injured but priority had now to be given to their rescue and fortunately Ron and his Squirrel were equal to the task. He even made an extra flight in the fading light and dropped another bag, which was retrieved by a blue-clad figure.

Ron Small now called on his friends on the west coast and they came over in their Squirrel. The next day the two helicopters flew in to a peak fortunately now in sunlight though from Mount Cook village a blanket of low cloud and snow spread eastward. Another radio had been dropped and Doole reported that he could be lifted out by the strop method but that his companion would need a stretcher. This problem called for the use of a Baumann stretcher-bag, developed by a Swiss rescuer. A large nylon bag opening its full length, it can be carried on a rescuer's hip, unpacked and the casualty rolled in while the rescuer remains attached to the helicopter strop – given adequate room and precision flying. This was achieved by Ron Small and first one, then the other, casualty was lifted out. As they landed cloud was spilling over the mountain.

Five months later the rescued pair were learning to walk on artificial lower limbs and both returned to climbing. Ron Small was awarded the MBE for his part in this and other rescues. (Inglis, 2002, Munro in MacInnes (ed) 2003)

The greatest ranges

In the Himalaya and Karakoram the growth of the tourist industry has stimulated the development of helicopter rescues. This is particularly so on Everest and the other peaks which are the objectives of so many trekkers and climbers, to deal with victims of pulmonary oedema and other high-altitude diseases and, of course, climbers and supporting Sherpas who have suffered accidents.

In the 1980s obtaining the services of a helicopter to carry out a high-altitude rescue in the Himalaya and other great ranges still posed many problems. Though more or less suitable machines, mainly military, were becoming increasingly available, and some crews were capable of operating at the extremes of altitude, terrain and weather conditions involved, rescue of climbers in distress was not their first duty. Costs and insurance to cover them were still uncertain. (Hunt and Gray, 1983, 61)

In 1986 Jim Curran, climbing cameraman on the British expedition to K2, was at base camp anxiously awaiting and watching for the return of members of his own and other teams engaged in attempts on the peak. On the morning of the 11th August he had resigned himself to the deaths of several of the climbers. A helicopter arrived unexpectedly and he hoped it would make a search. However, it soon became apparent that the colonel who jumped out was there merely to buy equipment no longer wanted by climbers. Appeals for a search, even of just the glacier area, met with no success. The colonel was annoyed because cloud prevented him from getting a good photograph; seven lives at risk appeared to mean nothing to him. The helicopter departed without help being given or promised. (Curran, 1987, 149–50)

The colonel's visit did eventually bear fruit but not immediately. In the deepening twilight, a figure emerged from the gloom, staggering and stumbling. It was Willi Bauer, who appeared to be the sole survivor of the storms that had been sweeping the mountain. Then came a porter who had gone up to fetch items from Advance Base. He had been firmly instructed to leave a tent in place but from his behaviour, Curran deduced that he had disobeyed orders and brought it down. The tent was Kurt Diemberger's and Curran knew it might have saved his life if left in place so he quickly organised a small group to go up with tents, sleeping bags and other items to replace those that had been removed. Not without difficulty in the darkness they got to the site of the camp and a little later Curran heard a noise and searched up the snow slope. There he found Diemberger, spread-eagled in the snow, weakly trying to kick in his crampons. He was helped to the tents and treated for frostbite. The descent to base camp next day was another desperate struggle. For several days Bauer and Diemberger continued to suffer from the frostbite they had incurred but were cared for as well as possible by those still at base camp and eventually a helicopter arrived and took them to civilisation. (Curran, 1987, 152–169)

As the years advanced so correspondingly did the number of helicopter rescues. A helicopter came to the rescue when Alan Hinckes, during his pursuit of being the first British climber to ascend all peaks of over 8,000m, suffered a most extraordinary accident. At Base Camp on Nanga Parbat he sneezed from the flour or dust on a chapatti crust and prolapsed a disk in his back. In agony, he could not even crawl and was stranded at 4,000m for ten days. Eventually he struggled down 700m to where a helicopter could reach him and he was flown to Islamabad for treatment, having lost 10kg. (Hinckes, 1998, 88) In the same

125

issue of the *Alpine Journal* another helicopter rescue was reported. Gimmigela on the Nepal-Sikkim frontier was the objective of a British services expedition in 1997. Roddy McArthur had fallen over an ice cliff into their Camp 3 and his survival seemed unlikely. However, a satcom call succeeded in getting a helicopter to fly to the scene and Roddy was rescued and made a full recovery. (Parsons, 1998, 132)

Conditions even at camps in the Himalaya and adjacent mountains are, however, often marginal or sub-marginal for helicopter operations and taking off near the limits of the altitude/weight-carrying capacity of the machine means that there may be no room for the medical staff that would normally accompany a patient during evacuation. On Everest, Kamler noted that the pilot picking up a seriously injured casualty said his fuel would allow only four minutes on the ground. He kept his rotors turning to avoid the risk in having to restart the engine. He threw out the patient's haversack that a Sherpa had put aboard – even that extra weight would add to the hazards. (Kamler, 2000, 105–6) In a subsequent evacuation from Camp II at 6,700m the pilot made a hazardous landing among crevasses, many of them hidden, with a bandanna tied to a ski pole making a rudimentary windsock. He took only one casualty on the first lift and ferried him over the icefall, then returned for another. From Base Camp, some 1,200m lower, it was possible to evacuate both together to Kathmandu. (Kamler, 2000, 284)

Another extreme Himalayan helicopter rescue was that of Stephen Venables in the Kumaun range in 1992. Venables was one of six British and five Indian climbers led by Chris Bonington. (Venables, 2001, 18–28) The British climbers had decided to round off the expedition by attempting the ascent of Panch Chuli V. The five Indian members of the expedition, who did not intend to attempt this hitherto unclimbed summit, were to leave a little food behind at the base camp for the British team when they came down.

The ascent posed many problems but the summit was gained, though much later than planned. With darkness approaching the climbers started on a series of abseils, accompanied by thunder and lightning. Using ice-screws until they ran out and then snow bollards, and with many problems with jammed and frozen ropes which necessitated climbing back up to free them, they struggled on down through the night. Venables took his turn at being last man down the ropes. Seconds later he was flying past the others who somehow managed to stop the fall. When he came to, it was to discover that both his legs were broken. With the aid of the others he eventually got back up the slope of some fifty degrees to a ledge and they got him into a tent and strapped up with makeshift splints.

For Bonington also it was not an easy task to hurry over fifty kilometres through the forests before he could even reach a telephone. Then came the need to use all his persuasive skills to get a promise of help from an air base some 400km away. There was no highly organised rescue service – this was not the Mont Blanc massif or the Eiger. However, the Indian Air Force agreed to make the rescue attempt. A first sortie had to turn back owing to dense cloud over the glacier – much to the disappointment of those still waiting on the mountain. The next morning, however, Squadron Leader P. Jaiswal and Flight Lieutenant P.K.Sharma were on their way again at 05.20. (Venables, 2001, 150) At 11.20 the pilot made his third approach to the glacier. The Lama was getting close to its service ceiling around 6,300m. Jean Boulet had, in 1972, coaxed one up to 12,442m. He had, however, taken out everything inessential – including the starter motor! On the descent the engine had stopped and he had had to rely on autorotation to get him back to earth in one piece. Jaiswal could not expect to hover safely at the height of the casualty, 5,600m. He swung away again from the menacing walls and reselected his approach. The waiting climbers were thinking in terms of a winch rescue but the rescuers were not equipped for that or, indeed, trained in advanced mountain rescue techniques.

The crew eased the helicopter in and pointed to the tent. Fortunately, the waiting climbers realised that the tent had to be moved so that the ledge could be used by the helicopter. In fact, Jaiswal could bring it in only until the starboard skid rested against the ledge, the tips of the rotor blades whirling to within a metre of the mountain. He was not satisfied and backed off four or five times before he finally committed himself to holding it steady at the ledge, then Sharma opened the door and shouted for Venables to get in. That was another mountain for Venables to climb – in intense pain. They all eased, pushed and man-oeuvred him until at last he was inside, screaming in agony but also in triumph. A moment later they were off, leaving the others to make their own hazardous way down. (Venables, 2001, 154–162)

There are still some areas where helicopter services are not always available. One example is Tanzania, which, like many African countries, is extremely poor and lacking in the sophis-ticated infrastructure and financial resources that would facil-itate such a service. In 2005 it was estimated that 26,000 visitors per year were attempting the ascent of Kilimanjaro, at 5,895m (19,340ft), the highest peak in Africa. This has risen over 40,000 annually. A basic rescue service is organised to meet the needs of anyone meeting with an accident or feeling ill. At that altitude there is ample opportunity for altitude-related problems and many of those who tackle this ascent are not adequately accli-matised. Fortunately, turning back and descending usually soon brings speedy relief to the sufferer but if for any reason a helicopter rescue is needed recourse to a private service is necessary. Arrangements will be made by the Tanzanian Na-tional Parks Authority in conjunction with the tour operator involved. At the time of writing (2011) the possibility of a dedicated service is being examined but trekkers should not underestimate the risks posed to those who undertake the ascent.

Where demand and money go together, the most difficult environments can be provided with rescue services, Antarctica being the prime example. A combination of helicopter and fixed-wing aircraft can normally be expected to reach accidents reported by mobile phone or satellite communication, though weather permits SAR operations only for very short periods. The American and New Zealand bases, McMurdo and Scott, collaborate and are prepared to mount a search if prearranged signals have not been received for 72 hours. Adventure Network International will also intervene as they did in 1995 when the British explorer Roger Mear, attempting the first unsupported crossing, faced serious equipment problems. His satellite call to England was relayed to ANI in Punta Arenas and they deployed a plane from Patriot Hills and the explorer's tent was spotted within two hours. (Trewby, ed. 2002, 151) Adequate insurance is obviously an essential part of every traveller's arrangements. This is also true in Greenland, another area that has become increasingly attractive in recent years to climbers who seek demanding routes and where a helicopter rescue is dependent on availability of a suitable machine from a fleet that is primarily intended for general commercial duties.

Mistaken signals on the Grandes Jorasses

A case where the rescuers came out – more than once – but rescue was tragically delayed because the helicopter crews misunderstood the situation, is described by René Desmaison. In February 1971 he and Serges Gousseault attempted a new winter route on the Grandes Jorasses. They had intended to tackle a route on the Croz Spur, previously climbed in winter, but finding another party ahead of them, turned to the new route on the Walker Spur. This was a very serious undertaking, so much so that they first went back to Chamonix to collect more equipment, including extra pitons and three ice-screws. After preparing the first pitches they retreated for a good night in the refuge, before starting up again next day. They maintained radio contact with Desmaison's wife, Simone, who kept them appraised of the latest weather forecasts, but a snow slide during the contact call put the radio out of action. Frostbite had caused Serge's hands to be very painful and he feared for them increasingly. Desmaison's hands were also in poor shape, suffering from abrasions and frostbite. Next day Desmaison suffered a fall but fortunately was able to continue leading the climb, despite prolonged snow. They struggled on through another day. A loose block fell and cut their one remaining sound rope. Desmaison reorganised the shortened ropes and led on. Gousseault was in great pain from his frostbitten hands, which made it extremely difficult for him to take out the pitons that Desmaison used to secure his lead and which were vital for the rest of the climb.

Their bivouac that night was a mere scoop hollowed out in the snow. The next day they managed to climb higher, to within around a hundred metres of the summit. This time the best that could be found for another bivouac was a foothold each, and there they perched, suspended from pitons, with no food left. The following morning, 20th February, when the storm had at last cleared, Gousseault was unable to continue. It was revealed later that he had been suffering all winter from a calcium deficiency but Desmaison had not known of this. All now depended on helicopter rescue. At 11.00 Simone made a formal request for a helicopter reconnaissance. The helicopter came up to them so close that the occupants must have understood, Desmaison thought, the plight of the climbers, but, to his astonishment, it flew away. Back in the valley they told Simone that all was well. They said that her husband had made a thumbs-up signal, which to a pilot would mean they were all right. Desmaison did not remember this though he admitted that he did not make the agreed mountain distress signal of waving an arm slowly up and down six times in a minute. This signal, he said, had never been taught when he was a Guide-Instructor. (Desmaison, 1973, 172–73; in Lewis, 2001, 249–50)

The next day was the pair's eleventh day on the face. Simone, convinced that all was not well, requested another reconnaissance. This was duly carried out. The weather was not so good and the wind was gusty. Desmaison could see that the pilot was having difficulty in controlling the machine near the face. This time, however, he did make arm signals. Again, however, the helicopter flew away and Simone was told that the climbers had waved happily. Simone was now convinced that this interpretation was quite wrong. If René was really refusing to be rescued, he must have gone mad. The next day she made an official

130

request for a rescue. Again a helicopter came, and again it went away. That evening a meeting was held in Chamonix and the pilot reported that he had tried to land on the summit but there had been serious air pockets and turbulence and the pilot and his passengers had had quite a fright. But meanwhile Serge Gousseault passed from a state of torpor through a period in which he thought he was down in the meadows to the finality of death. On Tuesday, 23rd February, there were attempts to organise a climbing team from the Chasseurs Alpins, the crack mountain troops, who were attached as instructors to the École Militaire de Haute Montagne, but this was turned down by the rescue organisation.

Then came another type of helicopter – an Aérospatiale SA330 Puma piloted by Jean Boulet, chief engineer and chief pilot of Sud Aviation, who had for some years held the world helicopter altitude record. The Puma was a much larger and heavier machine than the Alouette – designed as a military transport, it could carry up to 18 personnel. Desmaison knew it was different when he heard it approach – the beat of the rotors was heavier and different. As it had wheels it could not land on the glacier so Desmaison thought it was to drop supplies to a climbing rescue team but the pilot turned back because of the wind.

On Thursday, 25 February, Alain Frébault, a CRS pilot, and his mechanic, Roland Pin, serving in the Dauphiné region, flew from Grenoble in his Alouette. He flew over Mont Blanc and the Col du Géant, where a CRS post reported the wind conditions to him. He flew in towards the brèche between the summits of the Grandes Jorasses and put the machine down there. Then he flew to Chamonix where his achievement caused astonishment and consternation. Thirty minutes after his first touchdown on the mountain, with the guide Claude Ancey added to the team, he again put down in the brèche, took off again to prove that he could take-off loaded, then returned. Another Alouette III now came and deposited another guide, and Frébault put down Ancey. Soon there were five guides there. They climbed to the summit of the Point Walker, a hundred metres higher. From there they called down to Desmaison. Gérard Devouassoux descended by cable to Desmaison, clipped him on and lifted him to where the helicopter could collect him to take him to hospital. Only after they got him down did they tell his wife. The next 48 hours were critical but Desmaison survived. He returned to the face with Georgio Bertoner, a Courmayeur guide and Michel Claret, and, on 17th January 1973, he led up through a blizzard to complete the route. When Desmaison was able to thank Alain Frébault for his bold landing on the bréche that was the key to the rescue, he answered 'Nonsense, what I did could have been done by anyone.' (Desmaison, 1973, 199–200) Sadly, the rescue had come much too late for Serge Goussault. He is commemorated in the climb on which he lost his life, the Desmaison-Goussault route, recognised as one of the hardest in the Alps.

When weather restricts the use of a helicopter the MRTs (mountain rescue teams) carry most if not all of the responsibility.

A Cairngorm victory

The Cairngorms in the Scottish Highlands are only a third as high as the Grandes Jorasses but formidable precipices border great elevated, almost Arctic, plateaus, and offer plenty of scope in winter for advanced ice climbing. The Cairngorm Mountain Rescue Team provides the ground-based search and rescue services for the northern parts, supplemented when necessary by other teams including the RAF Mountain Rescue Teams.

On a cold New Year's Eve (Hogmanay, the most celebrated day of the year to the Scots) a mobile phone call from a narrow ledge high on a Cairngorm climb led to the MRT and a Sea King from Lossiemouth heading out into the dusk. The leader of the climb had dislodged a boulder on a part-frozen ice route and this had smashed into his father who was acting as his second.

At 15.45 the Sea King flew into the corrie but the turbulent and gusty conditions made it impossible for it to hover close

132

enough to the cliff for the rescue to be effected, so the pilot flew down the valley and picked up the Cairngorm rescue team members:

> '. . . the pilot performed a minor miracle of the flying arts by riding the wind on the lip of the corrie to lower both Team and equipment onto the plateau above the casualties.'

By 16.00 the leader on the ground had started the rescue operations. The easiest way to lift or lower a stretcher is vertically but in the case of spinal injury, which was suspected in this case, every effort must be made to keep the casualty horizontal. Double the usual number of ropes are needed and rope management is complicated. Two strong climbers abseiled down and made the casualty secure on the narrow ledge. When all was ready another rescuer went down with the stretcher, keeping it away from the wall to avoid dislodging more rocks. For fifteen minutes the three rescuers cut away with their ice axes to make the ledge a little wider. Then the stretcher was lowered, with one rescuer between it and the cliff to keep it away from the rock. This was the crux of the operation and extremely nerve-wracking for all. To help the operation flares were lit by members of an RAF MRT, who had also rushed to the spot to provide extra manpower, then the son was lowered while the father was carried down to safe ground. When the helicopter pilot again tried to fly into the corrie to lift out the casualty the weather made it impossible. He had to be carried on a stretcher all the way to the road where an ambulance was waiting. It was 23.45 before the teams stood down and too late to join families for greeting the New Year so they made the best of it at the team's Inverdruie base. (Allen with Davidson, 2009, 248–53)

SAR dogs and helicopters

Along with the human rescuers and helicopters, dogs often have an important role to play. The value of dogs to searches on the mountains and moorlands, usually in bad weather, became

133

apparent to Hamish MacInnes when he was invited to attend a Swiss Avalanche Dog Rescue Course at Davos in 1965. He was sponsored by the Scottish Red Cross. On his return he started the Search and Rescue Dog Association and the first training course was held in Glencoe the following winter. (MacInnes, 1980, 46)

Often the initial search is carried out by land rescue teams with dogs. It is now a matter of routine to take dogs to the search area by helicopter in Britain as in the Alps. They soon become used to entering the helicopter on the ground despite the noise of the engines and the rotors whirling above them. They are frequently winched aboard or lowered to the site with their handlers. The dog is put into a specially designed harness, hooked on to the cable and reassured by the handler and usually quickly becomes used to the experience. Bob Maslen-Jones, in his account of rescue work by the Llanberis Mountain Rescue Team, writes that often when out walking, the dogs hear the distinctive noise of a helicopter 'and watch the machine longingly, as it flies past.' (Maslen-Jones, 1993, 208) A bearded collie named Bobbie who won many prizes as a show dog but was equally at home on the hill with the Cairngorm MRT 'loved helicopters and used to sit with the winchman and look out of the open door.' (Allen with Davidson, 2009, 275)

Problems and disasters can occur on any mountain routes!

On some occasions the role of the helicopter has to be limited to flying in a rescue team to as close to the scene of an accident as possible and returning, if practicable, to pick up the rescued persons and, hopefully, members of the team. This restriction is particularly true in the British hills because of the high incidence of cloud cover and high winds and the belief, widespread among hillwalkers, that they can go out in almost any weather. Many are the tales of inexperienced, ill-equipped and ill-clad walkers who have come to grief on British hills in summer as well as in winter, or have been rescued only by the unquestioning devotion of the mountain rescue teams. In practice, helicopter crews as well as rescue teams composed of volunteers turn out whenever help is needed, irrespective of whether or not there is a threat to life – but it must be remembered that they may at any time be committed elsewhere.

CHAPTER 8

Mountain Rescue by the Pilots and Crews of Military Aviation

We have already seen that military aviators have played a major role in the history of aviation in the mountains, as in many other branches of flying. Army pilots and aircrews, as well as air force personnel, have loomed large throughout these pages, particularly in the field of rescue in the mountains – and here it must be remembered that the French gendarmerie are classified as military. Other service personnel have played a large part in innovation and development of techniques of general importance – such as the Swiss military officers in landings on glaciers and successes in early rescue work. Their achievements in the Alps are paralleled by the RAF and RN mountain rescue missions at home and in distant regions.

It has, of course, been the case that since the air arms of military forces were first created they have been in action whenever and wherever required and whether or not mountainous terrain has been the scene of the operations, the flying crews have undertaken the necessary and frequently very dangerous work to the best of their ability, often pushing their aircraft far beyond their design limitations.

A Pre-First World War concept of air strikes

Even before actual flying operations in the mountains entered into the prosecution of war, the possibility of using aircraft to control rebellion in colonial territories had been envisaged.

Emile Driant was a former officer who, as a civilian, wrote novels that, like those of H.G. Wells, anticipated the role that aircraft would play in forthcoming wars. In 1911, in his *Au-dessus du continent noir*, he conceived the use of an aircraft with adjustable wings and pontoons, giving it the advantages of a helicopter to land almost anywhere. It was projected as having a range of a thousand kilometres and a speed of 140km/hr. He postulated its use to attack dissident tribesmen in the mountains of North Africa. Driant returned to the army and was killed in 1916 at Verdun. (Driant, 1911, quoted by Wohl, 1994, 86–89 including illustration)

Mountain flying operations

It was, in fact, to be many decades before helicopters could attack opponents in such a manner. They did so in Malaya, Vietnam, Afghanistan and other campaigns from the middle of the 20th century, but long before that pilots were including mountain flying in their military tasks. The Spanish, Italians and French all used aircraft in their pre-First World War attacks on dissident tribesmen in the North African territories that they sought to control. Sometimes the aircraft were flying at a lower level than the rebels perched on commanding heights. There is a record of one Spanish officer in a Lohner biplane in 1913 being wounded by a bullet that entered through a shoulder and exited through his lower body but he was able to return to base.

As well as being of flimsy construction, the machines were powered by unreliable engines, which were at their best inadequate for mountain flying. The pilots had to learn as they went along, lacking in specific instruction and, indeed, commonly with minimal flying training. As the 1914–18 war raged, casualties were inevitably heavy as crashes in dangerous and inaccessible locations among peaks and glaciers were added to the toll of those shot down. Certainly this was the case with many Austrian, German, Italian and Balkan flyers in the fighting in the Alps. Some who survived became outstanding pilots in the world of post-war aviation, such as the German ace, Ernst Udet.

137

Others, including Italo Balbo, who became a general in command of the Italian air force, and Hermann Goering of the Luftwaffe, after making names for themselves during hostilities, literally talked their way up through the political scene and became dominant players in national and international affairs in the inter-war years.

The Second World War saw, of course, much more involvement of military forces in mountain areas, beginning with the German invasion of Norway and continuing with the deployment of parachute troops in other theatres of war, notably Greece and Crete. Allied aircrews had regularly to contend with the added dangers of exceptionally inhospitable mountain terrain as they flew over regions as widely separated, and as geographically contrasting as Greenland and the Arctic territories on the shortest route between North America and Europe and over 'the hump' between Burma and China. A few years later they were again often involved with mountain dangers in Korea, where helicopters proved their worth as rescue aircraft, a role to be immensely expanded by American forces in Vietnam.

Military rescue services

It was when the helicopter came into general use that the armed forces emerged as powerful agents of life-saving, far beyond their role on behalf of their own aircrews who had come to grief in crashes where helpers could not readily reach them by conventional means – in the mountains and at sea. The British services provide the perfect example. RAF rescue helicopters, like the RAF Mountain Rescue Teams, were originally conceived as providers of rapid help for military personnel but it was not long before they were authorised to afford help to civilians in life-threatening situations. It was recognised at an early stage that such work could be regarded as practice that was far more effective than training exercises in developing the skills needed by the services.

The system that developed was a mixed one in that civil helicopters were occasionally called on when there was no RAF or naval helicopter available. Firms that were servicing oil rigs and platforms in the North Sea had obvious skills in this direction, and could be drawn on for 'outside' jobs and the Coastguard was seen to have an especially valuable contribution to make. Air ambulances became common throughout the country and could handle much of the emergency transfer of patients to hospital but the rescue work that was needed in maritime disasters and mountain accidents called for special training and equipment, for which military personnel, along with the Coastguard in appropriate areas, were especially suited.

By 1963 RAF helicopters were being called out eight times as frequently to deal with civilians in trouble as they were for military purposes – in the UK on 348 occasions as compared with 45. Civilian callouts rose to 664 in 1966, with helicopters going out to 76 cases. (Air Historical Branch) The non-military callouts declined somewhat in the late 'sixties but rose again in the 'seventies as outdoor leisure activities became more popular and easier to undertake with increasing car ownership and disposable income. The Royal Navy became especially busy as holidaymakers around the coast became more ambitious in their exploration of cliffs and caves. RAF and RN callouts together topped a thousand a year.

Naval helicopters in Antarctic mountains

The Falkland War in 1982 broke new ground in the involvement of naval helicopters, normally engaged in search and rescue work around British coasts and nearby hills and mountains. They were precipitated into some of the most difficult and dangerous missions ever undertaken. In his history of the Royal Navy's search and rescue service, John Winton describes at length an operation that began as a military venture intended to initiate the freeing of South Georgia from Argentine occupation, but which rapidly turned into a desperate rescue mission.

The Mountain Troop of D Squadron, Special Air Service (SAS), was to be landed on Fortuna glacier in the north of South

139

Georgia by helicopters from the destroyer *HMS Antrim* and the Royal Fleet Auxiliary tanker *Tidespring*, a Wessex HAS3 of 737 Naval Air Squadron (NAS) and two Wessex HU5s of 845 Squadron. The latter were essentially transport aircraft with unsophisticated equipment such as the radio altimeter, which would maintain flying altitude but not position. In bad visibility, such as was to be expected on the glacier, they would have to rely on visual reference points or follow the Wessex 3. This was an anti-submarine aircraft that could fly guided by computer to a particular location and hover over it, maintaining heading, height and position. After a reconnaissance in the Wessex 3, familiarly known as 'Humphrey,' the troops were embarked in the three helicopters but they encountered a snowstorm and had to return. In a second attempt, a break in the gloom enabled Lieutenant Commander Ian Stanley to penetrate the mountains – which were 'like jagged teeth' – and up the glacier by hover-taxiing about thirty feet above the ice.

Captain John Hamilton, the SAS troop commander, was not enthused by what he saw – a deeply crevassed glacier over which the SAS would have to find their way. Lieutenant Chris Parry heard Major Chris Delves say 'Well, you've got to get on, John,' – which became a popular catchphrase on *Antrim*. 'OK. We'll do it.' said Hamilton and they returned for the troops. The weather, however, forced them back to the ship. In the afternoon they were again at their chosen spot and Stanley led the way down – nearly putting one wheel into a crevasse. Parry wrote:

'Today was not pleasant. We certainly would not have considered doing that sortie in anything short of operational or SAR [Search and Rescue] conditions . . . I've never worked so hard on the radar in my life. It's not designed for the terrain-following role which we were called upon to perform and the 30 degree blind arc through the nose doesn't help when you are running towards a mountain.'

The sixteen SAS men and their equipment were put down through the blinding, swirling snow. As 'Humphrey' took off

140

they saw that they had landed between two crevasses on an ice bridge that was rapidly disintegrating. Unfortunately, this operational flight had to be followed the very next day by a rescue mission.

During the night the weather deteriorated to a Force 11 storm. Hamilton made contact with *Antrim* and the three helicopters took off with emergency supplies but had to return. After refuelling they climbed up to the glacier bivouac and managed to land and embark the troops. Unfortunately, just after Lieutenant Mike Tidd lifted off his Wessex 5 he entered whiteout conditions in a snow squall. With no horizon, he sought a rock outcrop that he remembered to serve as a reference point but suddenly lost height and struck the glacier. The helicopter was thrown across the ice, breaking up as it went. As the squall passed, the other two helicopters took off and hover-taxied to the scene of the wreck. Fortunately there had been no serious injuries and all personnel were taken aboard, fuel being dumped to compensate for the extra weight. Unfortunately another squall caused the Wessex 3, which was leading the way, to disappear and the following Wessex 5, deprived of its guidance and reference points, touched the ice. They almost got away with it but the wind slewed them round and a wheel went into a crevasse. Remarkably, despite entanglement in the wreckage, all the occupants were got out again without serious injury. Stanley could take only his own survivors back to *Antrim*. He then took on enough fuel and blankets and made two attempts to rescue the others and narrowly escaped crashing, first into a mountainside and then on to the glacier. He had to return to the ship and wait for an improvement in the weather, meanwhile going through a period of self-analysis, asking himself if he had made mistakes but having to conclude that the weather alone had defeated them.

Lt. Cdr. Stanley was left with only 'Humphrey', the Wessex 3 helicopter, and it had only one engine and a rather poor record for reliability – Stanley himself had previously experienced two engine failures, once having to ditch in the sea off Dorset.

141

Moreover, 'Humphrey' had been five times up to the glacier in the past twenty-four hours. Before the 'sombre briefing', Stanley wrote a letter to his wife, enclosing his wedding ring. Almost subconsciously, the crew shook hands before they climbed into the aircraft. Stanley decided to risk icing and climbed to 3,000ft, 600ft above the glacier but still getting no view over the peaks. In a sudden clearance he saw the survivors and dived down to land, with the violent wind shifting every second. He realised that he could not expect to do a second trip that day and decided to cram everyone into the Wessex. All equipment was abandoned except the sidearms, which the SAS insisted on keeping. They piled twelve survivors on top of each other and Stanley took off with arms and legs projecting from Humphrey's door and windows. Three SAS men were in the sonar well and another lay with his head in the side blister while Parry sat on his chest reading the radar. The engine coped with the overloading but Stanley did not risk the usual landing approach of hovering by the ship and moving in sideways, he went straight down in a long descending slide. None of the men was injured, though all were very cold. Some had survived two air crashes on the glacier. (Winton, 1992, 206 – 212) Mountain rescue by helicopter had come a long way since the early trials in the 1940s.

Brabant Island rescue operations

Another challenge of mammoth proportions was presented to the helicopter crews stationed in the Falklands three years later. Lt. Cdr. Clive Waghorn, leader of a Joint Services Expedition to Brabant Island in the north-west of Antarctica had fallen from a snowbridge into a crevasse and suffered a broken leg. Two of 826 Squadron's Sea Kings left their anti-submarine patrols in Royal Fleet Auxiliary *Olna* to join the Wasp helicopters already embarked in HMS *Endurance*. Attempts by aircraft from the British Antarctic Survey team and a Chilean group had already failed in the face of blizzards and temperatures down to –30 degrees C. When the Sea Kings, now stripped of their normal operational equipment, got to the 8,000ft mountains of Brabant, 55 knot katabatic winds were roaring down from the peaks to join 40 knot surface winds in a maelstrom of turbulent updrafts and downdrafts. The search went on for hours without locating the tent in which Waghorn lay in great pain. On a repeat sortie, after picking up a doctor from the outpost at Minot Point – itself no easy operation – at 16.00 the tent was spotted at about 3,800ft – 1,500ft higher than had been under-stood. The turbulence, however, defeated them and they re-turned to *Olna*, dangerously iced-up and in deteriorating visibility that required radar approaches.

Next morning they picked up another doctor from Bulls Bay on the southeast coast but were beset by technical problems. Meanwhile, the camp was found by a Wasp from *Endurance* to be located between two wide crevasses on a steep slope, making a landing very precarious. The Wasp had fuel for only ten minutes left but fortunately the Sea Kings had been able to get off from *Olna* through the fog bank and were now ap-proaching. While the Wasp returned to *Endurance* on its last drops of fuel, the first Sea King flew straight in at low level and lowered a stretcher and five men from a high hover, to avoid disturbing the snow and causing a whiteout. Then cloud came in and forced them to climb and orbit while waiting for another clearance. When this occurred the rescue of all the men was completed. The approach to the *Olna* was made in thick fog and the ship was rolling more than ten degrees each way but the landing was successfully achieved. As they returned to the Falklands, the Sea Kings went ahead to take Waghorn and his colleagues to hospital. Even then one of them had to make a diversion and an emergency landing because of an oil leak. As with the South Georgia rescue operation, these missions were recognised by well-deserved awards and must be rated among the boldest and most professionally executed of rescues, despite the crews not being experienced in mountain rescue. (Winton, 1992, 252–254)

143

RAF rescue on Kinabalu

On 15th March 1994 the RAF Mountain Rescue Service was called on to help rescue ten army personnel who had disappeared while trying to make the first complete descent of Low's Gully on Kinabalu (4,101m, 13,455ft), in Sabah (North Borneo). Alister Haveron, Chief Instructor of the RAFMR, assembled a 17–man rescue team from the six RAFMR teams then operating in the UK. A Nimrod took the Kinloss members to Brize Norton, collecting other members from Leuchars and Leeming on the way. A Wessex helicopter took the Valley contingent to Brize Norton while the Stafford and St. Athan team members travelled by road. At Heathrow they were joined by an ex-Royal Navy Outdoor Instructor, who had first-hand knowledge of Kinabalu, and an army doctor, both from the RAF School of Combat Survival. They were then flown in a Malaysian Airlines Boeing 747 to Kuala Lumpur and on to Kota Kinabalu airport in a Boeing 737. Five of the soldiers had succeeded in getting out of the gully. Three of them were in hospital, the other two gave the new arrivals what information they could. (Carroll, 2003, Harveron et al, 2004)

The army expedition had started the descent of the gully on 27th February. On 17th March – only 34 hours after the call-out – the rescue team started up the mountain. Jet-lagged and with little rest, the rescue team was glad to accept the offer of a lift in a Malaysian Sikorsky army helicopter up the mountain to 11,000ft but after flying around for three hours at around 2,000ft, with cloud swathing the mountain and the helicopter showing a bad hydraulic leak, they were landed in a jungle village. The general in charge then asked for a lecture from the rescue team – this was apparently in order to get information to help with reorganisation of Malaysian SAR services. After a couple of hours slightly improved weather permitted take-off. Cloud around the mountain persisted, however, and the weary team finished up facing 5,000ft of ascent with all their gear. At first light they started out from the resthouse on the final 1,300ft to the col, from where the climb down difficult and dangerous slopes was made to Low's Gully.

The Malaysian Air Force provided helicopter searches. An Alouette covered the lower parts of the gully but was restricted to 6,500ft owing to severe turbulence and downdrafts near the mountain. Improved weather made possible use of the Sikorsky S61, which was able to reach 11,000ft but these searches did not reveal the whereabouts of the missing men. The RAF team was, however, making good progress in the lower parts of the gully and found various traces, including a bivouac site. Then further reconnaissance flights were made by the Alouette and on the last planned sortie one of the missing men was spotted at about 5,900ft, very close to where the RAF team had penetrated. The Alouette could not hover until its weight had been reduced but then a pick-up was made. The S61 lifted out two more men before the weather closed in and the last two were winched out the following morning. (Carroll, in MacInness, 2003; Haveron, 2004)

Mountain Search and Rescue in the UK

Already by 1983 the use of the helicopter had become almost routine for rescue work throughout the British Isles as well as all around its coasts and far out to sea. The Sea King had become the most used aircraft, though the Wessex was still in service. The greater range of the Sea King speeded up long-range operations as it reduced the need to refuel en route to distant incidents. It was a little large for operating in confined spaces and because of its weight and momentum it could not be brought to the hover quite as smartly as the Wessex (Winton, 1992, 276) but it brought new standards of service to rescue work and the time to respond to an alert was reduced progressively.

From 1986 onwards, RAF helicopter callouts from UK bases never fell below 100 per annum and by 1992 had risen to almost 1,500 with an input from the Royal Navy of over 500 (665 in 1995). (DASA statistics) The latter specialised in helping ships in distress, often flying to the limit of their fuel reserves in atrocious weather, far out over the Atlantic. Their operations are vividly described by Dr. James Begg, who flew with them as one of the doctors who unselfishly committed themselves to this exhausting, uncomfortable and hazardous rescue work, often between their normal surgeries with their civilian practices. (Begg, 2003, 2006) Many of the missions, especially those far out over the sea, were watched over and guided by RAF Nimrod surveillance jets, flying at great heights above the weather but able to locate, with their more specialised equipment, the vessels to which the Sea Kings were flying, keeping the rescue pilots informed of their exact position. Over seventy such sorties were flown by Nimrods in several of the years in the 1990s, reaching 80 in 2002. (DASA) Even on sorties to vessels in distress and people needing help in some of the non-mountainous areas on the western coasts and in the Hebrides, the helicopters on their mercy missions from Prestwick had to add mountains and hills to the hazards they had to face. This was especially so when flying low through the short-cut route by the Crinan Canal to reach the sea as quickly as possible.

It was considered that an SAR helicopter on permanent standby could be airborne in seven minutes – but a doctor might not get to the helicopter in this time. It had always been a race to get to the base and into flying kit before the helicopter took off. Sometimes the doctor was left behind as the aircrew sought to keep to the departure target time – but with a risk that they might then lack the full medical support needed when the casualty was reached, since the more extreme cases might well be beyond the competence of members of the crew, despite increased medical training. (Begg, 2003, 69) This was remedied as time progressed and now all members of SAR crews receive advanced pre-hospital life-support training. This is on a tri-service basis, i.e. Navy, RAF and Army personnel who might possibly be involved attend the same course, which is run by the RAF, so training is now uniform across the services.

146

Improvements for SAR Sea Kings

Up to 1995, the Sea Kings at Prestwick were heavily laden with military equipment – about a tonne of sonar gear for anti-submarine warfare. This was a severe handicap and very dangerous when flying in mountainous areas, especially when hovering in downdrafts near cliff faces. In 1995 – some 25 years after an SAR unit was first based at Prestwick – a dedicated, stripped-down Sea King was finally made available, meaning that naval pilots were no longer burdened with risks additional to those they were bound to take. The saving of weight also made it possible to carry additional, specialised medical equipment. The RN SAR unit at Culdrose had for some time benefited from having three SAR-designated Sea Kings. It was, however, the Prestwick medical team who took a lead in pressing for specialised medical equipment, which eventually became authorised for regular use. Stripping out the sonar equipment also made possible the positioning of two stretchers side by side in the back of the fuselage, where the casualties could be easily monitored, plus seating for up to eleven 'walking wounded'. Previously only one stretcher could be crammed into the narrow cargo bay aft of the sonar, where it was almost impossible to treat a patient. (Begg, 2003 and personal communication)

Dr Begg tells how Medical Assistant Gill Dorman, on her first duty as a member of the SAR crew, had to cope with a female hill walker who had been reported missing in the Cairngorms in a blizzard. They located her at four o'clock in the morning, lying frozen rigid in deep snow and found no pulse. Having got the casualty on board the aircraft, the 'backseat' crew applied cardio-pulmonary resuscitation (CPR) for the 30–minute flight to Ninewells Hospital at Dundee, their Heart Start monitor having not yet been authorised for defibrillation purposes on board a flying aircraft owing to possible interference with the aircraft's electronic equipment. However, on arrival at the hospital, ambulance paramedics came aboard, and, without asking, defibrillated the patient with their machine and restarted her heart. This combination of CPR and defibrillation undoubtedly saved her life, and the fact that the Sea King flew home to Prestwick with its systems intact was written up and possibly helped to obtain official approval a few months later, in August 1995, for defibrillator use on in-flight helicopters. Such progress was always slow and it might take several years of trials at Boscombe Down Research Establishment before any electronic equipment was passed as safe for use on military aircraft. (Personal communication)

The RAF and RN rescue record in the decade to 2010

The number of times the RAF and RN helicopters were involved in search and rescue missions fluctuated around 1,700 to 1,800 per annum between 2002 and 2005 including overseas interventions of about 70 on average. In 2009, however, a new peak of 2,418 callouts (including mountain rescue teams) arose from 2,262 incidents. Each incident may result in more than one unit being called out so the number of callouts is slightly higher each year than the number of incidents. There were 2,237 helicopter callouts in the UK in 2009 (1,963 in 2008). Of these the RN handled 758 (586 in 2008). The RAF's mountain rescue teams turned out on 86 occasions, slightly lower than the 91 callouts in 2008.

Regional distribution of search and rescue incidents

Year by year Scotland accounts for around 25% of the callouts. In most years Wales comes second and in 2009 accounted for 17.5% (357) of the total. South West England is responsible for almost as many callouts as Wales. North West England comes next, obviously because it includes the Lake District. It is clear that it is the mountainous areas that require most interventions, with coastal cliffs and hazardous paths no doubt responsible for many of the callouts in other regions. It should be remembered that these figures do not include search and rescue operations by

148

the Coastguard, police, fire, ambulance and other helicopter-operating authorities.

The records do not attempt to classify interventions by type of terrain, so there is no official separation of mountain incidents or of those in mountainous and hill areas, whether concerning climbing, farming or indeed any other kind of activity. Such information may be recorded on the details of each individual case but this data is confidential as names of individuals are entered on the record sheets and hence these are subject to the Data Protection Act. However, the geographical coordinates for each emergency are given so it is possible to plot their distribution in relation to the relief of the land and that is how the figures for interventions in the mountains given here have been derived. The nature of this method must be stressed as it indicates the reliability level of the figures given here – very limited it has to be admitted, but offering some overall guide to the volume and distribution of the search and rescue work by the RAF and RN in the hills and mountains.

The result of the above plotting of the coordinates of the callout locations suggest annual totals of 600 -700 RAF and RN helicopter SAR missions required in the mountains and major hill areas of the United Kingdom. The hills and moors south of the Bristol Channel are not included in this total. These statistics show up to 50 callouts to Ben Nevis, almost equally divided between the Sea Kings from RAF Lossiemouth and HMS Gannet, Prestwick. The latter also took on about half of the 20 or more calls to the Glencoe area. The Navy is clearly now very much involved in the mountains. There are about 40–50 callouts to each of the Lake District and Snowdonia mountain areas. The high total for interventions in Wales in 2009 is reflected in higher totals for Snowdon and surrounding hills than found for previous years. The North Wales calls were answered mainly by the Sea Kings from RAF Valley (Anglesey), as would be expected, but calls were answered, especially in the Lake District by the Sea Kings from as far north as Prestwick and as far south as Chivenor.

149

Rescue mishaps in the Lake District

SAR crews will always be at the sharp end when it comes to natural and technical hazards. In May 2004 a climber fell on Pike O'Stickle in Great Langdale and suffered a broken arm, saved from a worse fall by his companions holding on to him. A Sea King from *HMS Gannet* picked up members of the Kendal Mountain Rescue Team, and Andy Dell and a crewman from the helicopter were winched down to a ledge a few feet above the injured climber. Another Kendal rescuer, Peter Munford, was descending the cable and had just reached the ledge when the helicopter's rotor blades touched the cliff. Fragments of rock and carbon fibre from the rotor blades were sent flying into the air. Munford was dragged off the cliff but managed to detach himself from the strop. He hit the ground while the helicopter spun off down into the valley. By superb airmanship the pilot kept control and managed to land the Sea King. Dell secured the injured climber, his team-mates and the crewman to the face, then abseiled down to find Munford who was lying lower down. Munford had been seriously injured and was airlifted out to hospital by an RAF Sea King from Boulmer. No less than 37 members of the Langland and Ambleside, Kendal and Coniston mountain rescue teams had been involved over a period of seven hours.

The RAF Leeming Mountain Rescue Team was sent to guard the aircraft and the damaged aircraft was later airlifted out, slung under a Chinook helicopter – Boeing's big 'workhorse.' The day after the first accident, unfortunately, a further accident occurred. An RAF rescuer, recovering the parts that had broken off the rotors, slipped and fell and sustained head and arm injuries and had to be rescued from the same spot by another Sea King from *HMS Gannet.* (*The Westmoreland Gazette*, 21.5.04 and DASA data) The sequence of events show the hazards that are undertaken by all those who willingly participate in mountain rescue work, whether as professional or voluntary members of mountain rescue teams. It also illustrates the cooperation between the two friendly rivals, RAF and Fleet Air Arm.

Disaster, gratitude and ingratitude

Many mountaineers and trekkers, even in a time of need and mental or physical agony, are generous in expression of thanks to the pilots and others on whom they depended for rescue. An example that will remain engraved in the minds of the rescuers occurred in 2005. Nearing the summit of Aonach Mor in the Scottish Highlands on 14th May on a relatively simple scrambling route, Amy Larissa Rudge, 29 years old, slipped and fell from the ridge. Her companion, Patrick Roman, climbed down to her and was in no doubt that she had been killed by the fall. Patrick had to leave her in order to report the accident. A Royal Navy Sea King was scrambled from *HMS Gannet*, and brought members of the Lochaber Mountain Rescue Team to the scene. The understanding of the helicopter aircrew as well as the team and their efforts to comfort him left an indelible impression on Patrick who within days set out to show his gratitude and to ensure that Amy's death should be marked by positive assistance to the mountain rescue team, always in need of funds. Within weeks he raised almost £10,000 in donations, which he handed to the Lochaber team. Finding that the RN rescue flight also raised money for charity, notably for children suffering from leukaemia, he went on to raise funds for that purpose, (personal communications) and in his letter to *Summit,* the journal of the British Mountaineering Council, he drew attention to the growing pressure on the mountain rescue teams as outdoor activities continue to grow, and the need to give greater recognition to their immense efforts.

On the other hand, difficult rescue missions sometimes receive only criticism. Rescuers are always at risk of unsympathetic reporting in the popular press. A rather extreme case occurred when a military helicopter, scrambled to help a man and a woman who had called by mobile phone, emerged from the clouds above the forbidding north face of Ben Nevis and a crew member was winched down to a couple on the cliff. He was told to go away as they did not want to be rescued. Later another call established the fact that there were indeed two different people on the face who did need to be rescued and the Lochaber Mountain Rescue Team were able to reach them and bring them to safety. A newspaper not content with reporting the facts made a front-page article of the affair, saying that the aircrew had 'blundered' and referred to the rescue operation as 'botched.' A complaint to the editor by an experienced member of a helicopter rescue team elicited a letter of apology but the hurt caused by a high profile newspaper in publishing such an article could not be reversed. As the newspaper's critic pointed out, the helicopter crew had flown in foul weather through a temporary break in the cloud to locate two small specks of humanity clinging to rocks somewhere along miles of sheer cliffs in poor visibility.

Some jobs take even longer

On 27th February 2006, an RAF Sea King from Lossiemouth flew in to Coire an t'Sneachda in the northern Cairngorms to rescue a fallen climber. A winchman was lowered but while he was attending to the injured man a storm, which the helicopter had already flown through, moved in and the pilot was forced to set down to wait. The casualty was secured to a stretcher by Cairngorm MRT members and carried to a position ready for the evacuation. Then, however, the storm worsened and as the situation continued to deteriorate more ground support was mobilised. The helicopter rotors iced up and the pilot realised he would not be able to fly out that night. The machine was secured and the crew were guided out of the corrie. The RAF Kinloss team was called out to guard the Sea King and help with the long carry out that was now inevitable. It was almost midnight – ten hours after the mobile phone call had alerted the Cairngorm MRT – before the stretcher party was off the hill. The storm continued for days and it was almost a week before the stranded helicopter, long since covered with multiple layers of ice, could be made ready for recovery. Nevertheless, the engines started at the first attempt. The machine was flown back to its station at Lossiemouth escorted by its sister Sea King. The pilot and crew were subsequently cleared of all blame for the incident as no other procedure was practicable, much less safe. (Allen with Davidson, 2009, 253–61)

A hoax in Glencoe

Sadly, there are occasional hoax calls, which not only divert aircraft and mountain rescue teams from genuine emergencies but can also be extremely expensive. One exceptionally mischievous call was made in Glencoe in the Easter period in 1987. The caller claimed to be a naval officer in charge of a group of trainees in trouble on the mountains but was vague about the location. A mountain rescue team turned out and a Sea King from RAF Lossiemouth, which had just been dealing with a tragic accident, was made available. The search was extended and other rescue teams were called out, including a team from RAF Stafford, 250 miles away, and a Wessex from Leuchars. Soon more than a hundred searchers were spread throughout the glen, combing both the long ridge of the Aonach Eagach on the north side and the mountains on the south side. Nothing was found. The mystery was solved later when a man dressed as a naval officer presented an identity card with a background of the wrong colour in Edinburgh. He was arrested and turned out to have a record of impersonations and frauds. The cost of the helicopter operations was £49,765 (MacInnes, (ed) 2003, 280) to which had to be added well over a thousand man-hours, road travel by the rescue teams and the frustration of so much wasted time and effort.

Only a little less annoying than hoax calls are those that are necessitated by people going out on the hills with totally inadequate preparation and clothing, to say nothing of too little training. One might have thought, some years into the 21st century and given the publicity freely available to everyone and the special efforts that have been and are continuously directed to youth groups and schools, that such careless folly would be a thing of the past. That this is certainly not so is illustrated time after time, for example by a rescue operation carried out by RAF Valley on 23rd February 2006 in Snowdonia. A number of young people were in serious difficulties out on the mountains in freezing weather in the middle of a very cold spell that had been already affecting the whole country for at least a week. The prolonged low temperatures should have made the dangers obvious to anyone, even if they did not realise that severe conditions must always be expected in the British mountains in February. The BBC reported that the clothing being worn was more suitable to a summer's day on the beach than the mountains in winter.

Anne Sauvy's studies at Chamonix

Mountain rescue has deservedly attracted many of the best writers in the field of mountain literature. Also there are a number of very good books on the work of the helicopter rescue services, though not a great deal has been written in book form for English readers. Recently, however, this deficiency has been at least to some extent remedied, especially for the military services, by the appearance of Begg's book on the Royal Navy's SAR operations, referred to above, and English translations of Anne Sauvy's account of the work of the Chamonix rescue services. (Sauvy 2005) and D. Cauchy's work, also with the PGHM, to which further reference will be made later. (Cauchy, 2005, 2009)

The writer of many books and novels set in the mountains, Anne Sauvy spent day after day throughout one complete high season (July to early September) at the PGHM base at Les Bois. During this time she took every opportunity to observe and discuss their work with the rescue crews, and was occasionally able to lend a hand to someone in difficulty. An example was the case of a Slovak climber who had been brought down from Mont Blanc suffering from altitude sickness. Typical of the many climbers coming from the former Communist countries he had ample courage and determination but so little money that just hiring boots had been a major item for his budget. He had walked from

154

Chamonix to Les Houches, then all the way up the mountain. Payment for a night on the floor at the overcrowded Goûter hut had further reduced his cash, but he made it to the summit of Mont Blanc. He had been very relieved to find that when rescue was needed it was free but he declined hospital attention. He had left his girl friend at a campsite (they had no tent but someone had let them use a tent awning) but in all his problems he had forgotten its name. He could not afford a taxi, certainly not one to search for the site, so Sauvy earned his immense gratitude by driving him around the area until at Les Pélerins he recognised it. She concluded 'I wish him a happy holiday. Resourceful as he is, I think he will have one!' (Sauvy, 2005, 65–7)

Sauvy's account of the work of modern rescuers makes fascinating comparison with a book written by another woman author half a century earlier. Like Anne Sauvy, Gwen Moffat was herself an accomplished mountaineer. She was one of the first women to gain a guide's certificate. She spent long hours out on searches and rescues, including many in which the RAF were involved. So her book was very much an account from the 'sharp end' with all its benefits of being able to recount vividly the moments – and hours – of stress, suffering, celebration of success and despair at failure. At that time all the work was done the hard way. Helicopters are mentioned in her book only for the help afforded to the RAF rescuers in Turkey, as described above, and, briefly, for searches in Britain and the transport of a team to the summit of Lochnagar to speed up a rescue. There could be no greater contrast in methods than those of the initially ill-equipped and largely untrained volunteers in the RAF teams and the highly professional and superbly equipped British or alpine rescuers of today. Moffat (1964) shows vividly how the RAF Mountain Rescue Service had been transformed into a highly skilled organisation by 1961, while from her perspective almost half a century later, Sauvy recalls those dark days of failures in the early days at Chamonix. Not that there are no failures today. Inevitably some occur, despite the skills, professionalism and risks taken by the rescuers. Sauvy, like Moffat, describes vividly the different atmosphere that there is in the team when they can bring back only dead bodies compared with bringing in live persons, even when they are seriously injured.

Sauvy recorded that after a particularly difficult month, such was the strain and sadness, she seriously considered abandoning the task she had set herself when in late July on 'Black Monday' one of the rescuers, Régis Mischoux, was killed. He had been on a training climb and he and his colleagues were descending the Whymper Couloir of the Aiguille Verte. There were six deaths in two days. She decided it needed a man to write the book. 'You can say whatever you like about equality of the sexes. Men are tougher . . . I fall apart . . .' (Sauvy, 2005, 187) Fortunately, she was persuaded to continue.

Sauvy had numerous criticisms of the journalists and photo-graphers who haunted the helipad waiting for a chance to record the details of tragedies and take pictures of dead casualties, including from the helicopter when they were permitted to fly with the rescuers on a reconnaissance flight in preparation for a difficult assignment. The gendarmes could not express their views in public but Sauvy was so incensed and distressed that eventually she could not help telling the journalists that they were 'revolting' and 'disgusting.' (Sauvy, 2005, 191) She did, however, praise, indeed 'pay tribute,' to Pioneer Productions. Making a documentary film for British television, Gilles Perret, the producer, and Bill Duncan, cameraman, did not ask for flights but, of their own initiative, chartered a Lama helicopter and also attached a miniature video camera to the helmet of one of the rescuers to film automatically a rescue, from the winching down to the care of the rescued person. (Sauvy, 2005, 269, 272)

Anne Sauvy observes that sometimes statistics enable one to see things in better perspective. That year, during June, July and August there were 415 rescues. These involved 36 deaths, 1 missing person, 84 ill, 281 wounded, 183 unhurt, these last being for the most part people in difficulty or the partners of the victims. She points out, however, that hundreds of thousands of people would have enjoyed the walking, climbing and all the other sports available. She is a firm advocate of free rescue services, which she regards as a necessary part of state and social services to society.

In the French Alps the PGHM at Chamonix is the service that attracts the greatest attention and publicity but it should not be forgotten that PGHM units undertake similar work in the mountains in other regions of France, in total exceeding the number dealt with by the Chamonix and Annecy units. Units are based in the Alps at Grenoble, Bourg St. Maurice and Briançon (with detachments at other critical points such as Bourg d'Oisans and Modane) and in the Pyrenees, the Jura, the Vosges and the Massif Central. Some of the rescues, especially in the Vanoise and Écrins massifs, are equally demanding.

CHAPTER 9

Mountain Flying for Excitement, Sport and Pleasure: Gliders and Light Aircraft

Gliders had preceded by a century the powered aeroplane in the conquest of the air by heavier-than-air machines. Sir Roger Cayley (1773–1857) had been inspired by ballooning but his study of all forms of flight provided 'the secure foundations upon which all subsequent developments in aviation have been built.' (Gibbs-Smith, 1970, 21) In 1853 his long-suffering coach-man made the first successful gliding flight in history from the slope of a hill at Brompton in Yorkshire. Many others contributed in the 19th century to the science of aeronautics, the dominant figure being Otto Lilienthal (1848–96) who, with a succession of his hang-gliders, made some 2,500 gliding flights in Germany. Unfortunately he was killed flying from the Gollenberg in the Rhinower Hills in 1896 but others went on to realise the potential of gliding, later in parallel with the development of powered flight. Clubs were formed to facilitate the activities of like-minded enthusiasts. In the alpine lands they included those at Bern, Basel and Geneva, where a gliding school was established as early as 1912.

After the First World War gliding developed steadily. It was relatively cheap and free of onerous restrictions. Hills provided obvious opportunities for launching gliders at minimum cost and with prospects of rising air currents to lift the glider and soar or at least make for a satisfying gliding flight. Techniques and aerodynamic improvements soon made it possible to fly cross-country, circling and climbing in the thermal currents under cumulus clouds. Gliders offered opportunities to soar above the more modest mountains, such as those of the English Lake District, the Pennines, Shropshire hills and Scotland. In Germany (prohibited under the conditions of the Treaty of Versailles from operating, owning or building military aircraft) gliders provided the means of training thousands of pilots as part of the developing Nazi war machine. There was ample scope for adventurous flying in the mountainous regions of southern Germany, Austria and elsewhere.

In 1931, the German pilot Grünhoff flew from the Jungfraujoch and, despite the failure of some of his controls at the start, landed safe and sound at Interlaken. A few days later the Swiss Willi Farner made an hour-long flight from the Jungfraujoch over Kleine Scheidegg and the Lauberhorn to Stans, 80km away. Switzerland had become a playground for high mountain flying as it had long been for mountaineering. Its first gliding competitions were held at Gstaad in 1922 and the international contests that became a feature of Swiss gliding attracted strong entries from many countries and in return other countries hosted international 'gliding weeks.' First to cross the Alps in a sailplane was the Swiss pilot, H. Schreiber, who flew from Thun over the Jungfraujoch to Bellinzona in 1935. (Dollfus, 1969, 35)

In the 1930s, the German gliding fraternity were keen to show the progress they were making and the advanced gliders they were constructing. Hanna Reitsch, later to be a test-pilot for German jet and rocket-propelled fighters, was among the visitors at the Anglo-German gliding camp held by the London Gliding Club at Dunstable in August 1937. (Welch, 1983, 21)

During the war years, when gliders became the tools of invading troops (as in the German attack on Crete and the allied invasion of Normandy) the Swiss were able to continue with their sports gliding. Though Graubunden canton alone remained relatively free of restrictions, summer gliding meets and national championships were held annually at various alpine aerodromes including La Blecherette at Lausanne, Vevey

and Rochers-de-Naye in the Valais and Samedan just north-east
of St. Moritz in the Engadine. All these were positioned ideally
for mountain gliding and soaring. To the existing competitions
for achievements in height, distance and duration was added a
new task: that of flying to a predetermined point, with or
without return to the starting point, with the winner to be
the pilot successful in the least time. Tasks set at Samedan
included the 70km route Samedan – Aroser Weisshorn and
back. Nine pilots started and seven succeeded in returning to
base. Max Schachenmann won this contest with a time of 97
minutes and went on to win a 'Tour of Grisons' to the Weiss-
fluhjoch (2,663 m) and Lenzerhorn (2,911m) and back, over
100km in 162 minutes. (Dollfus, 1969, 50)

Two years after the war ended, the Swiss hosted at Samedan
an ambitious international championship meeting complying
with the rules of the Fédération Aéronautique Internationale
(FAI). In 1948 this was repeated and enlarged. A British team
was among the eight European countries represented. Ann
Welch was appointed team manager. In her autobiography
she wrote in some detail of this event which provided entirely
new experiences and challenges for British glider pilots, whose
previous flying had not taken them into high mountain country.
Many of the fields that were used for landings had in them
stakes for haycocks, providing a very considerable hazard. A
Fieseler Storch was used to provide aero-tows. One task was to
fly a 100km triangle, the first such route ever set. It was won by
a Swiss pilot, Sigbert Maurer, in a Moswey glider at an average
speed of 70km/hr, which made him also a world record holder.
In a subsequent task the pilot had to try to reach a destination of
his own choice. Pelle Person from Sweden won the championship with a 295km flight to Geneva. Sadly, a British pilot, Kit
Nicholson, crashed on the top of an Italian mountain as he
attempted to clear the peak in mist and cloud. Another British
pilot, Donald Greig, was killed flying into an unmarked cable
used for transporting logs on the same mountain. (Welch, 1983,
89–90) Both victims had survived wartime flying; their deaths
were a fearsome reminder of the hazards of mountain flying.

160

There are now many gliding clubs and schools throughout the Alps, North America, New Zealand and elsewhere with regular competitions and record-breaking flights, facilitated by the configuration and extent of the mountain chains and the meteorological conditions. In 2004 a new distance record for gliders was set up by Terry Delore and Steve Fossett over Argentina. Using an ASH 25M high performance sailplane they covered 2,186km (1,358ml) in 15 hours 42 minutes. (*Aerospace International*, Vol. 32, No.5, 2005)

The minimalist approach: hang-gliders

In the search to make ever-more exciting and demanding ascents, descents and other achievements in the mountains, recourse is had, not surprisingly, to the employment of all new developments and opportunities. The development of the hang-glider led to new exploits in the mountains. In 1973 the American pilot, M. Harker, jumped off the Zugspitze and reached Ehrwald, 1,980m lower and 12 kilometres away, in less than 12 minutes.

Also in 1973 R. Epper descended 2,550m from Mount Haleakala in Hawaii and landed 15km away after 19.5 minutes. Terris Moore, pioneer of Alaskan aviation and climbing expeditions as described previously, noted that Denali (Mount McKinley) was the scene in 1976 of:

'an entirely new event. . . . Three men successfully carried their light foot-launched gliders to the summit of Denali and then . . . at least one of them soared the full 13,000ft down to his Kahiltna Base Camp, landing gracefully at the very spot from where he had begun his climb'. (Moore and Andrasco, 1978, 27)

The Andes, Kilimanjaro and the Himalaya were among the ranges that soon saw hang-glider descents. The Austrian expedition of 1978 to Mount Everest, on which Reinhold Messner and Toni Habeler made the first ascent of the mountain without artificial oxygen, took hang-gliders along but did not use them on the mountain. Jean-Marc Boivin and Patrick Berhault climbed the south face of the Dru, used a two-seater hang-glider to descend and then climbed the American direct ascent on the same mountain, the same day. (Griffin, 1983)

In 1986 an American expedition overcame great obstacles to show what could be achieved with hang-gliders with a launch from Everest's west ridge. (Unsworth, 2000, 489) The Chinese bureaucracy placed incredible difficulties in the way of the Americans. The customs officers denied that the gliders had ever been seen, even when the determined Americans penetrated the customs cargo area and were able to point out the clearly visible 13ft tubes containing the machines. They resorted to threats that risked them being thrown into gaol to get the gliders released. Then it was another month before they reached Everest Base Camp in the truck the expedition had been forced to pay for. By that time they had lost the benefit of a month-long window of good weather, during which the members at Base Camp could only look at the blue skies and friendly cumulus clouds in frustration. They did get a glider up on to the west ridge and despite the jetstream having come down on the mountain, Steve McKinny made a flight but crashed on the moraine. He had, however, become the first person to fly a hang-glider on Everest. Larry Tudor endured the winds for another four nights and Bob Carter stayed yet another night before final retreat. Chinese officialdom had defeated their hope to achieve an entirely successful flight. (Internet: 'Over Everest,' 2005)

Microlights

Hang-gliders and paragliders provide obvious attractions to those who want to make their mark at relatively modest costs as compared with sailplanes. So do microlight aircraft. Depending on their engine power and other design characteristics, microlights can provide exciting opportunities in the mountains. In 1986 a three-man British team set out to make the highest landing achieved by any aircraft, taking two Southdown Raven microlights to Kathmandu. It is thought that Simon Baker was the first person to take-off in a microlight in Nepal. He and David Young flew the two microlights to Lamadanda en route to Lukla. Unfortunately, Baker's machine suffered a cracked exhaust and they took it in the other machine to Dharan, where a British Ghurka camp offered a chance to get it welded. Unable to climb over the hills with their 440cc engine they had to follow a circuitous valley route but both machines performed well later.

The repaired three-cylinder Robin two-stroke engine of 60hp enabled Simon Baker to take passengers up from Syangboche at 3,800m (12,467ft). With the smaller 440cc (only 38hp) Robin, he made a solo landing on a makeshift 150m landing strip on the dry bed of a lake near Gorak Shep, just below Everest Base Camp at over 5,300m. It was deemed too risky to take off at that altitude in a bowl so they dismantled the aircraft and had it carried it down. Baker had not used oxygen and felt unwell for 24 hours. The larger engine suffered several more cracks, requiring repairs at Dharan. Returning with the repaired exhaust, David Young encountered severe turbulence – he was flying after midday when the wind brought in cloud and turbulent conditions – and crashed at about 14,000ft. He was seriously injured but fortunately was near a first aid post and two American volunteer doctors kept him alive until he could be evacuated to Kathmandu. (Internet, 'Over Everest', 2005, 1–2) In November 1993 Ziri Zitka and Pavel Krizan made separate flights over Ama Dablam (6,855m, 22,493ft) (Internet, 'Over Everest,' 2005, 6–7)

Hang-glider and microlight over Everest – and an eagle

The Italian hang-glider champion, Angelo d'Arrigo, and Richard Meredith-Hardy, an experienced microlight pilot and engineer, achieved a remarkable flight over Everest in 2004 after several years of preparation. Angelo, who had achieved record-breaking flights in many regions, including the Sahara and between Siberia and the Caspian Sea, did not only want to fly over Everest. He wanted to study the flight patterns of the

Nepalese Stone Eagle and, to that effect, acquired one of these impressive birds, which he called Chumi (after the Tibetan name for Everest, Chomolungma) and set about training it in Sicily to accept the company of a human being on its flights. Later he obtained a companion Nepalese eagle from Moscow Zoo, which he named Geija. After winter training on Etna, he underwent tests for altitude, including his oxygen requirements, and commissioned wind tunnel research for his specially constructed hang-glider for flight up to 9,000m in winds of 130km/hr and temperatures of –40 degrees C.

In 2003 Angelo went to Tibet and climbed to 7,814m before being defeated by days of storms, then resumed training of himself and his eagles. The next year saw him in Nepal. He and Richard set up their base at Thyangboche but immediately Chumi contracted a virus and died. Angelo overcame this blow and continued preparations with Geija. In the end, however, the weather, especially the strong winds, caused him to abandon his ideas of flying in company with Geija and settled for an attempt to make a hang-gliding flight over Everest. Richard towed him up but Angelo had to abandon the flight. Bad weather prevented another attempt until the very last day they had available, but that day dawned clear and they took off. Nearing the summit they encountered severe turbulence and after separation through a broken cable, Richard flew the microlight over the summit of Everest and returned to base through cloud, making a hazardous but successful landing. Angelo found his way from close to the summit down through a hole in the cloud to an Italian research station and was able to put down there, eventually being collected by a helicopter and taken back to base and a triumphant reunion with Richard. (Meredith-Hardy, personal communication, also Internet and ARTE/BR TV, 2005)

Parachuting and BASE-jumping

Parachutes were first developed for descents by choice or necessity in the early days of ballooning. After many delays because generals thought that having them would induce pilots to unnecessarily abandon their aircraft in combat, parachutes became standard equipment for military use. Inevitably they also became of sporting interest and aircraft have launched many parachutists on to the summits of mountains, such as Mont Blanc in 1961 and Kilimanjaro in 1962. In the Pamirs, Soviet parachutists jumped from about 8,000m on Pik Lenin in 1968. Unfortunately of the ten that undertook this adventure, four were caught by the winds as they descended and blown over a precipice and killed. (Pyatt, 1980, 55)

An unusual use to which a parachute can be put was illustrated in a report in the *Alpine Journal* in 1983. On the summit of the Aiguille Verte a British party met a French soloist lightly clad and carrying a minuscule rucksack. Invited to join him in his bivouac shelter they expressed surprise that such a small rucksack could hold a 'three-man' bivi sack, whereupon the Frenchman unfurled a silk parachute to wrap around them. After also sharing a welcome brew the lone climber announced he must be going and politely asked if they would mind holding out the parachute to maximise the effective wind-catchment area. A few moments later he was drifting gently down to the valley while the British party began the long and dangerous descent down the Whymper Couloir, which they would be lucky to complete in daylight. 'There is,' the report concluded, 'no moral whatsoever to this story; just a difference in attitude!' (Griffin, 1983)

Free-fall parachuting, or skydiving, led to BASE-jumping. This less-than-obvious term is derived from the initials of the alternative types of launching points – Buildings; Antennae (or Aerials), such as pylons; Spans (bridges), and Earth, (i.e. precipices), from which the parachutist jumps.

A predecessor of the modern BASE-jumper, Dr. Erich Felbermayer, an Austrian dentist, is credited with the first such jump from the Giallo precipice in the Dolomites in 1965 but it was over a decade before much attention was given to this as a new sport. In 1978, a skydiving photographer, Carl Boenish, led a group of skydivers up the Yosemite peak El Capitan and filmed their spectacular descents. When this led to others

165

following suit, the National Park Service banned the practice. However, illegal jumping continued and the sport was eventually permitted, subject to regulations. These were spectacularly ignored, fatalities occurred, there was disruption and danger to other park users and after only three months the ban was reinstated. Illegal jumping, however, continued, despite arrests, seizure of equipment and fines. A federal ban was instituted when threats to wildfowl were cited. The activity by this time had spread to other areas far beyond the USA – the Troll North Wall in Norway and the French Alps providing notable challenges. Erich Beaud pioneered the free-fall jump in France from a cliff at Ayères, sites in Haute Savoie, including the Dent du Géant, and Dévoluy. The Cima Grande and other peaks in the Dolomites and Switzerland were soon added. In the Bernese Oberland, the north face of the Eiger offers a spectacular jump.

BASE-jumping grew steadily in the 1990s and early 2000s. Its adherents enthuse over the combination of mountaineering with the extra excitement of the free-fall element. There is particular appeal in making a jump from a point that has not previously been used. It is, of course, essential to ensure that there is no obstacle to the descent and the BASE-jumper seeking new locations has to accept that a particular excursion may yield no suitable site, but with the consolation that the climb and normal descent will make the day worthwhile. The BASE-jumper has to accept the need to carry an extra heavy rucksack, especially if reaching the chosen site requires alpine equipment. Erich Beaud writes of being 'loaded like mules.' He also comments on the invaluable aid provided by his partner at the base of the cliff, guiding him and his fellow-jumpers to the take-off point, often involving extensive rappelling (abseiling). He introduced the term 'paralpinisme,' understandably thinking it more evocative than 'BASE-jumping.' He pays tribute to those who have taken the sport further, such as Eric Fradet, 'the Reinhold Messner of the free jump' who introduced new techniques, including getting further out from the wall and facilitating longer periods in free fall. (Beaud, 2004)

166

Fatalities have been numerous. Having achieved in 1988 the parachuting feat of jumping off Everest and descending to Camp 2, as described later, J.M. Boivin, was killed in a jump at Angel Falls, Venezuela, in February 1990. He had already made several successful jumps – for a French television film about BASE-jumping – when a sudden wind gust blew him into the rock face. (Tabin in Gilmore, 1993, 176)

Paragliding

It is, however, the paraglider (or parapente) that has provided the greatest aeronautical lure for adventurers in the mountains in recent years. It is now a major sport. Paragliding provides excitement for many who have never wanted to climb mountains for the sake of climbing and also for climbers seeking an alternative but associated sport. The origins of the paraglider may be found in the early 1960s in the Para Commander parachute, which was developed to make it possible to reverse (in the early stage of a flight and until a descent has to be made) the usual purpose of a parachute. Towed aloft behind a land or water vehicle, para-ascending led to parachutes with canopies modified for gliding and control in flight. A rectangular canopy formed by a number of aerofoil-sectioned cells, which are inflated during the launch or pilot's take-off run, is the essence of the paraglider. A steerable reserve parachute was introduced in 1992. (Whittall, 1995, 10) Improvements in design and performance have been rapid.

The sport became popular in the late 1970s, the French Alps between Annemasse and Chamonix being one favoured area. A championship was initiated at Wengen in the Bernese Oberland in 1981. The sport is bracketed with hang-gliding by the Fédération Aéronautique Internationale (FAI), its Commission Internationale du Vol Libre (CIVL) regulating it and coordinating championships. (Whittall, 1995, 13)

For some, such as Joe Simpson and his former climbing partner, Ian Tattersall, paragliding seemed to offer comparable thrills without the element of danger inseparable from extreme climbing. Sadly, however, Tattersall was killed shortly after he had made the decision to give up climbing in favour of paragliding. (Simpson, 2002, 61–2)

Simpson describes how friends had praised the technical developments that had revolutionised the sport since he had previously tried it. They reminded him that previously they had, for harnesses, only 'glorified webbing bra straps' with wooden planks to sit on. The equipment that had been introduced included air bags, pre-formed foam padding and reserve parachutes as well as variometers to indicate rise and sink rates, wind and ground speed indicators and many more specialised items. Also, of course, global positioning satellite systems and light, reliable radios are used. (Simpson, 2002, 59)

Maria Coffey gives other examples of climbers who have found flying of one form or another to be an alternative to climbing. She cites Carlos Carsolio, a Mexican mountaineer with an outstanding record in the Himalaya, as going paragliding almost every day after giving up climbing temporarily to be near his young family, and writing that 'a whole phalanx of British climbers', like Simpson, have taken up the sport. (Coffey, 2004, 24)

A paragliding descent from the summit of Everest was one of the objectives of a post-monsoon French expedition in 1988. Five Frenchmen and three Sherpas made it to the top on 26th September. Jean-Marc Boivin, who had also taken up skis, chose to glide down from the extreme summit. He thus reduced his descent to a matter of minutes, reaching Camp 2 in the Western Cwm, 8,000ft lower, in eleven minutes. Geoff Tabin was at Camp 2 when he landed on his feet 'as light as a feather,' hat and glasses off, six feet from the camera crew. He responded to the applause from a group of twenty Sherpas, climbers and cameramen with a shy smile. (Tabin, in Gilmore (ed), 1993, 176) On 7th October 1990, Jean-Noel Roche and his son Bertrand 'Zébulon' Roche, who, at 17, became the youngest person to ascend Everest, descended by paraglider from the South Col. (Band, 2003; 2005, 218–219) He then made the next flight after Boivin's from near the summit. He had married the three-times female world champion paraglider, Claire Bernier-Roche, and the two climbed Everest with a double paraglider. On 22nd May 2001 they found a launch site about one hundred metres below the summit and made a ten-minute flight down towards the North Col and landed at Advanced Base at 6,400 metres (20,990ft). (Band, 2005, 219)

In 1994, Ivar Tollefsen, leader of a Norwegian expedition to the Antarctic, which climbed 36 peaks in Dronning Maud Land, paraglided off the summit of Ulvetanna (Wolf's Fang), a great spire of red granite. It had involved eleven days of climbing. (Trewby, 2002, 127)

Paragliding could also be termed 'parasoaring' since by using thermals and winds to rise, it is often possible to travel long distances. By soaring, rather than gliding, the flyer can rise far above the start point and much of the attraction is to fly over passes and attain the summits of high peaks. Television viewers were treated to an outstanding display of paragliding skills in 2000 when Toni Bender (a test pilot for the equipment) was filmed flying over the main Alpine chain and the Inn valley to the Dolomites. His equipment included the usual variometer to show rates of ascent and descent, compass and satellite navigation system. Cameras were mounted on the banana-shaped canopy, and directly in front of him. A cameraman in a two-seater took pictures of his flight showing him soaring dramatically up the big walls. After a six-hour flight he passed over the Achensee, often travelling at 40–60 km/hr. He made an intermediate glacier landing on the Olperer at 3,310m then flew on in the evening light to the Dolomites. He made a moonlit landing near a cow-herder's hut and enjoyed a calm night outside. He also commented that when there was no turbulence he was as comfortable in the air on his paraglider as when he was in bed.

On 13th August 2003, five members of the French Alpine Club made the first paraglider *ascent* of Mont Blanc. David Casartelli, Yvan Boullen, Jean-Paul Bonfanti, Alain Finet and Pierre Denambride took off from Planpraz at 1,900m. On the Chamonix side of Mont Blanc flying is restricted so that rescue services will not be endangered, so the prohibited zone had to be avoided. The five therefore contoured along the lower slopes. Meteorological conditions favoured the ascent, with warm air providing lift at altitude, where snow cover had been greatly reduced. They rose to land on the summit one after the other, one-and-a-half hours after take-off. For Bonfanti it was his first time on the summit of Mont Blanc. *(Montagnesinfos* No.27, Oct. 2003, 29)

After the success and popularity of paragliding a natural development was the addition to the paraglider of a motor to facilitate ascent, increase range and generally extend the scope of the sport. Giles ('Gilo') Cardoza developed a powered para-glider, or paramotor, which he called the 'Parajet,' to attempt a flight over Everest. On 21st May 2007 he and Bear Grylls, after a long wait at their base camp at Periche in the Khumbu Valley, fortunately got suitable weather and took off. At 28,000ft Gilo's supercharger belt failed but he made a safe return. Bear Grylls continued and reached an estimated height of 29,000ft. His instruments had failed but he was able to look out over Lhotse and Everest. They had decided to make a concession to safety by not attempting to fly over Everest, leaving that 'to be attempted by other protagonists' as they put it on the website, 'Wingover'. The expedition, which had been supported by the aerospace and engineering company GKN, raised over $1million for charities operating mainly in Africa.

Light aircraft on snowy summits and glaciers

As with both mountaineering and with flying, taken separately, there is with mountain flying no shortage of new exploits. It was, however, almost forty years after the landing of an aircraft on the Dôme du Goûter that a similar exploit was achieved on the summit of Mont Blanc. Henri Giraud, a Grenoble pilot who was a pupil of Hermann Geiger, achieved it on 23rd June 1960. He set out in his Piper Cub 'Chouca' at 04.30. After one hour he landed on the Col du Dôme, precisely where Durafour had landed in 1921.

Jean Moine, whose first landing on the summit of Mont Blanc has already been described, took Giraud in a helicopter from the col to the summit of Mont Blanc, where he marked his intended landing strip with flags and charcoal powder. Moine then took him back to his aircraft and took the prefect of Haute Savoie to the summit. Giraud soon appeared, cut his speed as much as possible and touched down at 100km/hr at 06.30. He planted a French flag in the snow and used his radio to announce his success to the French President, General de Gaulle in 'un message déférent d'affection et de gratitude.' He said that, from this highest point of their country and Western Europe, he understood the pride the president felt when looking at France from his own 'summit' to which the people had carried him. He dedicated 'cette victoire symbolique' to the glory of God, his mother and France. (Kossa, 1971, 16) After an hour he took off with a run of 80m and was back at Grenoble in fifty minutes, having established a new altitude record for landing a fixed-wing aircraft in Europe, 140 years after the peak was first climbed. (Borrel, 1983, 22)

Altiports and altisurfaces

The first 'altisurface' was, in effect, the more or less level area on the top of the Puy-de-Dôme chosen for his landing by Eugène Renaux. With the coming of pilots like Firmin Guiron, in the case of Mont Blanc, and the Swiss pioneers of glacier landings, such selected landing places high in the mountains became much more common for purposes mainly connected with maintenance and construction tasks and rescue work. However, the possibilities for sporting purposes soon became evident. From an early date, bush pilots were taking climbers into the Alaskan and Yukon mountains and skiers were lifted into many parts of the Alps and other ranges, while many pilots explored the possibilities simply in order that they themselves could enjoy mountain flying.

In this sport, much is owed to Léon Élissalde's pioneer work in the Pyrenees. After serving as an engineer in the giant six-engine Latécoère 631 flying boat he found life as an ordinary motor mechanic unsatisfying, even with skiing and mountaineering in his leisure time. He formed the Bagnères-de-Luchon flying club in 1954 and became a leading exponent of flying in the mountains. Having himself opened up some of the landing surfaces he participated in the creation of a network of 'alti-surfaces.' These were generally from 150 to 200 metres in length, sloping at an angle between 8 and 25 degrees and convex, concave or a mixture of both. Located in middle and high mountain zones, the highest of these landing areas in the French Pyrenees reported by Terrancle in 1992 was at Roc d'Aude at 2,350m. There were even higher ones on the Spanish side – over 2,700m. Reluctance by the Spanish government to recognise them, however, meant that their use was illegal. (Terrancle, 1992) Dollfus noted in 1969 that there were 42 high mountain landing strips in Switzerland, of which 18 were in Valais (Wallis), 12 in Graubünden, and seven in the Bernese Oberland. In 1968, these landing strips served 5,377 passengers on 1,607 flights. (Dollfus, 1969, 54)

Some altiports are virtually high-altitude aerodromes. An example is the one at Peyresourde-Balestas in the Pyrennees. It was provided with a hard-surface runway of 340m, open all the year round with full radio facilities. Altisurfaces have been controlled since 1963 by the authorities but have constituted one of the few remaining types of operating spaces to which pilots were allowed freedom of access by the Direction Général de l'Aviation Civile (DGAC). Pilots had to hold a special 'mountain' qualification, obtainable after a course flying dual-control at first with the centre for mountain flying at Grenoble-Saint-Geoirs. (Terrancle, 1992)

Pilots flying in the mountains have created regional, national and international organisations to further their activities. Thus the Pilotes Pyréréens de Montagne are affiliated to the Association Française des Pilotes de Montagne, which is supported by the Fédération Française Aéronautique, with local aero clubs functioning in many areas. The AFPM organises an ambitious programme of meets throughout the year. In 2006 there were 21

172

meets in the Alps and Pyrenees. Several events were arranged in conjunction with Swiss, Austrian and Italian organisations, with the collaboration further extended through a European Mountain Pilots organisation, including national groups in Spain and Luxembourg. (AFPM, no. 64, 2006) The number of altiports is being constantly extended but many hurdles have to be negotiated including local and environmental interests that are concerned at this spread of motorised activity and consequent noise.

Undertaking this kind of flying necessitates familiarity with the special and treacherous conditions that obtain in the mountains, especially understanding the nature of the snow that masks relief details, confusing estimation of distances and obscuring landmarks and reference points. Élissalde, like his predecessors such as Hermann Geiger, developed a well-rehearsed procedure for landing on an altisurface. If the pilot thinks the snow is in a suitable condition for landing, he makes two or three 'touch-and-go' manoeuvres and a final circuit. Even then, if he is not to find himself with four or five hours work with a shovel, caution remains essential. Élissalde described how, with one hand on the throttle and the other on the joystick, he approached the slope uphill – uphill because, with skis instead of wheels, no braking was possible – and lightly touched the surface, caressing the snow with 'une delectation toute sensuelle.' He considered that a good skier had a good chance of making a good pilot because to make a turn on the snow necessitated edging the skis properly if the aircraft was not to be turned over.

On one occasion when he made a 'cheval de bois' ('wooden horse'), as a serious accident is called, he had a ski dig in, causing a wing to tip down into the snow on the glacier. He made a temporary brace with the rope that was always on board, and flew back to Luchon. In 1992 he was able to claim proudly that he had never abandoned an aircraft on the mountain. (Terrancle, 1992)

One of the most striking developments in sporting aviation in recent years has been the revival and spectacular growth of ballooning. This has enabled immense numbers of people who could only imagine the fascination of silent flight, wafted by whatever winds may blow, to experience it for themselves. This will be the subject of Chapter 13. Before that, however, some more serious aspects of the interface between aviation and mountains will be examined.

CHAPTER 10

'Pull-up! Pull-up!'

The heading of this chapter will perhaps mean little to many readers, but a great deal to an aviator. Before explaining it, a short digression is proposed, commenting on the visual attractions of mountain scenery. There was a long period in history when most people regarded mountains with fear and horror, though for others they were the unapproachable home of the gods, many peaks in Asia and other continents still being regarded as holy today. Slowly, however, from the 14th century onwards they began to appeal to a few savants as places of beauty and spiritual uplift. In the 18th century, the Age of Enlightenment saw the cult of travel to the mountains evolving and leading to the first ascent of mountains in Switzerland and Savoy, including Mont Blanc. The name by which it had once been known, Mont Maudit (The Evil Mountain') became transferred to a neighbouring, lesser, peak in the range.

Once adventurous artists and writers penetrated the alpine valleys appreciation of the beauty and fascination of mountain landscapes became more widespread and attracted many more visitors, ranging from the dedicated climbers and explorers to the tourists who provided employment for couriers, coachmen and, of course, hoteliers.

Man's achievement of flight, first in balloons and later in aeroplanes, led to the exploration of mountain regions from the air and the revelation of the fascinating patterns of the great ranges and glaciers, as described in Chapter 1. Sightseeing flights by Thoret and other pilots who dared to fly deliberately close to the mountains enabled a few fortunate passengers, to whom expense was no barrier, to enjoy these panoramas. When airliners flew at moderate altitudes the views were often stunning and, even at present-day cruising heights they can still be impressive, with added magnificent close-ups as the aircraft descends on approach to nearby airports.

In Switzerland there is a railway tunnel known as the 'Ah and Oh tunnel.' From an interesting but relatively undistinguished climb up a green hillside the train enters a tunnel and emerges to a sensational view of the snowclad giants of the Bernese Oberland – the Eiger, Mönch and Jungfrau. This view obtained approaching the upper station of the Schynige Platte mountain railway can, however, be replicated hundreds of times in sightseeing trips by aircraft of all kinds, with the added attraction on many excursions of threading a route deep into the heart of the mountains, revealing views otherwise known only to mountaineers. 'Ah and Oh' must be heard very frequently indeed in the cabins of such aeroplanes and the baskets of alpine balloons.

However, from the pioneer days of the early balloonists who flew into mountain areas with only gas and ballast control to avoid crashes, aviators have had to face dangers from hills and mountains. In the jargon of modern air accident investigation, collision with a mountain is included under the classification of 'Controlled flight into terrain' – CFIT for short. The term covers any crash into land or sea while the machine is under full control

Airliners and mountain hazards

When an aircraft has disappeared in flight over the mountains, usually it is because it has been flown into a peak or mountainside. The work of the RAF Mountain Rescue Service to deal with such early accidents in Britain has been referred to earlier, as has the spectacular Swiss aid to the crashed Dakota in 1946. That episode ended happily but such was not the case when Air India's Lockheed Constellation *Malabar Princess*, flying from Bombay to London in 1950, crashed into Mont Blanc some 200m below the summit. (Cuvelier, 2004) Astonishingly, Air India suffered a virtual repeat of this disaster, when sixteen years later a Boeing 707 crashed on the same part of Mont Blanc. The progress made by 1966 enabled helicopters to be quickly at the scene but 117 people on board died in the disaster. Both these accidents are discussed in more detail in Chapter 14.

In November 1952, Dr Terris Moore, president of the University of Alaska and a skilled glacier pilot, received a request from the United States Air Force to undertake a mission to the site of the crash of one of its aircraft, a C-154 Globemaster transport which had struck Mount Gannet, some 30 miles east of Anchorage, with 52 people on board. The crash was at about 8,000ft and the Air Force did not have the resources to land an aircraft on the ice-covered slope to find out if there were any survivors. Moore took an Air Force expert in survival techniques with him and landed within a few hundred yards of the crash. They could do nothing for the victims, the collision having occurred probably at full cruising speed. Relatives of the victims wrote to Moore asking for details – the Air Force had given out little information, probably not wishing to publicise the fact that to get to the site it had had to turn to a bush pilot, even though he happened also to be a university president. Moore and his secretary wrote to the relatives of each of the casualties, assuring them that the deaths would have occurred instantaneously. In 1954 the Air Force conferred on Moore the Distinguished Service Award. (Moore, 1999, 201)

In even more remote areas it has sometimes been difficult to locate a crashed aircraft. All kinds of wild explanations have been advanced to explain some disappearances. One in which there were rumours of sabotage, fuelled by the information that one of the six passengers was a King's Messenger, as well as suggestions of extra-terrestrial forces was the disappearance in 1947 of the Avro Lancastrian *Stardust*. A British South American Airways flight, it was crossing the Andes on the route that was the scene of Guillaumet's heroic survival described in Chapter 2. The Lancastrian could, however, fly well above the peaks. The radio operator reported as it passed over Mendoza, bound for Santiago, that the ground was in sight and they were climbing to a safe altitude to clear the terrain ahead. When he thought he was safely over the mountains the pilot began the descent. Though still in cloud he believed he was only three minutes from Santiago when the transmissions from the aircraft ceased. Search operations began on the approach to Santiago and were extended over the mountains but no trace of the aircraft was found.

Fifty-two years later the wreckage of an aero-engine was seen on the surface of a glacier on the flanks of Tapangato, 80km from Santiago and on the east side of the range. This turned out to be one of the four Rolls-Royce engines fitted to *Stardust*. A team of accident investigators and one hundred soldiers trekked into the mountains and located the traces of the accident – a few more parts were found but not the main structure of the aircraft. Glaciologists were called in and provided the explanation that the aircraft had crashed much higher on the glacier, had been soon covered by snowfall, perhaps initially by an avalanche, and absorbed into the glacier. It was then carried down in the gradually moving ice until some parts were spilled out. The wheels were found to be intact, proving that they had been retracted at the time of the accident, whereas the propellers were bent from striking the ground while still revolving. It would seem that the aeroplane was flown into the mountain under power. Why was the descent commenced before the aircraft had passed over the mountains? It was suggested later that *Stardust* had probably encountered winds of 100mph or more at around 24,000ft, which would have so slowed it down that all the navigational calculations were rendered inaccurate. This might have been the first encounter of an airliner with the southern jetstream, which encircles the earth from west to east in the same manner as the great 'river of wind' previously described in relation to Mount Everest. Neither enemy agents nor Martians were involved.

In an analysis of all accidents occurring between 1975 and 1994 to transport aircraft in the UK or to UK-registered aircraft abroad (including those classed as 'general aviation' but ex-cluding balloons) the writer found that weather was a causal factor (there is usually more than one factor) in 28% of all accidents, excluding those occurring in taxiing or at airport ramps. Of the total then listed one-fifth were associated with lack of visibility but of those that resulted in fatalities the visibility-related cases accounted for two-thirds of the total. (Symons, 1997) Most crashes involved small numbers of fatalities but an exception was the loss of a Boeing 727 on approach to Tenerife in April 1980. Unclear instructions from air traffic control contributed to the aircraft being flown in cloud into a mountainside at 5,500ft with the loss of all on board.

The Air New Zealand Antarctic disaster

Quite astonishing in its causes was the accident on 28th November 1979 when a Douglas DC10 of Air New Zealand, with 257 crew and passengers on a sightseeing flight to the Antarctic, was flown straight into Mount Erebus (3,795m, 12,450ft) in broad daylight, with the mountain not obscured by cloud cover. The assumption was made officially that the disaster was caused by pilot error, but the persistence of Captain Alwyn Gordon Vette, one of the senior pilots of Air New Zealand, who voiced the concerns of those who considered this an unlikely and inadequate explanation, was followed by the appointment by the New Zealand government of a Royal Commission, which it thought would confirm the verdict of pilot error. In fact, after long and arduous research, the Royal Commissioner, The Hon. P.T. Mahon QC produced a report that vindicated the crew and accepted the facts brought out by Captain Vette and his associates.

It was revealed that Flight Operations Division of Air New Zealand had made an error in altering the pre-programmed flight path of the aircraft. The alteration had been made as a result of a misunderstanding. An expression of concern by another flight crew had led to the track selected being changed back to one previously used and properly discarded. This information was not given to the aircrew flying the route the following day. The crash occurred at the low level of 1,500ft. The crew had been cleared to descend to that level and had let down in a carefully selected 'safe approach' area and, though now flying below a layer of stratus cloud, felt confident that forward visibility was entirely adequate.

Captain Vette uncovered, however, a problem that had been observed in early flights in the Arctic regions, the lack of a clearly defined horizon. The problem of whiteout, when snow and cloud produce a confusing visual effect, is well known to mountaineers as well as to aviators. Vette became convinced that this phenomenon could explain the apparently inexplicable behaviour of the pilot and crew as they flew at 1,500ft in apparently good visibility towards a mountain of 12,450ft, which lay directly in the track along which their computers had been programmed to take them. Vette made a thorough investigation of the phenomenon and his findings were accepted in full by Justice Mahon, destroying the conclusions put forward by the government's air accident investigator and the operating company. Pilots with experience of flying in the Arctic and Antarctic may be surprised that the pilots selected by Air New Zealand for these flights were not fully briefed on these risks. Furthermore, although it had been made mandatory for the commanders of the sightseeing flights to have flown previously into the region, this rule was allowed to lapse after the first two flights and none of the flight crew on the fatal excursion, Flight TE901, had been given such experience. In their briefing the subject of whiteout had been mentioned only in relation to snow showers.

In his book, Peter Mahon wrote:

'I could not help but reflect that, in spite of the worldwide resources of the airline and of Civil Aviation and their access to all information on this topic, neither of the two organisations had proposed to bring forward one word of evidence on this vital point.' (Mahon, 1984, 154)

Vette admitted to being surprised to learn that even experienced 'ice pilots' could lose the surface definition under what would normally be considered very good visual flying conditions. (Vette, with Macdonald, 1983, 170) A light layer of cloud could so diffuse the direct rays of the sun that the crucial mental ability to define the surface would disappear. Only if there were an object such as a black rock breaking the snow surface would effective visibility be maintained. As the flight proceeded along the set track there were at first such indications to left and to right but ahead these were absent and Captain Collins and his co-pilot were unknowingly flying into what is known as 'sector whiteout' (meaning whiteout localised in one area). Soon this was replaced by full whiteout, though the sun was shining into the cabin of the aircraft and passengers were taking photographs right up to the moment of impact.

Expert witnesses testified to the accuracy of these interpretations and Peter Mahon, being flown along the fatal track in a helicopter, on 28th November, one year after the crash, actually had the experience of seeing Mount Erebus disappear before his eyes and this was recorded in photographs, one of which was reproduced in Vette's book. (Vette, with Macdonald, 1983, 80) The whiteout problem was demonstrated to him by the pilot of the Hercules in which he was being flown back to New Zealand after his visit to the scene of the crash. As they flew at low level towards a ridge distinguished by an outcrop of black rock, he raised a hand and blocked out the rock and could no longer distinguish the ridge. The pilot confirmed that the conditions were very similar to those that would have been experienced by Captain Collins and his crew. (Mahon, 1984, 208–210) The command to pull-up would have come far too late for the pilot to clear the peak.

First Officer Rhodes, acting in the capacity of air accident investigator for the airline pilots' association summed up these facts in the statement:

'The matt surface of the snow gives no depth perception even in conditions of fifty miles visibility and causes the wall of snow ahead to appear as a flat plateau with a distant horizon.' (Mahon, 1984, 155)

The crash site on Mount Erebus has been declared a tomb by Antarctic Treaty nations.

Such extraordinary errors apart, modern aircraft flying with the aid of sophisticated instruments should not be in danger from mountains as they can normally be crossed at a completely safe altitude Most transport aircraft are now equipped with terrain awareness and warning systems that alert pilots to the danger ahead if the aircraft is flying towards a mountain below a safe altitude. Visual warnings based on radar interceptions are supplemented by automated oral calls to the crew to 'Pull-up, pull-up.' Then, of course, the pilot has to respond immediately. Occasionally it is too late. The risks, however, are much reduced compared with the past. A worldwide study by the International Civil Aviation Organisation (ICAO) in 2007 found that fatalities from CFIT visibility-related accidents fell from 1,818 in the five years 1997–2001 to 1,143 in the period 2002–2006. (CAA, 2008, 1)

CFIT, however, still constitutes one of the major causes of aviation accidents and there is continuous research and training to reduce it. Smaller aircraft, including air taxis and other general aviation aircraft are exposed to higher risks because their routes vary from day to day and pilots will often undertake operations in marginal weather conditions to try to meet the needs of clients. Older machines and light aircraft are least likely to be equipped with the more sophisticated warning systems, if any.

Clouds, mountains and light aircraft

Light aircraft without sophisticated electronic equipment and flown by pilots of often limited experience are especially likely to encounter problems caused by bad weather in unforgiving terrain. The introductory lines in a book on the causes of accidents by Ann Welch put the question 'Why do light aircraft pilots fly into clouds stuffed with mountains?' (Welch, 1978)

One example she gave of a typical situation was encountered by a French pilot flying his family to Lyons in the Rhone Valley.

Because of cloud ahead he turned west seeking another way round. That put him heading towards the Massif Central. He then found himself in cloud and climbed to 9,500ft to find clear skies. Unfortunately he was now lost but established radio contact with air traffic control in Marseille who referred him to Montpellier. He then concentrated on maintaining this re-assuring contact rather than trying to fix his position from a radio beacon. He repeated his original estimated time of arrival and was cleared to descend. He had in fact been facing a strong headwind and was much too far north. Suddenly his wife saw houses through a hole in the cloud and he pulled up into a climb but the aircraft crashed at 1,500m. Had the aircraft been a few metres higher it would have cleared the mountain; a few metres lower and the results would almost certainly have been fatal. As it was, the pilot and his passengers had suffered relatively minor injuries and he was still able to speak to Montpellier. Unfortu-nately he could not report his position and failed to mention that they were surrounded by snow, which would have immediately identified their location as it was the only area in the region with snow cover. A large-scale search failed to find them because it was centred 100km to the east. Next morning the pilot under-took the descent, leaving his passengers in the aircraft. He managed to reach a farm and a rescue was initiated. (Welch, 1978, 21–23) In such a situation, a modern terrain avoidance system (if fitted) might well avoid a collision with gently rising ground.

A case when there was no option but to collide with the mountain

On 10th July 2006 an accident occurred in the Scottish moun-tains when a warning to 'pull-up' would have been no help to the pilot. John Russell, an experienced glider pilot, was taking part in a competition over the Grampian Mountains in his Ventus high-performance sailplane of 18m wingspan. The set task was to fly north from Aboyne in the Dee Valley over as many as possible of twelve designated lochs. The forecast was that there would be a front approaching later in the day but the morning was fine and Russell got away early. After release from his tug he quickly found a wave and climbed to 10,000ft above mean sea level (amsl.) When he reached the most northerly point, flying at 12,000ft, there was rather more cloud about than he liked so he turned but decided to earn some more competition points on the way back. He arrived over Feshie Bridge as the last of the gaps in the cloud closed below him and, with high mountains on each side and a strong cross wind he thought that to land there would be risky. He had plenty of height in hand to get home to Aboyne. He had to cross the Cairngorm range which rises to over 4,000ft, but he was flying at 9,000ft.

Unfortunately the weather continued to deteriorate and he was swept into cloud at about 7–8,000ft and torrential rain beat down on the glider. The noise was fearsome and disorientating and he realised that he was caught in the downside of the wave and the glider was being literally washed out of the sky. His altimeter showed that he was losing height rapidly so he expected to crash into a mountainside. He levelled the wings and suddenly glimpsed sloping ground ahead. There was nothing he could to do to avoid striking the ground at some 55–60 knots. His left leg was trapped in the wreckage and he realised that it was broken. The aircraft's radio aerial was in the tail, which had broken off, as had the wings. He failed to find his mobile 'phone. He could only wait for the search parties that he knew would be alerted to find him. Unfortunately nobody knew he was high up on Beinn a'Bhuird, just below the summit (3,924ft), half-way between Ben Macdhui (4,296ft) and Braemar.

The altimeter showed that he was at about 4,000ft amsl with the mists swirling around and it was bitterly cold. He managed to reach a sweater and the cloth canopy cover, which he spread over the upper part of his body but he continued to suffer from the cold. It was about 14.15 and the cold got worse as the hours wore by. He was soaked through and the wind shook the glider. It was the longest night of his life.

The glider was reported missing about 21.00 and a search was initiated early next morning that eventually involved a Sea King from *HMS Gannet* (Prestwick), RAF Sea Kings from Lossiemouth and Boulmer, and RAF Mountain Rescue Teams from Kinloss and Leuchars. It was, however, from the cockpit of a Tornado strike aircraft that was diverted to the area that the sailplane was eventually spotted. The cloud had fortunately cleared during the morning and at about 10.30 a Tornado approached and banked in front of him so that Russell thought he had been seen. But the hours passed and nothing happened. He resigned himself to another night in pain and suspense, aware that having survived the crash, he now faced a serious risk of death from hypothermia. Then came a second Tornado about 17.30, which circled low several times and he knew that this time he had been seen. He still had to wait another 30 or 40 minutes before a Sea King arrived and a paramedic jumped out and rushed towards him. He had been trapped on the mountain for over 27 hours. The helicopter went off and brought firemen from Braemar to cut him free and the helicopter took him to hospital in Aberdeen but all this took another 30 hours. He later said that no praise was too high for all those who had cooperated to save his life and this gratitude was extended unreservedly to the members of the surgical and medical staff of the hospitals at Aberdeen and Leeds who did everything in their power to help him overcome his injuries – he lost six inches of his tibia from infection but in time he was able to take up hill walking and other activities. (Personal communications)

Given the conditions that had forced the glider to lose height, Russell could not have responded to any warning device that could have told him of the imminent approach to the ground. However, in the accident investigation report it was recommended that gliders should carry emergency locator beacons that would be triggered in the event of an accident and Russell fully agreed with this recommendation. (Personal communications and BGA Accident report) Unfortunately these devices are sometimes triggered falsely, perhaps owing to a hypersensitive switch, or they may fail when needed because of corroded batteries or wrong fitting but they have saved many lives. Flares or even an ordinary flashlight are useful back-up items and the latter at least should always be carried.

One of the factors that help to create a dangerous situation is the error in altitude reading of an altimeter that occurs as a result of a change in air pressure. A normal altimeter is an aneroid barometer and since clouds and hill fog are the result of condensation their presence is accompanied by a drop in air pressure and the altimeter then reads too high. Frontal cloud often approaches gradually and deceptively, slowly thickening and with the base dropping nearer the ground, then suddenly it arrives and the pilot loses all visibility, with the altimeter becoming increasingly unreliable. A mountaineer using a pocket aneroid barometer must always be prepared for such a possibility but any climber should always be trained to cope with hill fog. At least he should have time to check his surroundings and take a little time to plan his next move but the pilot does not enjoy the luxury of time and is in immediate danger if he is anywhere where the terrain rises around him. A radio altimeter will make for much greater safety but, like terrain avoidance devices, is not usually part of the equipment of a light aeroplane

Even a very modest hill can still catch out a low-flying pilot and lead to a somewhat similar situation and a helicopter is as vulnerable as any other aircraft. In January 2005, the pilot of a Bell 206B Jetranger, en route from the Exeter area to Staverton airport near Gloucester, made a decision to re-route his flight because of bad weather. Unfortunately the valley he flew up was gently rising into the Blackdown Hills, south of Taunton, and he crashed at about 980ft. Lack of continued contact led to 'overdue action' being initiated. ARCC Kinloss was informed and scrambled a search helicopter at 17.55. At 19.00 it was stood down owing to the unsuitable weather. An all-night ground search by the police, friends of the pilot and his passengers, and others also failed to find the missing aircraft. Rain had turned to snow and this probably made the helicopter, predominantly white in colour, difficult to see. It was spotted next morning in a copse by a member of the public, whose two dogs alerted him.

Tragically all four occupants had been killed in the crash. A meteorological aftercast indicated that the cloudbase was scattered at 200ft, reducing to ground level in rain, with visibility falling to 100m. The pilot was partially trained in instrument flying but had not completed his course and had not been issued with an instrument rating, so was not qualified to fly in cloud. The helicopter was equipped with two GPS systems but was not approved for operations under Instrument Flight Rules (IFR). (*AAIB Bulletin* No. 1/2006)

Hazards are always present in the mountains

Lest it be thought that only exceptional conditions and low cloud bring difficulties and dangers, it is appropriate to review the problems that are an integral part of all flying in mountainous and hilly regions. Norman Bailey, a former Army Air Corps pilot, has published a specialised book on mountain flying. He lists many adverse factors that are peculiar to, or exacerbated, when flying among mountains. Some of these are classed as medical. They include the loss of the normal horizon, vertigo and apprehension. The normal horizon is lacking when flying below the level of nearby terrain, necessitating frequent reference to instruments. Sudden and dramatic changes in height may produce vertigo and disorientation, as with the approach to a pinnacle with a sheer drop on all sides. Apprehension and tenseness at the controls are quite normal until adequate experience is gained. Insufficient oxygen may be a problem with helicopters and light aeroplanes not fitted with oxygen systems; leading to the symptoms familiar to mountaineers – shortage of breath, confusion, poor judgement and a false feeling of confidence. (Bailey, 2002, 3–4) The experience of these symptoms by Zeppelin pilots in the First World War was mentioned in Chapter 2.

Actual weather information is usually lacking in the mountains and conditions vary rapidly in space and time. The pilot must allow for turbulence and rolling winds with either a horizontal or vertical axis. The venturi effect may cause the altimeter to over-read because of a reduction in air pressure, especially in a valley or on a col. Winds blowing over an uneven slope may produce strong turbulence on both sides of a ridge. Rolls may form in the wind between multiple ridges, so that downdrafts may be found on upward slopes where updrafts are normally expected.

What may seem to be straightforward to the uninitiated passenger may require considerable care from the pilot. For example, there is a risk of becoming mesmerised when flying along a slope and failing to spot a protruding buttress. When it is necessary to climb over a ridge, it is recommended that updafts should be sought to reduce the time spent in the climb but, when approaching the mountainside with this objective, the approach should be done not directly but by taking a converging course. An updraft on the far side of a ridge should not be relied on as the turbulence on that side may be dangerous. Landings on lee slopes are likely to be acceptable only in emergencies because of turbulence and downdrafts. These are likely to endanger even a reconnaissance on a lee slope. The crossing of a crestline should always be made much higher, if possible, than the height of the crest itself – a point that would have been of great concern to Lieutenant Colonel Madan already flying at his altitude limit in the rescue, as described in Chapter 14, of Beck Weathers.

Cols are natural routes of passage (though not necessarily easy) for the traveller on the ground. For the aviator they offer the possibility of crossing a range that may be otherwise too high for the aircraft. There are, however, special hazards to be guarded against. A col almost always has currents of air passing through it and the funnelling of the wind will increase their speed. Rocky outcrops give rise to extra turbulence. Norman Bailey summarises the situation:

'The passage of a col combines all the techniques of slope flying, flight through a valley and the passage of a crest. Always approach with a good margin of height, and always approach along one slope and never fly across the axis of a col.' (Bailey, 2002, 36)

The pilot flying towards a col must also pay close attention to the last point at which a turn is practicable and not fly beyond that point if there is doubt about the exit from the valley. It is obvious that, when cloud base is low, or intermittently obscuring the target area, it is sometimes impossible to carry out a mission, though pilots will often do their best to find 'windows'. Rotary circulation (rotors) below a layer of stable air or associated with lee waves may lead to a strong increase in wind strength downwind and severe turbulence. (Bailey, 2002, 7–15)

Many of these problems that are especially relevant to helicopter operations, now used for most aerial tasks in the mountains, were first experienced and slowly came to be understood by the pilots of fixed-wing aircraft. In the 1940s, the rapid increase in wartime operations, including regular training exercises over hostile terrain in whatever weather came along – when forecasting was still a very uncertain exercise – led to a large increase in the accidents to aircraft occurring amongst British hills, as described earlier.

Air currents at Gibralter

One of the reasons why British pilots were among those who went to Thoret's pioneer school of mountain flying, referred to in Chapter 1, was the need to be better equipped to deal with the dangerous air currents at the Rock of Gibraltar. (Kossa, 1971, 14–15) These currents are still regarded as dangerous and requiring absolute precision at all stages of the approach and landing, as a recent incident emphasised.

In March 2006, the crew of a Boeing 757 carrying 186 passengers had a problem sufficient to lead to a field investigation by the Air Accident Investigation Branch based at Farnborough. Recognising the special features at Gibraltar, it was company policy to require the landing to be made only by a nominated pilot; hence the commander was in control. The forecast had been within the required limits of 1,000ft cloud ceiling and 5,000m visibility but likely to deteriorate and the crew had taken the precaution of loading extra fuel. At 19.45

during the final approach to Gibraltar airport the crew lost visual contact with the strobe lights and the commander elected to 'go-around' and divert to Malaga. As a turn was initiated, the air traffic controller considered from his radar returns that the aircraft was turning towards the 'Rock,' which rises to 1,420ft. He issued a warning together with an instruction to tighten the turn, which took the aircraft out of danger. The planned diversion was then carried out. The report notes that 'The local topography can result in wind variations resulting in strong turbulence and rapidly changing visibility and cloud conditions.' (AAIB Bulletin No.8/2006, 10–17) That such conditions can still cause problems, despite all modern safety aids, emphasises the risks faced by pilots when such aids were non-existent and can only lead to admiration for those who have deliberately sought out and learned to deal with such natural hazards.

In 2006 a joint Anglo/American programme called T-REX (Terrain-induced Rotor Experiment) was sponsored by the National Environment Research Council (NERC) and the Meteorological Office to measure gravity-wave activity and associated rotors in the lee of the Sierra Nevada range, based at Fresno, California. A British aeroplane, the prototype of the four-engine BAE (Hawker-Siddeley) 146 which became the Avro RJX airliner, was converted to an exceptionally refined research machine, which was allocated to this work between other tasks in Europe and Africa. The findings of this research were expected to have considerable value for pilots operating in mountain areas. (*Aerospace International*, Vol.33 No.4 April 2006)

The examples that have been quoted of dangers associated with air currents and turbulence have been largely related to machines that were underpowered in relation to the demands placed upon them. Deliberately flying into the mountain environment, whether or not engaged on legitimate and important business, can still be dangerous for even large and adequately powered airliners because of the risk of encountering clear air turbulence (CAT). On 7th March 1966 the pilot of a Boeing 707 on departure from Tokyo airport, bound for Hong Kong, asked permission from air traffic control to deviate from the direct route to enable the passengers to enjoy the view of Mount Fuji. The aircraft encountered a rotor on the lee side and broke up. (Taylor, 1988, 87–8.) 124 people lost their lives.

Volcanic dust

Occasionally mountains are the cause of even more bizarre accidents, erupting volcanoes being especially liable to entrap the unwary. On 24th August 1982 a Boeing 747 en route from Kuala Lumpur to Perth, Western Australia, was well established in the cruise at 37,000ft, about 130 miles southeast of Jakarta, when strange phenomena were noticed by the crew. The windscreens glowed as if in a brilliant display of St. Elmo's fire then the engine intakes started glowing as if illuminated from within. A few moments later the flight engineer called out 'Engine failure number 4.' Moments later the remaining three engines failed. All attempts to restart the engines failed and soon the cabin pressurisation and oxygen-delivery system failed so the captain had no alternative but to actually increase the rate of descent that was occurring naturally. At 14,000ft Captain Moody felt it necessary to inform the passengers and uttered the memorable words:

> 'Good evening, ladies and gentlemen, this is your captain speaking. We have a small problem. All four engines have stopped. We are doing our damndest to get them going again. I trust you are not in too much distress.'

Fortunately the crew were able to restart number 4 engine, the first to have failed, and ninety seconds later the others restarted. Captain Moody headed for Jakarta and as he came in to land he found that the windscreens and windows had turned almost opaque. Nevertheless he made a good landing to loud cheers from his passengers who had thought their fate was sealed. Two days of investigations revealed that the engine failures and the damage to turbine blades and the surfaces of wings and fuselage had been caused by a thick cloud of volcanic dust in the earth's atmosphere. Captain Moody received six awards for his achievements and international arrangements to locate and track clouds of volcanic dust were added to those for reporting severe storms. (Taylor, 1988, 96–98) In this case, Gunung Agung, an Indonesian volcano of 10,309ft (3,142m) and therefore some 27,000ft below the flightpath of the Boeing 747, had erupted earlier that day.

In 2010 when volcanic dust from an eruption in Iceland led to widespread closure of airports in most European countries, search and rescue operations were also affected by the restrictions imposed by the aviation control authorities but, though non-urgent operations were suspended, rescue helicopters were allowed to continue their mercy missions. The decision as to whether or not to undertake the flight was for the pilot to make, as is normal in hazardous circumstances, but it is believed that there were few, if any, instances of a requested rescue operation not being carried out.

As the 19th century drew to a close balloonists were not only flying over the Alpine ranges but were making a photographic record unprecedented in the geographical features revealed. The impressive glaciers with their complicated systems of crevasses and moraines were for the first time made available for cartographers, geographers, geologists, alpinists and others to study in detail. Taking these views with the bulky plate cameras of the period from the balloon baskets in temperatures low enough to cause technical problems, as well as numbed fingers, was no easy task. The flights conducted by Eduard Spelterini, described in Chapter One resulted in many such images to delight not only contemporaries but also later generations. The quality

1. *Spelterini preparing balloon 'Stella' at Jungfraubahn-Station Eigergletscher, 1904.*

may not be high compared with modern photographs but the record is unique. There is also no better way to compare the extent of the glaciers at that time with their shrunken forms of today.

2. *Monte Rosa and glacier confluence taken from Spelterini's balloon.*

3. *Georges Chavez preparing to take off in his Bleriot XI at Brig in 1910.*

4. *The DH50 in which Cobham flew to India to survey the projected airship route. Cobham is seen here with Arthur Elliott (flight engineer) on his right, Sir Sefton Brancker (Director of Civil Aviation) on his left, and the Maharajah of Datia.*

5. *A philatelic cover flown by Charles Lindbergh in a De Havilland DH4M, as shown on the special stamp, on the inaugural mail flight by Robertson Air Transport.*

6. *An airmail cover flown from Valparaiso to Santiago, then by Jean Mermoz over the Andes to Buenos Aires.*

7. *Powered by a supercharged Bristol Pegasus 9-cylinder engine,*
the Houston-Westland approaches Everest over the mountains of Nepal in 1933.

8. *Westland Whirlwind over Cwm Idwal in North Wales.*

9. *A Westland Whirlwind makes a landing at high altitude in Austria, 1961.*

10. *Westland Wessex on mountain operations.*

11. *RN Westland Sea Kings deployed in the Norwegian mountains.*

12. *The Pilatus P4 first flew in 1948 and was used as an ambulance and for parachuting rescuers, search dogs and supplies.*

13. *Pilatus SB-2 Pelican, STOL design, predecessor of the Porter.*

14. *Pilatus PC-6 Porter 'Yeti' supplied to the Dhaulagiri expedition.*

PICTORIAL MAGAZINE 2ᴰ

Airborne over
the Himalayas
1924-1925

The postcard sent by
Alan Cobham to his wife,
showing the DH.50 parked
on the Maidan at Calcutta.

MY AIR ADVENTURES
By ALAN COBHAM

*15. The De Havilland DH50 piloted by Alan Cobham on the survey flight
to India in 1924 as depicted on a contemporary magazine cover.*

16. *Austers of Mount Cook Airways, New Zealand, 1950s.*

18. A Pilatus PC-6 Porter on an Alpine glacier.

17. A Cessna 180 of Mount Cook Airways with skis retracted,
being prepared for a tourist flight from the Mt. Cook airstrip 1960.

19. PGHM rescuers with an Alouette III in the Mont Blanc range.

20. A Eurocopter EC145 poised for a rescue on a glacier in the Mont Blanc range.

21. *A rescuer with search dog boarding a Rega Agusta A109.*

22. *A rescuer on a longline descent from a Rega Agusta A109.*

23. *A Rega Da Vinci helicopter being signalled to a landing on a Swiss glacier.*

24. *Rescuer with stretcher landing from a Rega Da Vinci helicopter.*

25. *A Rega Da Vinci swoops down over the Bietschhorn, a peak in the Bernese Oberland to the southwest of the Jungfrau.*

26. *A Eurocopter Lama heavy-lift helicopter of Chamonix Mont Blanc Helicopters, showing the fuselage construction which helps operation in high winds.*

27. *A Eurocopter Lama heavy-lift helicopter of Chamonix Mont Blanc Helicopters.*

28. *A Sea King of* HMS Gannet *landing on a mountain in the Scottish Highlands.*

29. *RAF MRT roping down a stretcher in the Black Cuillin of Skye.*

30. *RAF Sea King landing to a flare on a rescue in the Cairngorms.*

31. *A Cairngorm MRT party carrying a casualty on a stretcher to an RAF Sea King.*

32. *Gliders on an airfield in the Pyrenees.*

33. *A Pilatus sailplane over the Alps.*

34. *A paraglider carrying pilot and passenger descending at Chamonix.*

35. *De Havilland Tiger Moth in a top-dressing role in the hills in Southland, New Zealand, 1960.*

36. *A Grumman TBM Avenger dropping fire retardant on a Canadian forest fire, 1972.*

37. *A Lindstrand hot-air balloon over the Alps.*

38. *An Air Zermatt Écureuil (Squirrel) at the Air Zermatt base near the Matterhorn.*

39. *Michel-Gabriel Paccard surveys from Chamonix the ridge rising from the Aiguille du Goûter past the Vallot refuge to the summit of Mont Blanc.*

40. *Georges Chavez gazes out from the centre of Brig towards the Simplon Pass over which he flew in 1910.*

CHAPTER 11

Air Support for Adventure and Exploration

Attempts to make use of aerial observation to help explorers extend the area of observation available to them go back into the balloon age before aeroplanes could be of practical use. In 1902 Captain Robert Falcon Scott used a tethered balloon in the Antarctic to extend the view available from his base. Lacking aeronautical training, he threw out too much ballast and shot up to the limit of his 800ft anchor chain. (Grierson, 1964, 181) He had an excellent view of the ice shelf and the mountains and on a second flight Ernest Shackleton took photographs. (Trewby (ed), 2002, 5) In Chapter 1 it was noted that de Saussure thought there might be a possibility of using a balloon in the early stages of an ascent of Mont Blanc but it was not until aeroplanes that were controllable in mountain conditions became available that there could be any significant help to mountaineers from the air. Their use in this role developed along with the use of aeroplanes to support mineral prospecting and other commercial activities remote from other means of transport, in which there was rapid development in the 1920s.

North American bush pilot and glacier operations

The growth in demand for flights into the boreal forest and tundra areas gave rise to a hardy and enterprising race of bush pilots, as they came to be called. In 1927 Fairchild made a major contribution to this branch of aviation when it introduced aircraft on which wheels, floats or skis could be easily inter-changed. Floatplanes were widely used in remote areas. The lakes provided ready-made landing opportunities, though with many hazards to avoid, including floating and semi-submerged timber and ice. In 1932 Bradford Washburn and a party of friends from Harvard University aimed to climb Mount Fair-weather (4,670m, 15,320ft) in the Alaskan 'Panhandle', from which Washburn had previously had to turn back. Supported by Hamilton Rice of Harvard's Institute of Geographical Explora-tion, they were able to hire a floatplane to take them to a lake near the mountain. However, they found the lake frozen solid and had to divert to an already familiar lake 'making a perfect pontoon landing in good old Lituya Bay.' They changed their objective to a reconnaissance of the nearer and hitherto un-climbed and unexplored Mount Crillon, 3,882m high. (Wash-burn and Smith, 2002, 81)

Also in 1932, ski-equipped aircraft took climbers to the base of Mt. McKinley, Alaska's highest mountain (6,194m). Throughout the 1930s climbing expeditions to many of the Alaskan mountains were supported both in this way and with airdrops. (Sherwonit, 1996, 12) The packtrains, operated by 'outfitters', became a thing of the past.

There were many hazards in glacier operations, as on the lakes. With the objective of climbing Mount Lucania (5,226m, 17,146ft) Bradford Washburn and Robert Bates were flown into the St. Elias Mountains in the Yukon on June 18th 1937, in a Fairchild 51 high-wing monoplane. Bob Reeve, their experi-enced bush pilot, had previously landed stores for them on the Walsh glacier but an unusual thaw had seriously changed conditions. There was a brittle crust through which the skis broke into soft snow and although they dug out the machine and he taxied it up to the camp he was unable to take off. Not until four nights had elapsed did the surface freeze enough for a take-off, even after he had thrown out everything he could to lighten the plane and changed the pitch of the propeller with a hammer. He than jettisoned his tools and emergency equipment to mini-mise weight and pointed the plane down the slope in the manner used in such circumstances to get maximum speed in minimum distance, gave the motor full throttle and just managed to lift off. Not surprisingly he was not prepared to return, either with the two other climbers who had been left behind to await a second trip, or to pick up Washburn and Bates after the climb.

Bates and Washburn decided to go ahead with their plans to make the first ascent of Lucania. After that was achieved on 9th July, instead of taking the direct way back, they decided to traverse Mount Steele (5,010m, 16,438ft), and then descend through territory they had been over before. This involved a 100km trek. They jettisoned gear progressively, even to tent guy ropes and most of their food, expecting to be able to replace it with food left behind by the previous expedition, only to find that most of the stores had been eaten by bears. The little that had been left, together with a squirrel and a rabbit that they shot, just got them to the point where they luckily met a pack train. (Roberts, 2002, Washburn and Smith, 2002)

Reeve continued to fly parties into the Alaskan mountains, including several glacier landings for Washburn but never landed again on the Walsh glacier. In 1938 Reeve flew over the Chugach Mountains and took photographs that suggested to Washburn a major new first ascent from the Matanuska glacier. Washburn had become well and truly 'hooked' on Alaska and was himself building up a remarkable collection of aerial photographs. A small expedition from the Harvard Institute of Geography was organised for 1938 and Reeve undertook to fly its members to a plateau high on the Matanuska glacier. Bad weather played havoc with the flight plans but eventually they were able to start the climbing and, though repeatedly delayed and nearly defeated by the weather, they eventually succeeded in reaching the 4,014m (13,176ft) high summit on 19th June. (Sherwonit, 1996, 120)

Washburn and Mount McKinley

By this time Washburn had established himself as a world-famous photographer of mountain and glacier systems from the air. In 1936 he had obtained support for the first aerial survey of Mount McKinley, including from the National Geographic Society. Washburn was able to borrow from Albert W. Stephens, a pioneer aerial photographer, a Fairchild F6 camera, which used rolls of film 120ft long and 9.5in wide, producing negatives 7 x 9 inches. Stevens had used it in the 1920s to photograph unexplored areas in the Andes and the Amazon basin. To make the best use of this huge camera – an advance on the Fairchild F-8 he had purchased himself and used on his Crillon and Yukon expeditions – Washburn sat cross-legged in the open doorway of the twin-engine Lockheed 12 that was hired for the McKinley work, tied by ropes to prevent him falling out. (Washburn and Smith, 2002, 106)

After the Second World War, air support operations began to be developed on a much larger scale. The landing and take-off techniques perfected in the Alps, as referred to in Chapter 4, together with development of reliable retractable ski-landing gear, enabled light aircraft to take off from city airports in Alaska and land on the glaciers directly below the steep rock walls that were the targets of the new breed of climbers. (Moore and Andrasko, 1978, 24)

A major step forward was taken when Brad Washburn directed a survey for the Office of Naval Research. He looked for a route to the summit of Mount McKinley that would be quicker and perhaps safer than the then normal route by the Muldrow glacier. From the air he spotted the possibilities of an approach on the western side of the mountain. After an article in the *American Alpine Journal* he was invited to lead the expedition, which succeeded in climbing the mountain by the West Buttress. In 1951 Dr. Terris Moore (as previously noted, a skilled bush pilot) flew in the four members of the climbing party, one at a time, in thirty-minute flights in his Piper Super Cub, despite bad weather. Wheels and skis being fitted, he was able to take off from a gravel airstrip and land high on the Kahiltna glacier, where base camp was established at 7,600ft. In addition, supplies were dropped from a US Air Force C-47 cargo aircraft for the advanced base camp at 10,000ft. They made at least a dozen passes and dropped 43 items, five by parachute, the rest free-fall. They now had the equipment to continue the survey work of two years earlier. (Washburn and Smith, 2002, 158–9) Moore also flew the successful climbers back but bad weather interrupted the ferrying and the last two had to wait a week before the weather relented sufficiently for the flights to take place.

This achievement caught the public imagination and climbing in the area expanded rapidly. This was the first major new route on a mountain planned from aerial photographs, and between 1954 and 1963 Washburn suggested nine further routes on the mountain, all of which were climbed. The West Buttress became the most popular route and by 1991 some 600 climbers had attempted it and the landing strip had become known as 'Kahiltna (or Denali) International.' Now it is the regular route for thousands of climbers. Talkeetna, a small outpost about half-way along the Parks Highway between Anchorage and McKinley, became the base for flights to Kahiltna. Before 1951, only 76 people had attempted to climb the mountain; by the end of 2001, the records showed it to have been attempted by 24,968 people of whom 12,830 reached the summit. During the same period there were 91 deaths on the mountain, an average of almost two per year, about one in 250 climbers. The combination of the height of the summit and Alaskan weather and low temperatures make it a particularly dangerous mountain. (Washburn and Smith, 2002, 171–2)

Supply dropping from the air

Dropping of supplies with or sometimes without a parachute had become accepted practice in the 1930s where a landing was not possible. There was always a risk of losses but it was remarkable what could be achieved by good packaging. In 1937 fresh eggs and warm biscuits were among the supplies dropped to Walter Wood when attempting the unclimbed Mount Lucania. (Roberts, 2002)

In 1938, the German expedition to Nanga Parbat received

197

some supplies by parachute on to the glacier ice, the first time a mountaineering expedition in the Himalaya had been given aerial support. This arose partly because the organisers had found it difficult to recruit enough suitable porters, the most experienced having been engaged by the British expedition to Everest. The aircraft was a Junkers Ju52, the three-engine transport machine that was the workhorse of the Nazi war machine. In 1938 the Ju52 had already many operations behind it in Spain in support of Franco's forces. It was to prove to be a very successful aircraft in the Second World War in its role as a transport machine and for dropping parachute troops, despite its obsolete appearance, with a fixed undercarriage and virtually no attempt at streamlining. Present-day tourists in the Alps often still see these elderly aircraft, a flight of them being maintained in immaculate condition by a Swiss company for operating nostalgic sightseeing and other flights.

However, by the end of the 1930s the need for an aeroplane better suited than existing aircraft to the demanding work in the mountains, involving flying into high and narrow mountain valleys, had become urgent.

The development of Short Take-off and Landing (STOL) aeroplanes in Switzerland

The Swiss firm Pilatus Aircraft Ltd. had begun work as early as 1941 on a new design. It had to outperform significantly the German Fieseler Storch high-wing reconnaissance monoplane in slow flying and load-carrying operations from short airstrips. A first attempt, the Pilatus SB-2 Pelican, was a more powerful machine with a Pratt and Whitney Wasp Junior air-cooled radial engine rated at 446hp and carried a much greater payload than the Storch. It first flew in 1944 and soon proved its worth in passenger and cargo work, photography, surveying and as an air ambulance. In 1947, a 300m landing strip was constructed between Täsch and Randa, 7 km below Zermatt, for Seiler-Hotels, but the service envisaged was not developed. (Pilatus, 1989, 2)

In 1958 Pilatus began to work on a new design for a specifically STOL (Short Take-off and Landing) design, the PC-6, which became the legendary Pilatus Porter. One of the early Porters was delivered to Hermann Geiger in December 1959 and immediately put to work in the alpine transport and rescue services operated by what was soon to become Air-Glaciers, based at Sion, as described in Chapter 4. Another was then allocated to the support of the Swiss/Austrian/Polish expedition to Dhaulagiri, led by Max Eiselin. The machine was named *Yeti*, the Sherpa name for the so-called 'Abominable Snowman,' and was flown by Ernst Saxer and Emil Wick to Nepal to be based at Pokhara. (Pilatus, 1999, 22, and Emil Wick, Internet, 2005)

Reconnaissance flights around the mountain revealed two possible sites for a landing strip, at 5,700m at the foot of the north east spur and at 5,200m on the Dambush Pass. At the time the record for the highest landing was 4,200m so even the lower site would create a new world record, but the higher site was used. (Emil Wick, Internet, 2005)

Each day from March 29th two or three flights were made from Pokhara to deposit supplies on the mountain before the daily build-up of clouds limited flying. Unfortunately engine trouble developed, causing the flights to be interrupted until a new Lycoming engine was obtained from Switzerland. Radio contact had also failed so the climbers did not know what was happening. After three weeks the flights were restarted but on May 5th the rubber grip on the control column broke off on take-off from the Dambush Pass and caused a crash landing. Fortunately the pilots were uninjured and were able to walk to safety. Despite the loss of the *Yeti* the support programme had achieved its main objectives and six members of the expedition reached the summit of Dhaulagiri on May 13th and ten days later two more reached the top.

Emil Wick, who had become something of a legend for his flying in the high mountains, was seconded to Royal Nepal Airlines as a training captain. During his twelve years with RNA he is reputed to have made more than a thousand landings at

Syangboche airstrip above Namche Bazar in the Sola Kumbu valley. At almost 4,000m it is the highest regularly used airstrip in the world, some 120m (400ft) long between the mountain at one end and a ravine at the other. He developed the art of flying into the Western Cwm – known as 'the hole' – and using rising air currents to carry the Porter up the Lhotse face to far above its normal ceiling. Before Reinhold Messner and Peter Habeler became, on 8th May 1978, the first climbers to reach the summit of Everest without oxygen, Messner, on a flight with Wick, insisted on not using the oxygen mask provided. His fellow passengers observed that he turned rather blue and his eyes crossed but he remained fully conscious. (Emil Wick, Internet, 2005, 4)

Easing tasks in the Alps

In the Alps, aircraft have transformed access to high glaciers, where before the advent of help from the skies, every piece of wood and other material required to build or maintain a refuge had to be carried by man or beast up mountain tracks, across crevassed glaciers and up rocky promontories. Frison-Roche recalled the tasks faced by the porters in the case of equipping and supplying the Couvercle refuge at 2,700m above the right bank of the Telèfre glacier. This involved crossing crevasses and steep ice slopes in which staircases had to be hacked so iron ladders were installed in the worst sections. Carrying loads of sixty or more kilos up these demanded the combined skills of a champion weight lifter with the surety of step of a skilled mountaineer and a total absence of vertigo. (Frison-Roche, 1981, 337) One porter carried the cast-iron body of a stove, weighing 110kg. Some would do a six-hour carry from the Montenvers first thing in the morning and then a second load of 85kg in the afternoon.

Parachute dropping and then glacier landings had eased the burdens in many locations, but only with the helicopter age came general relief. Helicopters could, in minutes, carry up pre-fabricated panels and, eventually, complete cabins, at least of the smaller kind, as well as pylons for cable-cars and electricity transmission and many other items to be lowered gently and precisely on to a prepared site. The time required for construction was reduced to a fraction of what was formerly accepted, and at the same time costs also tumbled, despite the high hourly operating costs of helicopters. Helicopters have become indispensable for a vast range of other jobs up to the scale of the building of a new dam. Commercial support operations loom especially large in the economics of private firms in countries like France, where the main rescue services are handled by government bodies. There have been similar revolutions in practices even in smaller ranges like the Scottish Highlands and Welsh hills, for tasks ranging from clearing bracken and reafforestation to carrying in electricity pylons and maintenance teams.

Support for climbers today

In the most remote mountain ranges where access for expeditions otherwise entails a long trek in, the use of aircraft has now revolutionised the approach and reduced the time involved to a mere fraction of what was formerly required. In North America it has made major climbs in Alaska possible to climbers with only a week or two available – or even a long week-end in the more accessible ranges, like Denali (Mount McKinley). More remote mountains in the polar and sub-polar regions generally lack other practical means of access, involving otherwise long sea and sledging expeditions. The ascent of Vinson Massif, at 4,897m the highest point of the Antarctic continent, is necessarily a favoured target since its ascent is essential for any climber trying to ascend the highest mountain on every continent. Antarctica has also a vast number of unclimbed mountains, as well as unlimited opportunities for making first ascents of new routes. Aircraft fly into Patriot Hills, where conditions make it possible to operate aircraft fitted with wheels as well as ski-planes. From there, Vinson is an ascent normally spread over five days. Patriot Hills is also the favoured departure point for the growing number of parties that cannot resist the lure of a trek to the South Pole.

Adventure Network International has made a speciality of flying parties for trekking and mountaineering into Patriot Hills. They charter big jets, such as the four-engine Ilyushin Il 76, complete with a Russian crew, normally based in Siberia, for a frequent service in the Antarctic summer months from Punta Arenas at the southern tip of Chile. High winds make the service irregular but it is still an easy option for getting into the Antarctic, compared with the days before such a service existed.

Onward from Patriot hills, parties can be taken nearer to their goals by small aircraft, the main workhorse being the De Havilland Twin Otter, with helicopters for shorter trips

Mount Everest

The best-known example of routine aerial support for mountain travellers is probably the journey to Everest, with travel to the region eased to a short flight to the simple but effective airstrip from where Everest Base Camp is easily attained. This is of great help to expeditions and also has opened up the region to trekkers and tourists. The downside for serious climbers is that if they avail themselves of this opportunity, they forego the degree of acclimatisation associated with the walk-in.

If acclimatisation is curtailed the risk of mountain sickness is increased. Climbers offset this by adopting suitable procedures, notably by making gradually higher ascents and limiting the time at each stage, returning to lower levels for rest and to benefit from the easier and more relaxing sleeping conditions available at the lower camps. For visitors who are not fit, going up to stay at even lower or intermediate levels such as Everest Base Camp can produce sudden and serious illness. In that case a helicopter is needed for immediate evacuation. After he had found increasing inability to acclimatise at altitude, Sir Edmund Hillary made use of a helicopter to enable him to continue his great efforts on behalf of the Nepali people. He worked during the day on the projects in hand and was flown down to lower levels after each day's work.

Once helicopters had the performance to lift supplies above Base Camp levels there was obvious attraction in having them ferry supplies into the Western Cwm. Guido Monzino, a wealthy Italian newspaper owner, took with him to the mountain a team of sixty-four climbers, supported by seventy Sherpas. Few luxuries were omitted in the planning. Even carpets and easy chairs were provided for the leader's tent. Italian air force helicopters provided a ferry service into the camps but one of them crashed in the icefall. Fortunately there was no loss of life but the Nepalese government imposed a ban on the use of aircraft above Base Camp except for emergencies. (Unsworth, 2000, 462, 746) This was a law, however, that many regarded as one to be circumvented or ignored.

Using a helicopter to escape responsibility

There have been cases of appalling failure of civilised human responses to crises involving trekking or climbing groups. Joe Simpson has illustrated this in a book that looks at a number of unattractive aspects of the expansion of climbing and trekking in the Himalaya and adjacent mountain ranges. These have included helicopter evacuation after a devastating storm or other serious problem, leaving porters to fend for themselves. (Simpson, 1997) Fortunately he was able also to give examples of completely different behaviour where porters were lifted out by helicopter along with expedition members.

Sherpas' homecoming by helicopter

A Polish expedition to Annapurna in 1996 recorded a case in which some Sherpas decided to pay for helicopter transport themselves. Thirteen members of the expedition left Pokhara with ten porters on 22nd August for the North Sanctuary. The final four days necessitated trekking in incessant rain, plagued by leeches, along isolated paths and building improvised rope bridges across treacherous rivers. On 5th and 6th September two other Poles flew in by helicopter with three tons of food and equipment. Noting that helicopter transport was often cheaper than hiring porters, Waldemar Soroka then commented:

> 'In our case the use of a helicopter was absolutely essential, given the harshness of the terrain and the fact that our porters were terrified at the prospect of returning over difficult river crossings without our help. So they decided to give up part of their wages in order to return by helicopter.' (Soroka, 1998)

One hopes they got special rates on a returning helicopter or they would presumably have earned very little indeed from their arduous and dangerous work.

Sherpas' earnings and family friction

Tourism has been responsible for significant though localised improvement in the lot of the poor in many undeveloped regions, and this, in the case of mountain regions, means predominantly mountaineering and trekking. The most spectacular case has been Nepal, following the extraordinary growth in demand from those who have the ambition, backed by sufficient money, to attempt the ascent of Everest. To a lesser, but still considerable, extent, this demand extends to other peaks in the Himalaya, Karakoram and other great ranges, so that employment in many other regions has also benefited to varying degrees.

According to a recent study of mountaineering in the world's highest mountains, aimed at revealing the experience and attitudes of the Sherpas, it seems that when the attempt to make the first ascent of Everest in 1953 seemed likely to succeed there was a view among the porters that this would lead to an end in the demand for their services. This had become an important source of revenue to many Sherpas, especially those who had succeeded in carrying to great altitudes. Tenzing Norgay claimed in his autobiography that he had repudiated this idea and that he had

204

foreseen that Everest would attract many more expeditions and there would be many more jobs. (Neale, 2002; 2003, 281) This has most certainly been the case and portering has become a road to riches – at least by Nepalese standards – for many Sherpas, with those who have been able to carry high being far more rewarded for their efforts than ordinary porters. The dangers, of course, have always been and will remain immense. Many domestic differences have arisen between men who want to do this work and wives who fear their menfolk will meet with death or serious injury. (Neale 2002, 2003, *passim*) However, the situation remains that the economy of the Khumbu valley and its surroundings is hugely bound up with tourism and is to no small extent dependent on air transport to bring in the travellers and the commodities needed to support them.

Long-range mountain rescue support

Mountain rescue is treated in this book as a separate major aeronautical activity, but in many cases its role is still limited to getting the ground-based rescue teams as close as possible to the site of an accident when weather precludes lifting out the casualty to a hovering helicopter. However, there have been some remarkable examples of extraordinary long-range rescue operations, made possible only by the supporting use of large transport aircraft. Such was the case with the rescue in 1970 of the Austrian climber, Dr. Gerd Judmaier. With Dr. Oswald Oelz he had reached the summit of Batian, the main peak of Mount Kenya (5,199m; 17,058ft), and had begun the descent when a block of rock came away and took Judmaier down with it. He suffered serious injuries, which Oelz treated as well as he could. Then, leaving with the casualty what little food and drink they had – some whisky and a tin of fruit – he started down to get help, with little hope of being able to save Judmaier's life. He reached the Kami hut and found some British and American climbers who at once volunteered to help. One of them climbed in darkness to the Top Hut at 15,700ft, from where he was able to use an emergency radio to call the police, who alerted the

Mountain Club of Kenya in Nairobi. The club had only a rudimentary rescue organisation but volunteers were soon on their way through the night to the mountain. They hired a light aeroplane from which they spotted the injured man, who waved to them. They flew around and decided on the best rescue route. This still, inevitably, involved difficult climbing and a long descent.

Oelz started up the mountain despite excruciating pain from his hands, which had been burned by the rope when he had tried to hold Judmaier. A companion had to give up because of mountain sickness and Oelz had to lower him, running the rope through several interlinked karabiners. Oelz went up again the next day, and forty-eight hours after he had left him, reached Judmaier, still alive but in great pain. Oelz injected morphine and, with others now to help, they moved him a little way but he was in too much pain for them to do more. The next morning (Day 4) a helicopter, piloted by Jim Hastings above its normal ceiling, landed near the Kami hut with plasma. This was carried up and another bitter night was spent on the minute ledge. On Day 5 Hastings came again to the mountain with his helicopter and tragically crashed and was killed. The following day a 600ft rope was dropped from an aeroplane but drifted away and was lost. Oelz continued to try to treat a rapidly worsening Judmaier in appalling conditions.

Then came the astonishing news that six Austrians were flying out to Nairobi. Their assistance had been requested by Gerd Judmaier's father, who had himself flown to Nairobi. The rescue team hired a Cessna to fly round the mountain to study the situation, then flew to Nanyuki, the nearest landing place to the mountain and trekked in over two high passes to the Kami hut and then climbed, on Day 8 to the place where the others had lowered Judmaier on a stretcher that had been hauled up. The experienced Austrians took over and demonstrated their professionalism, developed in the Alps, quickly organising the difficult and dangerous task of lowering the stretcher, largely by moonlight. Eventually they reached the Kami hut. From there Judmaier was carried to the airstrip and flown to Nairobi, where

206

he was successfully operated on. (Oelz et al, 2003) This summary gives little indication of the immense climbing skills that were displayed, its main purpose being to demonstrate the role of the aircraft, without which the rescue would almost certainly have failed.

Even longer flights were involved in the rescue on Kinabalu, on Borneo, at 4,101m (13,455) the highest peak in South-East Asia, described in Chapter 8.

Helicopter equals quick bath!

To close this chapter on a lighter note, Catherine Destivelle made a new route, solo and self-belayed on the left flank of the Bonatti Pillar in the Mont Blanc range in the summer of 1991. She sat out a four-day storm and survived a fall of some ten metres. She did have some degree of back-up by radio contact with Chamonix and frequent observation from a helicopter. She had intended to go on over the summit and descend to the Charpoua glacier but ended up accepting a helicopter lift back down. She said that she afterwards regretted doing so 'but at the time all I wanted was a hot bath.' (Griffin, 1992/93)

Yet to be considered, there is another most important role for aviators in the mountains, closely allied to support flying and often performed partly by the same people – the work of environmental care and protection. There are also negative effects to be weighed in assessing the environmental relationships. It is these aspects of mountain aviation that form the subject of the next chapter.

CHAPTER 12

Mountain Aviation and the Environment

In the 21st century the environment is receiving the attention – though not often the actual protection – that it deserves, and that we owe to future generations. The issues of climatic change and global warming have become major subjects in world discussions and arguments. Aviation is one of the sectors much attacked because of its role in adding substantially to environmental pollution and other undesirable effects but it is less widely appreciated that there are many ways in which it actually contributes to conservation and improvement and has done for many decades. This is particularly true in the mountains where aircraft have made major contributions to controlling damage caused by man and his economic activities. This chapter will attempt to set out some of the actions and effects that are to be considered in any assessment of its role.

One of the most outstanding examples of economic and social changes to a region, deriving from mountaineering achievement, began in the Himalaya in the 1950s. At that time if aircraft were called upon to give help in any mountains with supplies, it could still be only through the medium of parachute drops, except in the landing of aircraft – mainly light aircraft – on glaciers. Both could, however, be of significant value, far beyond most previous achievements of this kind for non-military purposes. The possibilities of transporting building materials were not lost on Sir Edmund Hillary when, in the decade following the first ascent of Everest by himself and Tenzing Norgay, he set out to build schools in the Khumbu region. Even to check on progress involved a month of travel and considerable logistic effort.

For his 1963 expedition, Hillary 'toyed with' the idea of constructing an airfield to service his projects and approached an American company to see if they would make available an aircraft for the project. The company replied that they could not undertake this and justified their decision with reference to a historic example from the American Civil War. They said that a messenger conveyed a warning to a threatened region by a famous night ride on a horse. In the USA, the company explained, 'everyone knows the name of Paul Revere, but no one knows the name of the horse. I feel this describes our position in regard to furnishing an airplane from our publicity budget.' So no help was forthcoming. (Hillary, 1964, 15)

Hillary did not give up the idea of aerial assistance and had most of the supplies flown into Kathmandu in a chartered DC3. It was, he commented 'not the cheapest but certainly the easiest way of getting anything into Nepal.' (Hillary, 1964, 17) Loads still had to be carried up by porters to the Khumbu, there being no helicopters available. The Soviet Union had given Nepal several large helicopters, with the loan of aircrew to fly them. Unfortunately the Nepalese government failed to pay the agreed costs after an initial period and the airmen were recalled. (Hillary, 1964, 113) Hillary's party found a smallpox epidemic raging in the Khumbu area, with many fatalities. Hillary appealed for an airdrop of vaccine and this request resulted in the successful dropping of parcels of vaccine only two days later; but Hillary received a bill for the mercy flight. (Hillary, 1964, 42)

In 1964, Sir Edmund Hillary was back in the Khumbu region with a team from the Himalayan Trust. One of them, Jim Wilson, was approached by a group of farmers from the small village of Lukla, tucked away in a tributary valley. They wanted to sell some land and thought it might be useful for an airfield, even suggesting that the wind always blew in the right direction. Hillary and his helpers were astonished that the local people should have worked this out but Hillary was able to satisfy his long-held conviction of the need for an airstrip (Hillary, 1964,

169). He was able to purchase the land on behalf of the Nepalese government. All the work was done by physical labour. The last stage of levelling was rushed through by recruiting fifty Sherpas and supplying them with quantities of chang, the native drink, which stimulated them to link arms and dance their way back and forth until a sufficiently firm and level surface had been produced. The first landing by a Pilatus Porter brought in two civil aviation officials who approved the landing strip and Lukla became the busiest mountain airfield in Nepal, serving trekkers, climbers and others who came to the Everest region. (Hillary, 1999, 230–32)

Sir Edmund Hillary wrote that, when he first went to the Khumbu region in 1951:

'the forests were superb – big trees up to an altitude of 13,000 feet and extensive areas of azaleas and juniper shrubs covering the rocky valleys up to 16,000 feet. In 1952 the Swiss Everest expedition cut vast quantities of juniper to burn at their Base Camp and there was still much of this left in 1953. We in our turn burnt the remainder of the Swiss firewood and cut extra ourselves. So the higher valleys after a succession of expeditions quickly became devoid of virtually all shrubs and it is only in more recent years, when the use of firewood in the high valleys has been prohibited, that there has been a modest resurgence of the high-altitude flora. In building Lukla airfield we were partly to blame for the tremendous increase in the number of trekkers that visit the Khumbu, now exceeding 17,000 each year.' (Hillary, 1999, 290)

That there was a downside to the work was thus not over-looked but the economic gain was of enduring significance in improving the lot of the local people.

New Zealand experience

Hillary, born and brought up in New Zealand, would have already seen, at first hand, the struggle to restore the middle and lower slopes of the mountains there to something like their former vegetative glory – the native tussock grasslands. New

Zealand, one of the most mountainous countries in the world, is also the one – apart from even more isolated islands – with the fewest native mammals and predators. Hence, when well-meaning but misguided Europeans introduced a variety of animals, which ranged from domestic and farm animals, including sheep, pigs and cattle, to deer, the balance of nature was seriously disturbed. The deer were turned loose on the mountains, thereby, it was thought, enriching the fauna for hunters and others. This, however, also launched the harbingers of destruction of the indigenous mountain vegetation. Multiplying rapidly, with no natural enemies to control their numbers, deer wreaked havoc on the forests and tussock grasslands (aided and abetted, of course, by the pastoralists' flocks of sheep) so that up to and above the treeline the mountains became deeply scarred by gully and sheet erosion. Other introduced animals, such as rabbits, also multiplied and caused similar destruction at lower levels. Farmers and pastoralists had almost no chance of reversing this trend until, after the Second World War, it was recognised that aircraft could become 'tractors of the air' in the attack on vegetation destruction and soil erosion.

Aircraft had been in use in North America for spraying chemicals to control pests and diseases of crops and forests from as early as 1920 and had also been successful in fighting forest fires. The Soviet Union had carried out similar operations from 1922 and was quick to develop the use of aircraft on the vast areas of the state and collective farms imposed on all the agricultural landscapes of the USSR from 1928. It was reported officially that there were 224 aircraft in use for agricultural and forestry work by 1932. (Symons, 1975) In later years hundreds of aircraft were in use, migrating according to season from one Soviet republic to another according to the varying tasks needed in different regions, supplementing regional fleets. (Grazh. Av; Trans. i Svyaz)

Soil erosion and forest denudation

Erosion is a natural process and is taking place continuously on all mountains – though much faster on some than on others, according to rock type, slope, climate and other factors. On the high peaks, ridges and steepest faces there is little that man can do to retard it as it is maintained by freeze-thaw processes, rock falls, avalanches and rivers, all contributing to the life cycle of the mountains. At more moderate altitudes, however, where natural vegetation normally provides a protective skin for the earth, it is altogether different. Here, the human race has been systematically – or chaotically, perhaps one should say – stripping the forests for agricultural and industrial purposes.

In the case of New Zealand over 50% of the South Island and some 10% of the North Island is mountainous, with some five million hectares covered with natural grasslands, mostly of a tussock nature. These hills are steeply sloping and particularly prone to accelerated erosion induced by over-grazing, a problem that did not exist before the colonisation of the islands in the 19th century. As the severity of the situation was realised in the 1930s and especially after the Second World War it was found that hill pastures responded positively to topdressing with phosphate fertilisers and trace elements and reseeding – all involving moderate quantities. Access for treatment to high and remote pastures was, however, too difficult until the possibility arose of using light, single-engine aircraft. Extensive trials and demonstrations to farmers led to rapid expansion of the new industry between 1947 and 1950. In 1949 the Soil Conservation and Rivers Control Board reported to the government that unless the large-scale erosion and denudation of the hills and mountains was reversed the country would face a large decline in production. It recommended aerial sowing of seed and fertilising, fencing and reafforestation. (James, 1969, 497) The first commercial company to specialise in this work was formed in 1949. (Steele, 1969, 368) Disposals from the armed services provided a cheap source of aircraft, the De Havilland DH82 Tiger Moth, designed as an elementary trainer, being the favourite for the new job. It could carry only about one-quarter of a ton of superphosphate – a granulated fertiliser – but that seemed a lot to farmers whose only way of distributing it where a tractor could not go had been by hand from horseback.

212

Fertilisers and seed had to be transported in large quantities by road and track to the aircraft, so in order that the planes would be operating from sites as near as possible to the area to be treated, airstrips were built in many unlikely places on the crests of hills and ridges, often little over 200m long and with a grade as steep as 25%. (James, 1969, 498) Pilots would routinely take-off with a full load of fertiliser from a hill-top strip and allow the aircraft to lurch alarmingly towards the valley while picking up adequate flying speed to climb to its target area. It was probably familiarity with the resourcefulness of such pilots – as well as his own service as a navigator in the Royal New Zealand Air Force – that would have made Hillary alert to the possibilities for creating airstrips in the Everest region. The Pilatus Porter, which Hillary had in mind to use those airstrips and which, in due course, was among the aircraft used in New Zealand, was designed to take off in as little as 180m with a landing run of only 130m. For fertilising work, it could carry over 1,600kg. An aircraft with similar characteristics, the Fletcher F-124, powered by a 750hp engine was adopted as the standard agricultural aircraft in New Zealand, built there, and called the Cresco. The 'ag pilot' could throw it into a procedural turn at the end of each run. This involves standing the plane virtually on its wingtip between ten and a few score feet above ground, hundreds of times a day, frequently landing to have the hopper refilled and taking off again within a couple of minutes.

Treatment from the air has made great improvements in restoring the vegetative cover. Cost is, of course, an important factor and normally there has to be the prospect of productive gains for the work to be undertaken. By the 1970s the tonnage applied from the air had exceeded a million tonnes, spread over more than seven million hectares. The work is still an important aspect of the economy of the New Zealand hill sheep farms and an entertaining description of it is given by an English visitor who went to New Zealand as part of a round-the-world trip. Martin Buckley found top-dressing flying a sensational experience even after sampling aerial work by bush pilots in Canada (where he himself qualified as a pilot), as well as beach-landing airline and postal services in the Scottish Hebrides and missionary activities in Africa. (Buckley, 2003)

Aerial treatment of British hills

In an attempt to increase production from hill and marginal lands after the Second World War experiments were made in Great Britain using Lancaster bombers to drop lime on the pastures, but such large four-engine aircraft were uneconomic and the quantities of lime needed on the acidic grasslands of the British Isles rendered the idea impracticable. In due course however light aircraft and helicopters became widely employed in forestry, fire-fighting and bracken control.

British hills have suffered less from erosion because the moist climate helps the vegetation cover to maintain itself, but care has to be taken to protect intermediate and lower levels from overgrazing and other detrimental land-use. The Brecon Beacons provide an example. Rising to almost 3000ft, they are very attractive to hill walkers, present no technical difficulties in their ascent, and are easy of access by road. The number of tramping feet throughout the 1960s and 70s produced a fearsome scar up the hill from Storey Arms to Corn Du and Pen-y-Fan, the highest points, and it was found necessary to construct a path, though this itself is all too obvious from nearby hills. On the peat-covered plateau land also there has been serious erosion and helicopters have been used to ferry up large bales of straw to place against the exposed faces of the peat hags in an effort to reduce erosion. Spraying from the air is also a recognised aid to controlling bracken infestation, which is a constant threat to heather and grass moorland.

Helicopter help to alpine livestock farmers

Helicopter operators can rightly claim that much of the other work of which they are capable is environmentally friendly including much needed transport, fertilising land and seeding

214

for forestry and agricultural purposes. Rega (Swiss Air-Rescue) as part of their services to mountain farmers organises helicopter rescue of cows and other animals that have fallen into ravines, been struck by lightning or are otherwise in difficulties, including the recovery of carcasses. The communes and owners have a legal responsibility to remove carcasses, the time when it was acceptable to bury them on the spot being long past, but removal from the high pastures to the valley was often beyond their means. Currently, around one thousand animals are lifted out annually to the nearest road. This is still free to owners that have a family subscription to Rega, otherwise Rega arranges with another non-profit organisation to complete the work.

Aerial forest fire control

Fighting forest fires is now an important role in which aircraft contribute to the preservation of the mountain environment. After the Second World War, as in crop spraying, the availability of ex-military aeroplanes provided an opportunity for enterprising pilots to offer their services economically for such purposes. Some government bodies with major forest fire problems, often occurring every dry season, became steady employers of private firms or even set up their own services.

It was in North America that the most dramatic aeronautical contribution to fire control developed. In both the United States and Canada, fleets of former bombers and transport aircraft proved the value of large aircraft in which tanks could be installed with capacity to hold considerable quantities of water or chemical retardants. Many of these machines were four-engine types, offering long range and safety in operation but some of the smaller aircraft, such as the single-engine Grumman TBM Avenger, developed to fight in the wide open spaces of the Pacific Ocean, had the space to install tanks of considerable size – 2,724 litres (600 Imperial gallons) in the case of the Avenger. In 1962 the forest service awarded the first contract for fire control from the air in the predominantly mountainous state of

215

British Columbia to the firm Skyway Air Services following four years of trials after fires had destroyed 850,000 hectares of forest and grazing land in 1958. Twelve TBM Avengers were stationed in four groups of three aircraft at Kamloops, Smithers, Prince George and Cranbrook. Each group was also equipped with a Cessna 180 Bird Dog lead and observation aircraft flown by a Skyway pilot accompanied by an officer of the forest service. This approach, using fire retardant chemicals or water, proved very successful in limiting outbreaks before they grew too large for ground operations to control. In the season when they were not required in this role, deployment of aircraft to eastern Canada to spray forests against the spruce budworm and other pests ensured maximum utilisation of the fleets.

After some years Skyways established a specialised subsidiary, Conair, which became the largest aerial fire-fighting company in the world. Bigger and faster aircraft were added to the fleet of Avengers, including other ex-military types and ex-airliners including the four-engine Douglas DC6 with its very large capacity. The large number of lakes in the Canadian forest and mountain regions led to the utilisation of the Consolidated PBY Canso (or Catalina) amphibian, which could operate from the larger lakes and therefore have shorter distances to fly from the water source to the fires to be attacked, as well as having flexibility for temporary bases in lakes or sea inlets close to the affected territory. The ability to scoop up water whilst on the move was one of the greatest attractions of such a machine and led to the design of the specialist Canadair CL215 which was soon adopted in Mediterranean lands, notably in the south of France.

The Soviet Union was another major user of aircraft for fighting forest fires. In the Russian Republic about 300 fixed-wing aircraft and 200 helicopters were used in the 1970s for seasonal control of forest fires. (Symons, 1976, 292) The more recently developed Russian Irkut-Beriev Be-200 large amphibian has been attracting a great deal of interest in many countries. Powered by two by-pass jet engines mounted on pylons above the wings to avoid water entering the engines on take-off and

216

landing it can operate from lakes in remote areas. It has tanks for twelve tonnes of water and auxiliary tanks for fire retardant chemicals. It entered service with the Russian Ministry of Emergency Situations in 2003 and has also been purchased by Azerbaijan. (Irkiut-Beriev website) It has been also used in Sardinia, Portugal, Greece and Indonesia. In Sardinia in 2005 the leased Be-200 completed 46 sorties in 90 flying hours, scooping up water on 255 operations. It dropped a total of 1,800 tonnes of water and chemical fire retardant. It was especially credited with being instrumental in extinguishing major fires in the mountains. (Laskina, 2005) In the summer of 2010 millions of TV watchers worldwide had glimpses of this impressive aircraft attacking the fires that swept Russia, causing immense destruction. The Be-200 can also be configured for search and rescue, maritime patrol, passenger transport and as an air ambulance.

Helicopter fire-fighters

As in other applications, helicopters offer special advantages offsetting their higher costs of operation. Equipped for transporting underslung loads, they can easily interchange fire-fighting with transport jobs. They can pick up from small bodies of water, such as reservoirs, among mountains that restrict the climb out, making such operations unacceptably hazardous for large fixed-wing aircraft. The huge Erikson Air-Crane, a modified Sikorsky S64, powered by two 4,500hp turbine engines, is fitted with a snorkel device to pick up water from a lake or the sea while flying at 30 knots. This method was developed to avoid the risks, after taking on water while hovering, inherent in climbing out fully laden, which requires much more power and risk of disaster if an engine fails. (Hunter-Jones, 2005)

The Russians also have a giant helicopter on offer for fire control. The Mi-26 can drop 18 tonnes of fire retardant or water and potentially could be the most cost-effective fire-fighting helicopter in the world. (Laskina, 2005) A comparable distinction can be claimed for another Russian helicopter, the Kamov

217

Ka-32. This, like other Kamov designs, is a coaxial machine – its two Klimov engines drive two rotors mounted on the same shaft. These rotors are counter-rotating so that no power is required to drive a tail rotor as is the case in more conventional helicopters. In 2009 the Kamov 32 became the first Russian helicopter to receive European type certification. It is used in a number of countries in forest fire-fighting and in aerial logging. (Robinson, 2010)

Even in countries less affected by great heat and drought and where scales and distances are small, forest, hill and moorland fires can still be a problem and helicopters a great help in controlling them. The Peak District in northern England, home to one of the oldest National Parks in Britain, provides an example. One of the many fires in 2006 lasted for 23 days. The dryness of the peat cover in summer causes fires to take a deep hold. The traditional remedy of beating actually adds oxygen so makes the fire worse. (*Summit*, 43, 2006, 46) Water bombing by a helicopter with water collected in underslung buckets from lakes and reservoirs offers a better solution. Key support personnel and equipment such as pumps, portable reservoirs and hoses can also be airlifted in, while other fire-fighters walk in. Financing the high hourly cost of employing a helicopter is, however, a problem for National Park administrators.

Scientific research and aerial mapping

Scientific work in the mountains has been helped immensely, as in all other environments, by the employment of aircraft. The work of geological as well as topographical surveying has benefited particularly from the rapidity and breadth of scope conferred by flying. The exploratory work by Brad Washburn in the Yukon and Alaska has received comment in Chapter 11. He later took his skills to the ultimate in mountain mapping when he turned his attention to Mount Everest. With the support of the National Geographic Society's Committee for Research and Exploration, which contributed $75,000 for the air photography, and the co-operation of Swissair Photo-Surveys, Washburn was able to have the services of a Learjet for the aerial surveys. A further input came from the space shuttle Columbia. As the area to be flown over straddled China and Nepal, agreement of both governments was required. The Chinese, surprisingly, came up with the permissions very quickly, whereas, despite early enthusiasm from the King of Nepal, it was more than three years before everything was settled. The expedition went to Kathmandu in October 1984. Unfortunately, Washburn's wife, Barbara, became critically ill and had to be evacuated to the USA and he went back with her. Notwithstanding this setback, the work went ahead and resulted in the publication of the most detailed map of the Everest region, covering 350 square miles. (Washburn and Smith, 2002, 195–6)

Antarctic discoveries

Many mountains in remote areas have been discovered in the course of exploratory flights, this being particularly true of the Antarctic. Ellsworth's flight over the mountains that bear his name was described in Chapter 3. Numerous mountains were first recorded and surveyed by the American expeditions led by Richard Byrd. Among those first recorded in his second expedition in 1933–35 were many peaks in the Transantarctic Mountains, including the Horlick Mountains, which he named after William Horlick of Horlick's Malted Milk Company, who supported the expedition. (Trewby ed. 2002, 99)

In 1946 a major exploratory research programme was begun under the direction of Finn Ronne, who had served with Byrd in the Antarctic in 1933–35. Ronne had also been involved with Antarctic survey work in 1940. A Curtis Condor proved to be invaluable to support sledging parties and for photographic work and Alexander I Land was found to be an island. When the Condor landed at Mikkelsen Island men from the support ship rushed out and started cutting pieces from the aeroplane's covering for souvenirs. 'In minutes the Condor was little more than a skeleton' wrote an astonished Ronne. (Ronne, 1979, 119)

The Ronne Antarctic Research Expedition 1946–8 did not suffer such wanton destruction. It had three aircraft: a Norduyn Norseman high-wing monoplane with a 650hp engine, familiar in the Canadian Arctic and Alaskan regions, and a twin-engine Beechcraft, both fitted with skis. Additionally, a small two-seater was available for reconnaissance. The Beechcraft was fully equipped for aerial photography and could remain in the air for nine hours without refuelling. New mountain ranges were discovered in the Antarctic Peninsula and West Antarctica. In some 45,000 flying hours, 450,000 square miles were mapped from 14,000 aerial photographs. The US Board of Geographic Names adopted the name of Edith Ronne Land for the newly explored area, later to be renamed the Ronne Ice Shelf. (Ronne, 1979, 163–178)

The highest mountain in the Southern Continent, Vinson Massif, 4,897m (16,067ft), was first reported in 1957 by US Navy airmen. It was named for Carl G. Vinson, a US Congressman who campaigned for expenditure on Antarctic exploration from the time of Byrd's second expedition. (Trewby ed. 2002, 193) The geographic location and conditions in the Antarctic result in virtually all mountaineering and trekking expeditions in its wilderness accepting aerial support, despite environmental disturbance and pollution. Though still relatively small in scale, added to all the other tourist travel now exploiting Antarctica, it is not without an adverse impact on this sensitive natural environment.

Controversial uses of aircraft in the mountains

Whereas the advantages of aerial topdressing and fertilising have been generally welcomed in New Zealand, another practice which developed with the increasing availability of helicopters later in the 20th century was that of controlling the numbers of deer over the vast areas of the mountains, where they accelerate erosion. This was formerly in the hands of a relatively small number of trained sharpshooters employed by the government, but such control was hard to maintain on the required scale. Helicopter 'gunships' are much more effective, especially enabling commercial exploitation of the market for venison to be exploited. This is looked on by many as a murderous practice and understandably there is considerable criticism of its use.

Skiing damage

Much more widespread practices can be cited as negative environmental consequences of the use of aircraft in other fields of activity, notable in the extension of off-piste skiing to mountain heights beyond the reach of ordinary mechanical access such as lifts and cable cars.

In many regions where snowfall is sufficient, the burgeoning skiing industry has caused severe destruction of natural vegetation and complete removal of topsoil and subsoil as well. When the winter snow has gone there are great bare areas scarred by access roads and networks of ski-lifts of various kinds, which lie abandoned in the summer and autumn except for maintenance work – and further scarring development.

During the winter and spring, skiing is directly responsible for a huge amount of aerial activity at the venues for major downhill, slalom and other ski races, such as those in the FIS Alpine World Cup series.

At the Swiss resort of Wengen, for example, the annual downhill event starts from the top of the Lauberhorn at 2,315m. Helicopters are the most efficient as well as the quickest method to get all that is required to support the race to the top of the mountain as well as to intermediate points. Among the items transported are the marker poles, safety fences and rubber mats to protect skiers who crash into the fences, plus first aid points, TV and radio equipment, temporary toilets and other facilities. Special guests are transported to the best viewing spots and others can pay for the ride – the charge in 2005 being 100 Swiss francs, to include skis and toboggans. Within 45 seconds of one group of passengers being dropped off a helicopter is away to collect the next group. Skis are carried up in batches in underslung containers. Air-Glaciers, the principal operator, and other firms, expect to lift about 1,100 passengers to the top on a race day. Many spectators will ski down to the valley but others will require to be brought back down. (Norris, 2006) Short sight-seeing flights are also widely available. Clearly, such an operation is of considerable financial importance to the community and to the helicopter firms.

Heliskiing

Fixed mechanical means of access extend high into the realms of permanent snow cover and the upper reaches of glaciers and are constantly being extended. Above and beyond these lie the domains of the mountaineer and ski-mountaineer, whose passage, given the adherence of the participants to good environmental practice, leaves few traces. These areas are now being increasingly exploited by skiers who have neither the desire nor energy to get themselves to these heights by their own efforts, or to become skilled ski-mountaineers. The en-piste downhill skier can go back up many times in a day in cable cars and gondolas to repeat a run or to sample another. Helicopters make it possible to do this on more ambitious off-piste runs.

In 2004 the influential French journal, *Alpinisme et Randonée* (No. 253), published a critical article on heliskiing and invited its readers to comment. The writer of the article, Daniel Léon, pointed out that although banned in France it was legal in Italy, Switzerland and Austria. The practice was condemned by Mountain Wilderness France, citing the view of the International Commission for the Protection of the Alps (CIPRA). Confirming its opposition to the use of helicopters for tourist purpose, the Commission had stated that they produce noise pollution for residents and other tourists and disturb wildlife, especially in winter. They claimed that there was no comparison with other sports and no excuse for exporting a practice deplored in the Alps to other areas.

It was claimed that, in Switzerland, there were more than 50,000 tourists transported by helicopter each year, using forty-three landing places. In Germany and Lichtenstein it was 'almost

222

banned'. In France it was banned but it was alleged that the law was breached without prosecution. In Austria, heliskiing was permitted only in parts of the Vorarlberg; in Italy it was common in the Dolomites and banned only in the autonomous province of Trentino. The practice was developing in Slovenia. The argument that the extension of heliskiing to Nepal was helping in the development of the country was offset, in the view of its critics, by the fact that only the relatively wealthy could afford it and it was of minimal benefit to ordinary people, unlike the widespread diffusion of expenditure associated with trekking.

Despite these views, the practice is spreading rapidly – perhaps one might be permitted a pun and say 'snowballing.' In the Alps, snowboarders as well as skiers are offered the services of mountain guides, whose services are stated to be obligatory if helicopters are used. A brief look at a French Internet site will reveal many organisations advertising the sport, the French ban being easily circumvented by taking parties over the border. A typical arrangement is for one helicopter to transport skiers over the border and then for an Italian helicopter to take them on to a peak from which they can ski back. Day tours are offered from Chamonix through the Mont Blanc tunnel to the Val d'Aosta to enjoy a helicopter ride to the Glacier du Trient, Pigne d'Arolla or Monte Rosa for the descent by ski or snowboard and return through the Mont Blanc tunnel or in some cases skiing back to Argentière. Some companies offer to take 'skiers, snowboarders "ou télémarkeurs"' to a mountain summit. One advertisement has offered the attraction of 'mountains virgin of all human and material presence!' Even allowing for advertising hyperbole, the threat to wilderness areas, previously accessible only to relatively few skiers with the necessary skill, strength and commitment, is obvious.

Prices are not sufficient to deter very many skiers in these days of high disposable incomes. In 2010 prices quoted in the Alps are around 400 to 600 euros per day with three-day trips for 1,800 to 2,500 euros, as compared with 1,000 to 1,700 for normal skiing. Such charges, even with added costs for meals will not be regarded as prohibitively expensive by those already used to spending highly on ski equipment, transport, accommodation, insurance, and après-ski entertainment.

In the Caucasus, development went ahead rapidly in the first decade of the 21st century. Vladimir Putin, the Russian prime minister, joined those who have participated in and promoted heliskiing. The modest ski resort created in Soviet times at Krasnaya Pol'yana was selected for a huge injection of state and private capital in the hope of developing it to be a future Olympic contender. Gazprom, the state energy corporation, undertook large-scale development with six ski lifts. Meanwhile, large helicopters were introduced to offer flights to an immense range of starting points. Foreign operators send skiers to the resort with claims that it is easy to find unspoilt conditions now rare in Europe. Advertisements include television coverage, notably in sports programmes, stressing the adventure elements seen in the opportunities presented by the helicopters. The liberal newspaper *Novaya Gazeta* expressed scepticism and saw the new investments as favouring the wealthy and diverting money from more essential needs

Unfortunately this is a problem that is unlikely to go away. Heliskiing is now offered by commercial companies in many parts of the world, such as Europe, Canada, Alaska and other parts of the USA, Russia including Kamchatka in the Far East, Abkhazia (Caucasus), the Himalaya and Karakoram, regions in Central Asia such as the Tien Shan in Kyrgistan, New Zealand and Greenland. Helicopters will be called on more and more unless their operation is severely curtailed by regulation and enforced by international agreement. As global warming causes snowfall to diminish and glaciers and snowfields to melt ever more quickly, relatively low skiing areas such as the Bavarian Alps will become impracticable to maintain except by using artificial snow, which is expensive and still dependent on conditions cold enough for the cover to be preserved. Pressure will increase on the higher areas and helicopters offer the flexibility that will be increasingly in demand.

Avalanche control

Avalanches are a natural process in mountain areas. Aircraft make an important contribution to limiting dangers of avalanches, such as described earlier. The construction and maintenance of the steel or timber 'avalanche fences' that are conspicuous on many mountainsides above villages, roads and railways is transformed from a formidable undertaking to a much more manageable task by helicopters. Control is also assisted by planned explosions. This practice has been undertaken widely in the past to bring down snow threatening patrolled ski slopes before normal downhill skiing can be permitted, as well as to remove danger from villages and transport routes. Now it is frequently extended to more remote areas where skiing from helicopters is offered. This involves further interference with the mountain environment where it may not bring the benefits to the wider community that elsewhere fully justify its use.

The noise problem and control of helicopter use

Noise continues to be a common and increasing cause of complaint and criticism of flying operations in the mountains. Helicopters are particularly noisy because of the disturbance of the air caused by their rotors, and many feel that uncontrolled access to the skifields and ridges by helicopters creates an intolerable noise situation as well as increasing pollution and other problems such as air traffic congestion and possible obstruction of rescue flights.

It may at present seem surprising that the Swiss introduced strict control over commercial helicopters operating in the mountains in the early 1960s. Swiss Air-Rescue (Rega) had to fight for access to the areas in which they needed to carry out training. They also wanted to help with the enormous costs of operating a helicopter on rescue work by taking skiers to the start of the most attractive descent routes. They found themselves opposed not only by some environmental interests but also by the Swiss Alpine Club. Swiss Air-Rescue found it incomprehensible that the Club, their partner in rescue operations, became their opponent in this matter. They felt that an alpine club should have understood the necessity for continuous training in techniques needed for rescue operations in the high mountains. (Itin and Rutchsmann, with Odermatt, 2002, 66, 70, 72) The inability to earn their own way by making fuller use of their helicopters was particularly hard on the rescue service because they experienced continual funding problems, with no financial help from the federal government. Although controls are still exercised, restrictions on helicopter firms from exploiting earning potential in the Swiss mountains have been much relaxed, as in the case of heliskiing, but with continuing controversy.

Although noise is still, of course, an inevitable by-product of all uses of helicopters, and thus also of modern methods of mountain transport and rescue, one could not expect people suffering pain from injuries, possibly life-threatening, to forego rescue from the air because of the brief period of environmental disturbance from the individual helicopter intervention. Nor would there be any sense in thinking of evacuation by any means other than a helicopter. Nobody could wish for a return to long and exhausting, often hazardous, carrying of stretchers by teams of volunteers, except where it is absolutely unavoidable. So for the foreseeable future, the noise of rescue helicopters must be accepted, but that does not mean that there will never be any improvement. Modern rotor blade design has already substantially reduced the noise 'footprint' and many of the newer helicopters are significantly less intrusive than their predecessors.

Technological advances will continue and may produce revolutionary solutions. As a current example, search and rescue is one of many tasks envisaged for a new design being developed by Eurocopter, the X3 ('X cubed: long-range, high-speed, hybrid helicopter.') It takes off, hovers and lands by means of a rotor, as in a normal helicopter. Forward propulsion is provided by two propellers driven by shafts running through stub wings (which contribute to lift) on which the propellers are mounted. A machine of this type should be much quieter as well as faster than an ordinary helicopter. (Norris, 2010, Europcopter website)

Meanwhile, for the SAR helicopter, exemptions from noise and other controls appear to be necessary, but for uses such as heliskiing and tourist flights a different approach is needed if the environment is not to suffer increasingly.

Military training over the mountains

Perhaps to the mountaineer the equivalent of the aeroplane that upset Lunn by disturbing his peace is today the military strike machine that hurtles across the sky at a speed close to the speed of sound, often at a height below the climber. It leaves behind it a roar that, if the climber has not seen the aircraft, or is otherwise unprepared, can be dangerous as a delicate move is made, or it may set off an avalanche on a treacherous snow slope. Such flights are restricted over many mountain regions such as the Alps in order not to shatter the peace unnecessarily but training necessitates some such disturbance. In some areas such as the Scottish Highlands and the Welsh hills there are frequent military sorties that cause considerable controversy and lead to many protests. Such disturbance is an essential part of training for modern warfare and is part of the price of maintaining an effective strike force for defence and retaliation in the interests of national and international security. Much of this training is carried out over virtually uninhabited areas in northern Canada and Scandinavia, but complete service training and also control over costs make it necessary to continue to fly over British hills and mountains and this activity must be expected as long as there is a military requirement.

Mountain-top development

The exploitation of mountain summits for commercial purposes is a long-established process, long preceding the present-day availability of aircraft to make the construction work much easier. In his thoughtful survey of the Alps, R.L.G. Irving, who took parties of his pupils, one of them being George Mallory, on climbing parties in the Alps, commented:

'The Zugspitze, which was the highest peak in Germany before the annexation of Austria [and is again so] and the Parseierspitze which is the highest point of all this part of the range, have been tamed by means of iron chains and blasting into mountain pets for the non-climbing tourist.'(Irving, 1939, 107)

Throughout the 1930s there was strong opposition in the Alpine Club and among British climbers generally to the practices of using pitons and other aids to climbing, though these made possible routes that would be impossibly dangerous without them and are now accepted as normal. Similarly by means of fixed ropes and ladders, climbers of moderate ability can now safely undertake climbs otherwise far beyond their capabilities.

The Zugspitze has a huge complex on its summit ridge, catering for hundreds of visitors, for whom a rack railway and two cable cars provide easy access. In the Bernese Oberland the Jungfraujoch has even more provision for tourists (much extended in recent years) accessed by the railway driven through the rock of the Eiger. At least, though on the ridgeline, in this case it is not on a summit. No such modesty restricted the building of the immense, though relatively graceful, tower complex on the summit of the Aiguille du Midi, proudly crowning the skyline of Chamonix. Probably few people find these edifices obtrusive and they enable thousands of people to enjoy the impressive views but the ease with which they could be replicated in the helicopter age demands the maintenance of firm planning controls.

Political considerations

The care of the mountain environment is a particularly sensitive issue politically, not only because it is very conspicuous with its obvious attractions for large numbers of tourists and its vulnerability, but also because of the strategic importance of many mountainous regions. From time immemorial mountain ranges have provided the most obvious boundaries between nations and smaller groups of peoples. The development of aviation posed immense political and strategic problems and revolutionised warfare. These issues have become exceedingly complex.

Global warning

There are still many who refuse to believe or are sceptical that man's activities are responsible for the observed increases in global temperatures that are taking place. In any case, even if there is in progress a natural evolution towards warmer conditions – just as in the past throughout the earth's history there have been ice ages and warmer periods – it seems impossible to deny that man's activities are exacerbating the present rise in temperatures. Between 1995 and 2006 there were 11 out of 12 of the hottest years ever recorded. It seems at least highly likely that the severity of the disastrous floods and fires that have recently swept across many areas of the world, especially severe in 2010, are connected with the rising worldwide temperatures. Scientists had predicted such developments and there is no reason not to accept the connection.

To summarise briefly the main facts relevant to aviation, it has been shown that global emissions of carbon dioxide (CO_2) in the atmosphere from air transport grew by 45% between 1992 and 2005, reaching an estimated 733 million tonnes a year by the end of the period. This arose largely from the burning of aviation kerosene. Between 2000 and 2007, air traffic grew by an average annual rate of 5.3%. (GIACC/4, 2009, together with Lee et al). CO_2 is widely regarded as the most significant greenhouse gas (GHG) because it remains in the atmosphere for about 100 years. In addition, nitrogen oxides (NOx) from exhausts, aerosols from soot and sulphate and increased cloudiness in the form of persistent condensation trails (contrails), and cloudiness from increased cirrus formation are also contributors to the total global warming impact.

The International Commission for Sustainable Aviation, whose figures are quoted above, deplores the lack of international agreement on action to reduce GHGs. It recommends a cap on emissions that is consistent with a broader global deal on reducing these, and urges the International Civil Aviation Organization (ICAO) to set a GHG standard that does not penalise new aircraft designs with reduced climate impact due to lower design cruise altitudes and speed.

In addition, there is a huge amount of fuel burnt by motor vehicles taking users to and from airports and providing technical and supply services for them; and the emissions from the fuel consumed within the airport structures themselves. The total global warming impact from aviation is probably around 10%. (Archer and Norman, 2010)

Mountain regions, because of relatively low permanent population density, do not originate large numbers of travellers but they do receive them for winter sports and walking and climbing, especially in summer. To these activities local low-flying aircraft add relatively modest additions to pollution and global warming effects in their services. However, while the adverse effects of the small and relatively low powered aircraft employed on these local services are of relatively low magnitude they should not be ignored.

It seems reasonable to make the judgement that, from what information is currently available, the direct effects of aviation taking place in the mountains are unlikely to be nearly as great a contributor to global warming and climate change as the effects resulting from travel to and from centres of population to climb, walk and practise winter sports in mountain areas. These effects are not only at present appreciable but likely to increase as the numbers of travellers to distant areas increases.

In 2007 *Summit*, the magazine of the British Mountaineering Council, published an article by David Strahan entitled 'Climate Criminals', drawing attention to the lack of awareness shown by climbers of the adverse effects of their activities, through the emissions created in the course of their travel to climb in distant regions and to fly internationally for week-end climbing to centres like Chamonix. Among the examples he cited was a scheme by a group of teenagers to raise money for an environmental group called Leave No Trace by climbing the Seven Summits – involving at least fourteen long haul flights. At the time of writing (2011) David Strahan's article is available on the Internet and deserves to be considered by all intending travellers. (Strahan, 2007).

It will be seen that aviation is a relevant factor in the environmental problems which are widespread and increasing as more and more people have the time and income to walk, climb, ski and otherwise enjoy the mountain environment and the pressure of increasing commercial development. Aviation brings both positive and negative influences to the mountain regions.

After this diversion a return to the adventures made possible by flight is offered in the next chapter

CHAPTER 13

Full Circle: Back to Balloons

The very first form of aerial travel, ballooning, has been enjoying a remarkable renaissance. In the mid-20th century it was a relatively obscure form of flying, though developed over generations in the course of scientific research, military observation, and establishing new records such as those for altitude and distance. Balloons were also used for commercial purposes, notably advertising. Hydrogen or helium provided the source of lift. Then in the 1950s the US Office of Naval Research initiated development for research purposes of hot-air balloons made of synthetic fibres powered by propane gas. Raven Industries accepted the task and P.E. ('Ed') Yost became programme manager. In the following years the modern hot-air balloon was born and became an important element in recreational flying. Sporting use spread from the USA to Europe and eventually to most parts of the world.

Before considering further these developments, it may be of interest to note that for the glider pilot and the balloonist, meteorological conditions offer very specific and sometimes very different opportunities and dangers. Fair-weather cumulus clouds (relatively favourable for mountaineering, at least as long as they stay away from the peak being climbed) are indicators of lift for glider pilots but are serious threats to balloonists. If a balloon gets sucked up into a cumulus cloud by the thermal currents that are the source of the cloud, it may be drawn upward in uncontrollable ascent.

As for cumulonimbus clouds, Don Cameron has pointed out that if a balloonist were to be drawn into one of the upward currents associated with this towering cloud-type which may generate vertical currents with speeds above 100 knots (185km/hr), there would be no means by which the pilot could escape. It would be likely that the balloon would be destroyed by the turbulence, and, if not, the occupants would probably die from oxygen starvation or cold. (Cameron, 1980, 36) So the balloon pilot must normally try to avoid thermals, whereas those same thermals are the means by which glider pilots gain their height and sustain their flights.

The balloon pilot seeks stable air in which ascent can be increased through heat input in a hot-air balloon, or, in the case of a gas balloon, dropping ballast, while descent is managed by venting hot air or gas. The more extreme the conditions, by and large, the greater the contrast between their suitability for balloons and gliders – though of course there are limits to this argument.

Mountaineers need to be watchful for the lenticular clouds that frequently form along the apex of a wave, much as a cloud forms on the summit of a mountain. They may herald the approach of bad weather, so mountaineers should be alert; and nearby pilots even more so. The cloud is stationary, or rather is continuously forming on the windward edge and dispersing to leeward. The higher the speed of the airflow, the greater is the risk of turbulence. On the sheltered site of the hill the wind is likely to curve back downwards, hence the term 'curlover' much used in ballooning and gliding circles. This may develop into a rotor, a form of air current particularly dangerous to all types of aircraft, as mentioned in earlier chapters.

Any hills or mountains may cause the airstream to develop rotors or lee waves. The nearer a pilot is to the mountains the more likely they are to cause problems. The pilot of a Lockheed P38, a wartime twin-engine fighter aircraft of distinctive twin-boom design, was in 1950 flying along the lee slope of the Sierra Nevada range in the USA. Finding very strong air currents, he feathered the aircraft's propellers and rose from 15,000ft to 32,000ft at a velocity of nearly 8,000ft a minute. (Harvey, 1955)

On the first successful round-the-world balloon flight by

Bertrand Piccard and Brian Jones in 1999 violent vertical movements of the balloon were experienced high above the mountains of Myanmar (Burma). Jones was in control and noticed the
variometer showing the balloon falling at a rate of 600ft per
minute. He thought they were dropping out of the sky and
immediately started burning propane gas but could not stop the
descent. Then they shot up again. He concluded that mountain
waves were the cause, something which they had not previously
encountered on their already long journey from Switzerland.
Eventually things settled down again to steadier flight over
China. (Piccard and Jones, 1999, 154)

Balloon and glider pilots must study also the less sensational
but very important air currents that are part of the daily pattern in
many hill areas, notably katabatic and anabatic winds. The effect
of solar heating on slopes facing south (north in the southern
hemisphere) is to produce localised wind patterns. During the day
the air near the slope is heated more than that further away so that
an uphill, or anabatic, wind results. The pattern is reversed at
night when cold air flows downslope – a katabatic wind. (The
name is derived from the Greek *katabatikos*, downward.) Glider
pilots make a great deal of use of anabatic winds, launching from
ridges, exploiting thermals and perhaps using an anabatic wind
to fly back up the slope at the end of the flight when the thermals
have died away. Sea breezes are similar, the air movement tending
to be in daytime off the cool sea and rising over the land that has
warmed up. Katabatic winds will help to keep landing grounds
on slopes free of fog but will make it difficult for a glider pilot to
return to a hill-top launch site and may force a balloon down very
suddenly, so a hot-air balloon pilot must be ready to counter this
with bursts of heat and a gas balloonist will need to reserve ballast
against such a need. In this case there is similarity in the effects on
gliders and balloons

Hot-air balloons in the Alps

The first crossing of the Alps by a hot-air balloon took place in
1972 when D. Cameron and M. Yarro took off from Zermatt in

the 3,970 m balloon *Cumulo Nimbus* and rose to 5,495m (18,030 ft). They flew over the Gorner glacier, the Matterhorn and Monte Rosa and landed at Biella in Italy, a distance of 60km. (Pyatt, 1980, 52; Cameron, 1980, 60)

For a traverse of Mont Blanc by hot-air balloon, three pilots from Lyon prepared for a year until, in the autumn of 1979, they at last felt ready. After three weeks of waiting at Chamonix for suitable meteorological conditions, they took off at 09.10 in two balloons, *Setrak* and *Dynastar*, on 20th October. The baskets were packed with ten bottles of propane for the continued supply of hot air and the appropriate navigation instruments, oxygen equipment and radio. A photographic record of the flight was made by other aircraft.

Setrak flew over the Mer de Glace and the Glacier du Géant, crossed the frontier into Italy over the Dent du Géant and headed down into the Val Ferret. The other crew took *Dynastar* up to 5,700m (compared with the 4,200m at which *Setrak* had been flown over the frontier), and crossed the range further to the east, over the Grandes Jorasses. They had to settle for a landing among rocks at a height of 2,000m. The recovery of the balloon was not easy but was carried out the following day with the aid of a jeep. (Borrel, 1983, 21)

The Alps today are the venue for many well-established ballooning centres, such as Chateau d'Oex and Mürren in Switzerland, Zell-am-See and Filzmoos in Austria and Meribel and Courcheval in France. In the Rocky Mountains and other American mountain areas there are a great many ballooning centres. The balloon festivals that are organised regularly at such centres attract large numbers of participants and enormous crowds of spectators. It was estimated that the 28th International Balloon Festival at Chateau d'Oex in January 2006 attracted 50,000 spectators. Balloons were brought from all over Europe and one was from Kazan' in Tartarstan in the Russian Federation, 4,000km away. In all 147 pilots from 18 countries took part in the event, clocking up over 500 flights and 740 flying hours. (Berry, 2006)

At many of these events there are facilities for tuition and it is usual for the public to be offered opportunities for short flights at much the same price as that of a sightseeing ride in a helicopter. The big difference in the experience is that the balloon pilot can normally return his passengers to the take-off point only with the aid of ground transport. Alpine valleys are cluttered not only with settlements, railways and roads but also power lines and ski-lifts, all restricting landing places. Inaccessible pastures without a road for the following balloon-recovery and passenger transport vehicles are to be avoided. To limit the problems, in the mountains small baskets are used, carrying typically six passengers and the pilot, whereas in areas where the potential landing places are less limited the basket may carry around ten or twelve passengers. Passengers must still be warned that the flight may have to be more protracted than intended because of the shortage of suitable safe landing places as well as the vagaries of the winds. They have also to inform passengers that although risks are small, landings may be rough if the basket bounces over the ground. Hence, it is desirable that passengers should be fit enough to adopt the recommended position, hold on firmly and evacuate the basket when the time comes. Many operators impose a minimum age of twelve, with the proviso that the child must be able to see over the side of the basket.

Ballooning over Mount Everest

As with other sports, the aim of the ambitious pilot is always to seek a more difficult target. In the 1980s and 1990s it was the turn of Mount Everest to receive attention from balloonists seeking to be the first to fly over its summit in a hot-air balloon. The first balloon flights in the Himalaya took place in 1985 from Kathmandu, organised by Chris Dewhurst. Two balloons were employed. They did not have permission to fly into Tibet and Leo Dickinson had to be content with photographing Mount Everest before the pilot burners failed. The balloon made a frighteningly rapid descent and a landing was made in the foothills. The other balloon was also forced down out of control and landed in a tree. The basket tipped up, caught fire and the crew narrowly escaped. Another flight was made towards Annapurna but there were problems again and another premature descent had to be made.

Five years later, a Japanese team comprising Michio Kanda, Sabu Ichiyoshi and Atsushi Saito, the cameraman, almost succeeded in flying over Everest from the Tibetan side. In the spring of 1990, watched by a jet aircraft engaged to fly overhead, they ran into a powerful downdraft, which forced the balloon down from an altitude at which they would have passed over the summit and, losing control, they struck the mountain at about 5,600m. Kanda and Saito cut through the envelope and dragged Ichiyoshi, who was seriously injured, to safety, just before fire broke out and the propane exploded, destroying their survival equipment. Leaving Saito to look after Ichiyoshi, who was protected only by their parachutes, Kanda set off for base camp. Ichiyoshi and Saito were rescued thirty-six hours after the crash. (Dickinson, 1993, 9–10)

Per Lindstrand, who was building record-breaking balloons at Oswestry in Shropshire, had already been engaged to attempt such a flight in 1989, sponsored by Star Micronics UK, part of a Japanese firm manufacturing computer printers. Dickinson was invited to join the project. With Peter Mason, another experienced balloonist, as manager, the expedition reached Nepal only to become spectators of the revolution that had flared up. The possibility of joining with the Japanese was considered but when that attempt ended in near disaster, Peter Mason decided things were more difficult and dangerous than he had previously thought and the project was abandoned. (Dickinson, 1993, 40)

Of critical importance to the chances of success of any plan to fly a balloon over the summit of Everest was the harnessing of the power of the jetstream. The discovery – or rediscovery – of the jetstream that flows like a mighty river of wind around the earth had come with the problems faced by American bomber crews when they were attempting precision bombing over Japan in 1944. At first their reports of encountering winds of well over 100mph over Japan were not believed but eventually they were proved to be right and it was found that this belt of wind was a variable but regular feature of the atmosphere in those latitudes. The discovery of this phenomenon by a Japanese scientist had been overlooked – he had published his report in Esperanto, the international language created in the 1930s but not normally used by scientists. The experiences of the Everest climbers in the inter-war period and of the crews of the 1933 photographic flight might have led meteorologists to realise that the regularity of hurricane-force winds over the summit of Everest, betrayed by its famous plume, could indicate a force of much wider significance than merely an obstacle to mountaineers. With the knowledge subsequently acquired by meteorologists and airmen, Lindstrand knew that with the aid of the jetstream a balloon could be blown over the summit of Everest into Tibet.

It was not long before plans were afoot for a very determined attempt. A new team was assembled and they battled their way through many organisational problems. They arrived in Kathmandu with the film crew they had had in 1985. (Dickinson, 1993, 64) A second balloon was financed partly by National Geographic and partly by Star Japan. When nearly ready, they went up to the monastery at Tyangboche to get blessings on the attempt, involving, as it did, a flight over the home of the gods. The blessings cost 3,000 rupees plus 30 rupees each for the scarves put round the necks of the three balloonists. One, Andy Elson, had stayed away because 'his god is the spanner carried in the bottom of his rucksack'. (Dickinson, 1993, 70) Retrieval in Tibet was under the control of Russell Brice, who was first to climb the pinnacles of the northeast ridge of Everest in 1988, where Joe Tasker and Peter Boardman had disappeared six years earlier. (Dickinson, 1993, 71)

Two hundred porters and about 30 yaks carried the gear up to Gokyo, at 16,000ft, chosen as the launch site. Eleven porters were needed to move the 400lb balloon. The need for a larger balloon than had been used for the earlier expeditions had been demonstrated by the inadequate performance of those then used. A diversion occurred when it was claimed that a yeti had been spotted on the ridge above. Dickinson suspected a trick but eventually agreed to the whole film crew going up the hill. He offered a huge reward for good film footage but not surprisingly they found nothing.

Dennison 'had a filming field day' when they arrived at Gokyo, believed by the Sherpas to be a magic place, with a lake into which to plunge to bring lasting fertility. Dickinson's comment was 'Judging by the temperature, I would have thought the opposite was true.' (Dickinson, 1993, 84) Other diversions included a report of seeing porters venting helium to lighten the cylinder. 'The porters,' wrote Dickinson, 'were last heard speaking in high voices.' (Dickinson, 1993, 89)

The helium was needed for the weather balloons. The meteorological research was in itself very impressive. Named Memex 91, the Mount Everest Meteorological Expedition was to collect data on the vertical structure of the atmosphere to contribute towards the study of global warming as well as providing information for mountaineers. Two weather balloons were to be sent off each day to supplement data received from satellites and the international weather centre in Berkshire. Martin Harris had two tonnes of equipment for this, temporarily the world's highest weather station. (Dickinson, 1993, 84–5)

Adverse weather caused delays which put great strain on the party – but also gave Leo Dickinson some more entertaining asides for his already fascinating book – it was decided that the next day (October 20th) could be launch day but twelve hours before lift-off it was decided to wait another day. Three radiosondes confirmed that they would have been flying too far to the south – not acceptable when the enterprise had cost 'nearly one million pounds of effort'. All was put in place for the next day. The radiosonde check at 18.00 was encouraging. The final hour before take-off was 'chaotic' for Eric Jones and 'very frightening' for Chris Dewhurst. (Dickinson, 1993, 102–6) It was still dark, with a faint glow in the east as final preparations were made. Dewhurst was worried because the temperature gauge attached to the top of the balloon was reading dangerously high. In fact the gauge was faulty. He could have sought reassurance but decided to launch. Leo Dickinson was taken by surprise, and

Elson didn't immediately realise they were airborne so the second balloon did not follow as quickly as planned.

Leo Dickinson was not even in the basket. He was outside on a plywood contraption attached by climbing tape to give him a clearer view for filming, free from flying wires and gas tanks. Not surprisingly, despite being roped on, he felt insecure 'hanging out from the basket 3,000 feet above the roof of the world.' (Dickinson, 1993, 113) However, he stayed at the post he had chosen for himself as they cleared Nuptse and approached Everest at 33,000ft, looking down into the Western Cwm. Temperatures around -56 degrees C had been predicted but Dickinson did not need his gloves because of the warm air spilling from the envelope. Suddenly he found himself without oxygen – ice had encased the regulator. Somehow things got sorted out and he went on filming. They sped over Everest's summit and the black pyramid of rock suddenly became white – a 'beautiful, illuminated summit of a fluted mountain.' (Dickinson, 1993, 118) At 58 knots they rushed on over Tibet.

In the other balloon Eric Jones was filming from a plastic barrel strapped to the basket. Suddenly the burners failed and he had to join Elson in a frantic effort to relight them. They succeeded, only for another failure to follow as they sank towards the Khumbu icefall. Jones thought they had lost control and prepared to parachute out over the Western Cwm. (Dickinson, 1993, 109–121) Far ahead, Dickinson also prepared to jump as the first balloon ran low on fuel. He wrote that when he climbed back into the basket it was a big mistake, because a few moments later they hit a moraine ridge and were dragged along at speed, scooping up boulders into the basket, then they shot up, then back again to the ground. A fire, such as the Japanese suffered, was likely. Dickinson was catapulted out, the movie camera still in his hand. Three of the remote cameras disintegrated. Dewhurst was dragged on by the balloon. (Dickinson, 1993, 136–8)

Meanwhile the crisis in the other balloon continued. Twice more the burners had gone out but were relit and with all five working they limped on towards Everest, only for a series of

240

loud twangs to announce the failure of one after another of the steel flying wires that secured the basket to the balloon. They were not high enough to jump with much hope of survival but for a time that seemed their only option. The bottom of the balloon melted but it cleared the top of Everest. Then they hit turbulence – the rotors swirling around the summit ridge. (Dickinson, 1993, 139–40)

As the first balloon bounced on across the barren Tibetan plateau, Dewhurst fell out and raced after the balloon. Dickinson sneezed and fainted from the pain of a cracked rib. A small crowd of Tibetans gathered. The other balloon had been rising but then spiralled downwards. Control was regained and a bouncy but safe landing was made. Tibetans gathered round, dispersed but later returned and appeared hostile. Fortunately the recovery truck, which had been following the balloons, reached them and the situation was saved. After recovering overnight in the camp, they set off for Lhasa. The authorities were suspicious of the video and film but fortunately let the adventurers retain them. (Dickinson, 1993, 141–9)

Over the Andes by balloon

In 1998 David Hempleman-Adams was on his third – and finally successful – attempt to walk to the North Pole when he conceived the idea of returning to the Pole but this time by balloon. He would thus finally achieve the target of the Swedish meteorologist Saloman Auguste Andrée, who, in 1897, with two companions, tried to reach the North Pole in a hydrogen balloon. All three lost their lives in the attempt. As a first step, Hempleman-Adams learned to pilot a hot-air balloon. To cross the Andes in one seemed to be a good way of preparing for his polar attempt. He had previously completed the ascent of the Seven Summits, the highest peaks in each of the continents, and therefore had climbed Aconcagua, 22,831ft, highest peak in the world outside the Himalaya and Karakoram ranges. After a mere four hours piloting a balloon he went to Chile and put in another half-hour in the second-hand balloon that had been

241

acquired for the attempt. He took off from Los Andes, sixty miles north of Santiago, in the early morning and at first rose rapidly but failed to find the winds that would blow him eastward even though he went higher and higher:

'I know that I face certain death if I venture beyond 34,000ft without enriched oxygen, so I level off just short of 32,000ft . . . I've never flown higher than a few thousand feet above southern England and here I am close to the jetstream.' (Hempleman-Adams, 2001, 2002, 37)

A necessary switch of oxygen tanks practiced thoroughly on the ground failed because the couplings were frozen. All he could do was switch off the burners and plunge downwards but when he came to re-ignite them they failed to respond. He narrowly averted catastrophe by calling up the support helicopter, with which he had lost contact but which was fortunately hovering nearby. He had the idea of getting the pilot to use the downdraft from his rotors to push the balloon away from the mountainside towards which he was heading. Fortunately this worked and he managed to relight the burners but took the first opportunity to make a relatively controlled landing.

Three days later Hempleman-Adams started off again. This time he was a little less ambitious, choosing to forego the opportunity to cross the highest peak in order to benefit from better weather-forecasting facilities. So he took off from a polo field on the outskirts of Santiago. At 10,000ft he picked up the westerlies and as he climbed the windspeed increased. He was flying at 25 knots by the time he reached his ceiling of 32,000ft. He passed over the 21,555ft volcano, Tupungata and headed into Argentina. When he had passed the mountains he began his descent and then encountered winds that blew him back towards the mountains. He put down hurriedly and found he was some forty miles beyond the frontier. (Hempleman-Adams, 2002, 41–43)

In May 2000 Hempleman-Adams achieved his long-term objective of piloting his own balloon, with helium to provide the main source of lift and propane to supply extra inflation when needed, to within a few miles of the North Pole. Like Andrée, he started from Spitsbergen, but with the invaluable help of modern science and technology, not least constant communication by satellite telephone to specialist weather fore-casters. They guided him from one height level to another to tap the winds he needed to fly in the required direction, without which he would have been unlikely to have had much more success than had Andrée and his companions in 1897. Hemple-man-Adams still found it a gruelling experience in which he came close to disaster but, persuaded to return when as close to the Pole as it seemed possible to steer the balloon, he made it back successfully to make a roller-coaster landing on an ice-floe, bouncing in and out of water for fifteen minutes before the basket settled on the ice. His hired helicopter from Longyearben was overhead and within minutes the crew were down and had slashed the balloon envelope to vent the remaining gas, then the helicopter transported him and his equipment to the small island where two members of his support team were waiting and all were soon back in Spitsbergen.

Inevitably, the balloons themselves have many characteristics that present hazards, even though, with approximately half a century of experience and development built into them since their rebirth, modern balloons have become vastly safer. Hot-air balloons have improved burners to control the necessary fre-quent jets of hot air from the propane gas. Gas balloons filled with helium are less exposed to fire hazards but valuable gas is lost to the atmosphere every time it is vented in order to control altitude, hence the appeal of modern 'Roziers' combining the use of helium and hot-air. All have the benefit of improved fabrics, especially in the areas most exposed to the heating process, as well as radios, mobile phones, GPS, variometers to show rate of ascent and descent and many other safety features and items of equipment. Nevertheless, there are still plenty of things that can go wrong and the weather is the final arbiter. Cameron con-cludes '. . . there can be no doubt that this must be ranked as a dangerous sport' (Cameron, 1980, 56)

It will be obvious, however, that all flying in the high mountains is fraught with special risks for aviators and it is appropriate at this stage to introduce the question, what do mountaineers and flyers owe each other in the pursuit of their hazardous activities?

CHAPTER 14

What do Aviators and Mountaineers Owe Each Other?

In the early interactions between mountaineers and flyers, if it was a matter of rescue, it was usually the airmen who needed to be helped off the mountain. When aircraft disappeared in remote country the search parties were often made up mainly or entirely of local people who were mountaineers in the older sense of the term – dwellers among the mountains. Local knowledge was of inestimable assistance in remote areas especially when the topography was complicated by forests – sometimes as difficult to deal with as ice and rock. Such would have been the case when, in the early days of air transport, a trimotor biplane was lost in the highlands of New Guinea. This machine, the sole example of the Handley Page W9a Hampstead, was one of a line of civil transports developed from the 0/400 bombers, built in 1925 for Imperial Airways, who named it *City of New York*. It had set up a record time of 1 hour 26 minutes between London and Paris. When replaced by new airliners in 1929 it was sold to Ellyns Goldfields and shipped to Port Moresby. (Clayton, 1970, 47) After the crash it was five days before the pilot and his mechanic were rescued but they had survived unharmed.

Not so fortunate were the nine-man crew and passengers of a flying boat who died in one of the highest-profile peacetime disasters suffered by the RAF. It having been decided that, for the first time, aircraft for a Far East squadron would be delivered by air, four flying boats flew out from Pembroke

Dock in the winter of 1935. They were of the Short Singapore III type with four Rolls-Royce Kestrel engines, representing the latest technology and described by the press as 'giant,' though today they would look small beside a modern aircraft designed for their type of job. After delays in Naples, caused by illness and technical problems, two of them left for Malta at 10.00 on February 15. At noon people near Messina in Sicily heard the aircraft overhead in cloud, followed by the noise of a crash coming from a spur of Peloritana, a 4,000ft mountain. Local people who tried to get near were defeated by fire so ran down to get help. Firemen and officials made the two and a half hour climb on the backs of donkeys, the fastest method available, but could do little more than search for bodies. The flying boat was assumed to be British because the name of Rolls Royce was still visible on the engines despite the fire. (*News Chronicle*, London, 16th February 1935)

When, in contrast to these accidents, a crash occurred in mountains that presented technical mountaineering problems, experienced climbers were obviously needed to get to the scene, as in the following instance.

The debt owed to the climbers

No accident is more sharply remembered nor constantly brought to the attention of the people of Chamonix than that which occurred on 3rd November 1950. A Lockheed L-749 Constellation airliner, *Malabar Princess*, powered by four powerful piston engines, was reported missing as it approached Geneva en route from Bombay to London, commanded by an experienced pilot who was completely familiar with the route. At 10.43 air traffic control received the message 'I am vertical with Voiron at 4,700 metres altitude.' Voiron is about 100km SSW of Geneva and a direct line linking them would pass some 70km WNW of Mont Blanc. No more was heard from the aircraft. Storms, low cloud and high winds hindered the aerial search and it was not until November 5th that the wreckage was spotted from a Swiss aircraft. Through a break in the clouds, it was seen lying on the French face of the Rochers de la Tournette, 4,677m, just below the final ridge on the normal route to the summit of Mont Blanc, not far from the Vallot refuge.

At that time climbing Mont Blanc was rarely undertaken in winter but a rescue attempt was quickly organised under the direction of René Payot, a guide of the École de Haute Montagne at Chamonix. Some thirty ski-mountaineers set out from the Glaciers station of the Aiguille du Midi téléphérique. Tragically, René Payot was avalanched into a crevasse and he died a hundred metres or so from where his brother had lost his life in an avalanche in 1939. A second rescue column, from the neighbouring commune of St.Gervais, defied official reluctance to risk more lives and reached the crash site but found there were no survivors. The crash had cost the lives of 48 airline passengers and crew and a leading mountaineer, who had not hesitated to risk his life in the hope of saving others, as, of course, had all the rescuers.

Pieces of the wreckage emerged from the Glacier des Bossons years later and continue to appear. Many, including an undercarriage wheel, disgorged by the ice in 1986, are displayed in the Chalet du Glacier des Bossons et du Mont-Blanc. The tragedy was studied intensively by Françoise Rey, whose book is always to be found in the bookshops at Chamonix. A novel, *La neige en deuil*, by Henri Troyat, was adapted in Hollywood for a film, *The Mountain*, starring the actor, Spencer Tracy. Another film, *Malabar Princess*, was shot in the Chamonix area. (Cuvelier, 2004) A work of fiction, it concerns the search by a 9-year-old boy for traces of his mother who had disappeared looking for the wreckage when he was an infant. There is some good photography of the mountains and glaciers and the modern helicopters of the gendarmerie. The film, however, does not attempt to depict in any detail the accident or the rescue work by the guides, which could be considered a missed opportunity to highlight their tremendous work.

The loss of the Air India Boeing 707, *Kangchenjunga*, occurred also as it was preparing to let down to land at Geneva, before continuing to London and New York. Contact was lost at 08.00 on 24th January 1966, the last report being from an altitude of 6,200m. The wreckage was found at almost the same spot on the French face of Mont Blanc. Helicopters arriving soon on the scene found no survivors of the 117 passengers and crew. The rescue column included René Payot's son, George, who had also become a guide.

Aerial rescue

During the years between these two disasters, as the role of rescuers from the air increased dramatically so did the risks they were likely to incur, as their capabilities increased from mere observation and reporting to direct intervention. In the Chamonix area the attempt to use helicopters with crews untrained in mountain flying to help to rescue Vincendon and Henry, as detailed in Chapter 5, had necessitated the rescue of the crew and led to the reconstruction of French mountain rescue services. Before the helicopter era was fully established the dramatic rescue of the Dakota survivors by Swiss pilots, as also described earlier, had been followed by many more daring rescues by Hermann Geiger and other pilots of the mountains. Technology has constantly increased the safety of flying and reduced the risk of collisions with high ground, though many still occur, especially during the approach and landing phases in bad weather.

How aircraft still get lost

Whereas cruising altitudes of modern transport aircraft are now much higher, light aircraft are often still flown at moderate heights. Some do not have the ability to climb clear of mountains, or if taken high are likely to suffer icing problems so pilots are likely still to rely on finding their way through passes. Or the aircraft may be flown too close to mountains for sightseeing purposes, or simply because it is the shortest route. If they go missing they can be difficult to locate. This was the case with one that was lost near the Matterhorn on 23rd December 2000. The

248

pilot, with two passengers aboard, filed a flight plan from Aosta to Milan via Valpelline, to pass close to the Matterhorn. Thus, although the final destination was to the southeast of Aosta, the pilot intended first to fly northward for a short distance close to the mountains before turning south. Take-off was at 14.30 but the aircraft failed to appear at Milan and at 17.00 the alarm was raised. There were severe winds in the area and it was considered that the aircraft could have crashed either in the Matterhorn – Dent d'Hérens area or near Monte Rosa. Unfortunately, the aircraft was not equipped with an automatic radio signal transmitter. Initial searches failed to locate the aircraft even though they were continued until midnight, using powerful searchlights.

Next morning the search was resumed with four Italian helicopters and two from Air Zermatt. The latter located the crashed aircraft at 3,200m near the Col de Valpelline but there was no sign of life. However, faint footsteps in the snow were detected and they were followed. Then, a flight chart was spotted lying on the Tsa de Tsan glacier. The footprints guided the searchers towards a deep crevasse. The pilot and one of the passengers had plunged down more than a hundred metres into the crevasse and had not survived. The other passenger had ploughed on down through deep snow and bitter winds and managed to cover about seven kilometres from the crash site and was picked up by an Air Zermatt helicopter at about 2,100m and was subsequently passed over to an Italian rescue team. (Air Zermatt, 2001, 10–11)

The advice generally given to survivors of aircraft or other vehicle crashes in remote territory is to stay with the machine as it is much easier for searchers to detect the wreck than human figures, especially from the air. Also, by staying with the aircraft the survivors in this case would have benefited from some shelter – they were inadequately clad and not at all equipped to traverse a glacier – and all would most probably have been rescued alive. This would almost certainly have been the case if the aircraft had been fitted with emergency signalling equipment.

Weather conditions may still necessitate rescue by ground teams. In May 2005, an experienced pilot flying a Cessna 150 equipped with GPS, which would have presented him with basic terrain information, set off on a flight from Inverness to Zurich via Newcastle. The pilot levelled out in cloud at 3,300ft, the freezing level, but soon found that the aircraft was losing height, presumably because of icing. He struck a mountain at approximately 2,600ft but suffered only minor injuries and was able to leave the aircraft. With his mobile telephone he contacted his family in Austria and they alerted their national rescue service. This, in turn, notified the UK Aeronautical Rescue Co-ordination Centre (ARCC) at Kinloss and the duty controller made contact with the stranded pilot at 09.47. An RAF helicopter was despatched from RAF Lossiemouth, while ARCC maintained contact with the pilot. Unfortunately, low cloud prevented the helicopter from visually locating the pilot and a mountain rescue team was flown to the area for a ground search. Under instructions from ARCC, the pilot used a whistle, which enabled the rescue team to find him at about 15.00. The pilot, on reflection, considered that he had not properly planned the flight sector and, with his experience of flying in the Alps, had not thought that the Scottish mountains would give him any trouble. (*AAIB Bulletin* No. 8/2005)

The hazards associated with flying over mountainous and largely uninhabited mountainous areas received worldwide attention in September 2007 when the adventurer Steve Fossett, first person to fly round the world in a single-seat aircraft non-stop and without refuelling, and first to fly a balloon solo round the world, vanished over the mountains of Nevada. He had taken off in a light single-engine Bellanca Super Decathlon to survey possible sites for an attempt on the world land-speed record, but he did not file a flight plan. It was reported that the aircraft was equipped with an electronic tracking device that should have been activated in an emergency but no signals were received. When he became overdue a search was instigated and several dozen light aircraft and helicopters, including Black Hawks with the latest thermal imaging and other search aids were deployed to comb the mountains and desert country. No trace was found of the missing pilot or his aeroplane. After 474 flights covering 20,000 square miles the Nevada Civil Air Patrol ceased its active search as did the National Guard. A private search with light aircraft was continued.

Other wrecks were sighted during the search. Some had been lying among the jagged mountains and deep canyons for decades. Risks in this area include flying into a box canyon in which there is not room enough to turn, or encountering an excessively strong downdraft, or rotor, as described in Chapter 10. In such country it would be very difficult for a survivor of a crash or forced landing caused by fuel or other problems to decide whether to stay with his aircraft or try to walk out, especially if a transponder was found not to be giving out signals. The complexities of the terrain are such that eventually it may be accidental discovery that reveals such an accident and that may be made by walkers or climbers rather than from aircraft. This was what eventually happened in this case, when walkers found the crash site and remains found later were tested for DNA and found to be in line with Fossett's records.

Most rescues of aerial travellers today are carried out from the air. Sometimes a helicopter is needed to pick up crews and passengers from balloons that have had to make a landing where the retrieval truck cannot reach them, which is especially likely in mountain areas, as noted earlier. In such cases there is also the collapsed balloon to be salvaged.

Mountain flying risks in the far north

Airmen operating in the remotest areas, such as the polar and sub-arctic regions, where there are few settlements and roads even in the lowlands, are very dependent on air rescue if they have to make forced landings or fail to get airborne again after a landing. The North American experience with Arctic and mountain flying is unparalleled in its volume and variety because of the numbers of both business and private flights that are carried out daily, in all kinds of weather conditions by pilots of vastly varying experience over very hostile terrain. The Transportation Safety Board of Canada found that both commercial and private flying in mountain regions leads to a high incidence of accidents. Most of these accidents occur on charter flights, on which many relatively young and inexperienced pilots are employed. Few of the aircraft were equipped to the standards required for flying in cloud under Instrument Flight Rules (IFR) and, in about one-third of the cases, the pilots involved in accidents were found not to have had a weather briefing and some had not used the facility when available – classic examples of 'flying by the seat of one's pants'. It was also found that private aircraft coming to grief in the mountains are commonly piloted by older-than-average pilots, reflecting the incidence of recreational flying by the equivalent of 'Sunday drivers', as the report succinctly puts it.

At the other extreme, helicopter pilots involved in accidents are usually more experienced than the average because they are more likely to be specially trained professionals. In the Canadian example, dominated by charter flights in the north during the spring period of snow melt and autumn freeze-up, vertigo and whiteout accounted for the majority of helicopter accidents – vertigo being cited in 54% of cases reported and whiteout in 39%. In over half the cases no weather briefing had been available. Whiteout is a problem that is particularly encountered by helicopter pilots because the rotors themselves can cause blowing snow conditions, giving rise to reduction of visual contrast while hovering, landing or air-taxiing.

It could be said, however, that the main debt owed by flyers to the various other groups whose life takes them into the mountains is nowadays simply one of employment, if that can be called indebtedness. Mountain rescue is only the most dramatic and most obvious of many tasks performed by flyers. Transport of constructional materials and regular supplies to mountain huts is valuable employment for many other pilots, which exists only because the mountaineers and others provide a constant demand. Servicing lifts and mountain railways of all kinds is also needed because mountaineers, skiers and general tourists provide the custom that calls them into being and keeps them operating.

The debt owed by mountaineers to airmen

The debt owed by mountaineers, skiers and others in the mountains to the air and ground crews who keep aircraft ready for rescue work is enormous and it is with rescue work that by far their most impressive contribution to social well-being lies. Where the helicopters have not been able to operate, things have been, and still are, much slower and more painful for the victim. Although there have been numerous references in this book to the difficulty of many of the tasks undertaken by rescue pilots, just how difficult and dangerous the work can be has not been adequately illustrated.

Those who have not paid much attention to the available literature may not appreciate that helicopters have not made the rescuers' tasks much, if any, safer. They have immensely widened the envelope of risks that surrounds the rescuers daily – and nightly. A few examples must suffice to illustrate this point specifically, though more occur elsewhere in this book.

In November 1977 in the Bernese Oberland, Markus Burkard undertook to attempt the rescue of a group of climbers who had been overtaken by a storm, unusually severe even for November, with winds that reached 140km/hr. As soon as a flight was practicable Urs Menet, the mechanic, prepared an Alouette 319 for take-off. Winds at 3,000m were forecast as 50 knots (57.5mph) with gusts to 65 knots. From a clear sky above Meiringen, Burkard flew into a dark, fearsome cauldron of storm clouds above the Rosenlaui glacier. Tossed up and down in winds he had seldom before experienced in thirteen years of flying helicopters, he circled low above the ice, desperately seeking the missing climbers and at last two figures were spotted higher up near an icefall. Flying in conditions beyond reasonable limits, he cursed himself and the profession he had chosen. He persisted and eventually managed to get the nose-wheel on the ice in a cloud of whirling snow. Blinded, with no landmark, he realised that he could not get the two men aboard and that he would have to get help. He radioed to base and flew back and picked up a guide, Fritz Immer.

Back above the glacier, Burkard used a blue, half-buried, rucksack as a marker and, after several attempts, succeeded in again positioning the nose-wheel on the ice and Fritz Immer jumped out and dragged the two men, both exhausted, one almost paralysed, in to the helicopter. After landing, the 17-year-old French boy they had rescued was able to tell them that two members of the party were already dead, but that a younger boy was still alive at the small Dossen hut. The rescuers went back yet again and flew over and around the hut without seeing any sign of life. Burkard managed to hover low enough for Franz Immer to jump out. He ran the fifty metres to the hut and found the boy and dragged him by his belt to the helicopter. The three survivors were taken to hospital. Two women and another 17-year-old youth had died, but there would have been six dead but for the skill and bravery of the pilot, his mechanic and the guide. (Burkard in MacInnes, 1980, MacInnes (ed), 2003)

The mention here of a mechanic as well as the pilot and a guide is a reminder that much is owed to the workers 'behind the scenes.' Behind every pilot and aircrew is a ground organisation to keep the aircraft available at a moment's notice. The mechanics are key personnel who will often work through the night to return a machine to serviceability in time for a take-off at first light. Furthermore, as indicated in the above report, they will often join the pilot and rescue team on a mission. This may be either because there is a possibility that their expert services may be needed during the mission, or because they are people of wide experience – including familiarity with their local mountains or other terrain – and their wish to back up the pilot in any way they can.

Accidents to rescuers

All too often the outcome of such missions has been the payment of the ultimate price by a brave rescuer and, especially since the advent of the pick-up by winch and longline, it has often been the rescuer descending to the casualty who has been the most endangered person. In 1968, when the techniques were still relatively new, in the course of an intervention in the Urbachtal in Switzerland, Kaspar von Bergen slipped out of the aluminium seat at the end of the cable as he was lifted away after a rescue. He clutched desperately at the cable but, exhausted, fell before the helicopter could lower him to safety and was killed. (Itin and Rutschmann, with Odermatt, 2002, 87)

Years later, in the French Alps, sheer misfortune led to the death of Pierre Nicollet, who had moved from the gendarmerie at Chamonix to the unit at Grenoble. He had been lowered to the scene of an accident on the Barre des Écrins, the highest peak in the Dauphiné. A girl with a fractured leg had already been taken off from the cliff and the helicopter had returned to lift out another climber, whose rucksack Nicollet attached just below the casualty as usual. As the helicopter rose an ice axe strapped to the rucksack caught Nicollet and lifted him too. The strap broke and Nicollet fell to his death. (Sauvy, 2005, 175)

The risks undertaken by rescue helicopter crews were made all too clear when in November 2010 a Eurocopter AS350B3 Ecureuil (Squirrel) operated by Fishtail Air of Kathmandu crashed while carrying out a rescue mission at the base camp on Ama Dablam in the Khumbu region of Nepal. Captain Sabin Basnyat and techician Purna Awale, having already evacuated a German climber, had returned for a Japanese climber. The helicopter crashed and the pilot and technician lost their lives. A second Ecureuil carried out the second rescue next day and dropped off a team to recover the bodies of the victims. (Internet, Fishtail Air Pvt Ltd)

Similarly, many mountaineers participating in rescue attempts have met with disaster, the example of the death of René Payot in the attempt to rescue any survivors of the crash of the *Malabar Princess* being but one example.

Rescue at extreme flying limits

In 1996, Seaborn Beck Weathers was brought down from the South Col of Everest after he had been abandoned above the col as already dead when other casualties had been got down after the most disastrous storm ever experienced by Everest climbers. He had then succeeded in struggling alone down to the South Col but was far too ill and weak to be brought through the dangers and technical problems of the icefall to Base Camp, where air rescue was now practicable. Lieutenant Colonel Khatri Madan of the Nepalese army flew a Eurocopter AS350 Ecureuil to the very limits of its flight envelope at just under 20,000ft (over 6096m). Madan studied his landing place carefully and eventually put the machine down. He then found that there was now another casualty waiting, the Taiwanese 'Makalu' Gau, one of those saved in the storm. Weathers selflessly ceded his place – for only one person could be lifted out at that altitude. Despite the fact that it was now evening, Madan repeated the dangerous flight and collected Weathers. Within hours, both casualties were being treated in hospital in Kathmandu. New records for rescue at altitude were created and it was an exceptionally hazardous mission.

The rescue of Beck Weathers illustrates both the hazards and the skill needed. Firstly, Madan undertook the rescue when the area contract pilots refused to undertake the mission because the casualty was at about 20,000ft and the prevailing weather conditions added to the dangers. Furthermore, he persisted even though the service ceiling of his AS350 helicopter was theoretically inadequate for the task. To reach Weathers he flew 2500ft above that ceiling to cross a ridge, which he was able to do only because he understood precisely the relationships between the engine power available and that required by the conditions. After several attempts to land he had descended to a lower area, put down his co-pilot and returned for the casualty. He had known that he would have difficulty in hovering and had decided to land without hovering, (Lobik, 2003, 3) hoping that he would find firm ice between the crevasses. When he took off he had followed the glacier downward until he could pick up airspeed. It was an exceptional demonstration of airmanship.

The altitude record for a rescue was pushed higher by Sabin Basnyat when, in May 2010, only six months before his fatal accident, he lifted out three Spanish climbers from about 6,900m on Annapurna.

It is clearly very relevant to try to enhance the capabilities of helicopters to fly still higher than appears at present possible.

Pushing the attainable ever higher

Ten years after the epic rescue by Madan, described above, a helicopter pilot achieved the outstanding feat of the first landing on the summit of Everest and it was in a later model of the same type of helicopter. On May 14 2005 Didier Delsalle put down a standard Eurocopter AS350B3 Ecureuil on the summit at 07.08, thus achieving, at 8,850m (29,035ft), the highest possible touch-down and take-off. The machine was a standard current pro-duction model, with a standard engine, though stripped of any unnecessary equipment to make it as light as possible. The flight was made from Lukla at 2,866m (9,403ft) and the pilot kept the helicopter on the summit for 3 minutes 50 seconds – comfor-tably exceeding the two minutes required by the Fédération Aéronautique Internationale (FAI) for the touch-down to be recognised as a record. The skids were in contact with the ground with the engines running to keep the machine stable and ensure the take-off in the extremely 'thin' air at that altitude. On his return Delsalle said that to reach this 'mythical summit' was like a dream and the aircraft had demonstrated its cap-abilities to cope with the difficulties and reach the target, 'sublimated by the magic of the place.' The following day he repeated the exploit.

Fabrice Brégier, president of Eurocopter, a division of the aerospace and defence group EADS, in congratulating Delsalle, also praised the machine, of which 3,670 examples had been sold to a range of countries and had logged 15 million flight hours. (Eurocopter web site, Internet)

Application was made at once for the achievement to be ratified as a new record, far surpassing the previous record landing altitude of 7,670m by a Cheetah, a variant of the Lama, also made by Eurocopter. The Ecureuil had previously climbed experimentally to 8,892m in France during training, but there is nowhere to land higher than the summit of Everest.

Perhaps, however, it was inevitable that doubt should be raised on whether the landing really was on the actual summit of Everest and that photographs taken from the machine did not confirm that it was on the summit of Everest. There was even the allegation that only the South Col had been reached, but the local police chief had been placed as an observer on a nearby peak, as instructed by the Napalese authorities. The FAI validated the record on 14th February 2006. The achievement was widely denigrated as a 'stunt' but that, of course, was the kind of reaction reported on other occasions when aircraft were flown to new and dangerous locations and heights – though these were often the testing and proving flights that had to precede the subsequent employment of aircraft for rescue work and other invaluable tasks. As least on this occasion there was some recognition that the way was being opened for rescues to be carried out high on Everest and other 8,000m peaks, hitherto regarded as likely to be beyond the reach of any helicopter for some time to come

It must also be stressed that the helicopter used was a standard production type. The Ecureuil had been chosen because it was one of Eurocopter's main high-altitude workhorses and the B3 had a lower empty weight then other versions. All the seats and electronics that were not needed were removed, the empty weight being then 11,000kg. With his equipment the pilot weighed 80kg and 100kg of fuel was added. So at the top the total weight was less than 13,000kg and this actually caused problems. Because of an updraft the helicopter was too light and Delsalle thought he could have had three on board and still succeeded in landing on the summit. The fuel was standard Jet A1 purchased in Kathmandu and flown to Lukla in a rented helicopter. Oxygen proved to be more of a restraint on time at the summit than fuel.

Delsalle's experiences on the approach to Everest make interesting comparison with those of McIntyre in his Westland biplane in 1933 described in Chapter 2. Delsalle also encountered severe turbulence:

'I was pushed away by the updrafts . . . though I was in a position of full pitch down and nearly overspinning the rotor and I was still climbing at 1000ft per minute . . . a few yards away you had a downdraft of more than 2000ft per minute.' (Norris, 2006)

McIntyre's problem was how to pass low but safely over the summit and enable his observer to get clear photographs, Delsalle's was to land:

'The approach I chose was a very flat one because the aircraft was at the limit of the known territory for the AS350B3 and I did not want to be too abrupt with the engine controls initially, so it was very difficult not to touch the collective, which was not so easy because of the turbulence there. On the day of the record climbers reported wind speeds of 60 to 70 miles per hour.'

When Delsalle returned the following day because he thought they had had some problems with the data recorded on equipment usually used for glider competitions, the wind had increased and he could not keep the helicopter's skid on the summit. He said he buried the nose of the helicopter in the snow. In fact the data the first day was satisfactory, unlike the photographs taken on the first of the 1933 flights that had led to an unauthorised repetition of those flights.

The wide range of mountain flying dangers

In any mountainous area, as compared with the normal aviation risks which result in most accidents occurring in the landing or take-off phase, in mountain flying a higher proportion of accidents occur, as one might expect, en route. Cloud-covered mountains present constant hazards, and the risk of icing of wings and engine carburettors is increased by the need to fly well above the ranges. As previously mentioned, only for soaring glider pilots may waves be good news. Along with thermal currents they provide the sources of lift that can lead to long flights and have been the main 'engines' for record-breaking successes. Nevertheless, waves are to be treated with great caution, since, apart from the turbulence, wind speeds in a wave may be around 80km/hr (50mph). This is too much for paragliders. (Whittall, 1995, 93)

Pilots who frequently operate and require to land in unpre-pared areas face many hazards every time they do so and again when they take off. Glenn Gregory, an Alaskan bush pilot, was asked to retrieve a Cub which the pilot had failed to get back into the air after putting down on a hunting trip in the Alaska Range. After abandoning the aircraft the pilot had sold it 'as is, where is.' When Gregory and a companion set off to retrieve it he took off with an extra propeller and a pair of skis tied to his wing struts, fuel, tools and other items making a two hundred pound overload. The job also called for greater appreciation of necessary technique than the Cub's pilot had possessed, espe-cially the action of the wind on the wings, as he had tried to take-off downhill with level ground below. He had been encouraged by the stiff uphill breeze. 'If he only knew' wrote Gregory:

'An airplane . . . has to have a good positive angle of attack in relation to the relative wind before it will climb . . . When an aircraft is in motion down a hill and the wind is blowing across level ground and then bouncing up the hill, it is, in effect, blowing downward on the top of the wing where the downward slope mets the level space. Because the hill is so steep the pilot cannot get his tail down far enough to create a positive angle of attack in relation to the flow of the air over the wings . . . If the downhill slope is long enough and the airplane is far enough up the slope to allow the wind to begin to flow up . . . parallel to the surface, flight can be attained.'

260

When they approached the area 'the wind was blowing so hard in the mountains that we would have two Cubs to retrieve if we were to proceed much further.' They had also loaded guns and ammunition so they went hunting wolves and left the retrieval to another day. (Gregory, 2006, 116–18)

In the case of rescue pilots, they must often fly in extremely marginal circumstances and land or hover in places and conditions where a pilot would normally not venture. A rescue helicopter pilot has therefore especially to be on the lookout for phenomena such as lee waves and rotor streaming, which can produce the most dangerous turbulence to be found even at relatively low levels and must be rigorously avoided by balloonists and most other pilots. For early rescue helicopters, which had relatively low margins of power, the hazards were particularly marked and although modern turbine-powered machines have much greater reserves, often conditions still present dangers. Yet rescuers have all too often failed to get thanks for their efforts, sometimes suffering criticism and even abuse for having come to the aid of someone who had not specifically called for help. Bob Maslen-Jones, member of the Llanberis Mountain Rescue team, gives many examples. (Maslen-Jones, 1993). Beck Weather's wife wrote to Madan after his rescue on Everest to thank him for his extraordinary act of courage. Weathers wrote in his book 'I later learned from Madan that in all the hundreds of times he had rescued individuals in the Himalaya, this was the first time he was so thanked.' (Weathers, 2000, 2001, 67)

Climbers may be excused to some extent since they are often, when rescued, in poor shape after their ordeal and possibly in a state of shock, even if not suffering severely from physical injury. They should, however, when they have recovered somewhat, give a little more thought to their saviours. A further excuse may be that they do not realise the extent of the hazards faced by the rescuers or how much skill has been involved.

Is the future remote?

The likelihood that piloted aircraft will ever be replaced for the transport of people into the mountains seems extremely unlikely. As for rescue work, there seems little possibility of substantially reducing the hazards that are faced by doctors and rescue teams in many of the tasks in their daily invaluable work in the mountains. Some aspects of flying in the mountains, including some searches may, however, be at least supplemented by pilotless aircraft quite soon. The Unmanned Aerial Vehicle (UAV) is already an important element in the aviation scene. Only a few short years ago, pilotless aircraft were restricted to drones used by the military as targets for training in gunnery and a few other tasks – apart from model aircraft. This situation has changed radically. They are now widely used for surveillance and other purposes. Military jargon classifies such activities as ISTAR – Intelligence, Surveillance, Target Acquisition and Reconnaissance. It was estimated in 2008 that some 60,000 UAVs of 60 different types were being operated by NATO countries, ranging from micro-appliances to sophisticated and very expensive reconnaissance machines that even then could fly halfway round the world. (*Aerospace Professional*, May 2008, 3) Helicopters present much more difficult engineering problems to be solved before many useful UAV versions can be developed, but developed they undoubtedly will be. In 2010 several aircraft manufacturers were making rapid progress with entirely new designs or adaptation of existing machines. For example, it was reported that Sikorsky planned to develop an unmanned version of its Black Hawk utility helicopter. (*Aerospace International*, 37.3, p10) Civil applications, as in the case of so many developments in technology, especially in aviation, are following and mountain rescue may eventually be one of them.

A critical view of the possible environmental impact of remotely controlled helicopters operating on Everest was expressed by a contributor to the British Mountaineering Council's journal *Summit*. He thought that such a development was 'a striking example of international market forces landing squarely in the middle of one of the world's wildest places' and asked 'Will quick aerial drop-offs at the South Col become common-place in future years?' (Pickford, 2007) Such objections are likely to be set aside, given the immense advantages that would accrue in humanitarian terms if the technical and financing problems could be overcome. It could open up the possibility of more equal treatment of porters and their employers who have hitherto received most of the benefits of helicopter opera-tions.

Any development that would reduce the risks incurred by pilots and crews of aircraft engaged in search and rescue must be welcomed. It has been demonstrated in several chapters in this book that there are acts of outstanding heroism being performed constantly by the teams responsible for mountain rescue, whether on the ground or in the air, and the men and women of the flying rescue services are now seen as in the front line of mountain rescue. They need all the technological as well as other help that they can be given. Likewise, any development which will ease the severity of the work of Sherpas and other porters in the arduous and dangerous tasks in which they find employment must also be welcomed.

Perception of risk by climbers and pilots

Paddy Sherman had some interesting comments to make after he and his friends had climbed Mount Fairweather in Alaska. They were flown out one at a time from a badly crevassed glacier. The pilot remarked that he would not even think of climbing such a mountain – it was far too dangerous. Sherman, however, found it awe-inspiring to see the small ski-plane bumping and swaying over the ice before staggering into the air. This view of climbing, wrote Sherman, came from a man who spent his life flying single-engine aircraft over some of the most dangerous country in the world, with no one to help him if he were to be forced down, in territory notorious for its rapid changes of weather. They each thought that the other was foolish to tackle the dangers they respectively accepted. After some more climbing on that trip, Sherman judged conditions too bad to continue and radioed for an early pick up by the Royal Canadian Air Force Canso amphibian that was laid on for this centennial celebration climbing expedition. Because of a weather threat, the Canso came in earlier than expected and the climbers had to rush to get their gear together. Just two hours and seventeen minutes after take-off the area was devastated by an earthquake and their camp site disappeared under a tidal wave. (Sherman in Sherwonit, 1996, 90–94)

It is not unusual for mountaineers, whose nerves are regularly tested in hazardous climbing situations, to express dislike of putting themselves in the hands of pilots for the flights that offer them so much convenience in saving the time and discomfort otherwise necessary. Sometimes there is good cause for nervousness, particularly when there are signs of inadequate maintenance, lack of availability of spare parts or simply a casual attitude to safety in flight.

Helicopters tend to produce more nervous reactions from passengers who are not flying enthusiasts than do fixed-wing aircraft. There is some justification for this, inasmuch as helicopters are extremely complicated in their engineering and greater skills are required to control them in marginal situations. These factors offset to some extent the helicopter's advantage that in the case of engine failure a descent may be possible by autorotation – the rotors being allowed to, as it were, freewheel, continuing to provide enough lift to make a safe, if hard, landing. The chances are less over rocky and steep mountain terrain. Noise and vibration unsettle passengers, much magnified if the crew seem to lack attention to firmly securing loose items being carried. Robert Macfarlane called his flight into the fastnesses of the Tien Shan in a Russian helicopter 'not a happy journey.' He and his fourteen companions on the flight were first weighed on 'an ancient set of abattoir-scales' and travelled with watermelons and a dead goat as company. He also had a heavy red gas canister placed between his legs and was told to hug it in the event of a crash. During the flight he 'felt lucky – at least I'd die first and fastest.' A pair of Americans told him that among the rocks on the south bank of the glacier they had seen the remains of three helicopters. (Macfarlane, 2003, 171) It should be added, however, that Soviet helicopters were actually very well designed and engineered and are still giving excellent service in many parts of the world, provided, as with all other aircraft, they are properly maintained.

It would seem to be inarguable that the position today is that mountaineers, trekkers and others who frequent or live in the mountains owe a great deal to the pilots and crews of SAR and transport helicopters and, in some places, also to those who operate fixed-wing aircraft. The reverse is still true when the weather makes it impracticable for SAR helicopters to carry out their normal procedures. Then the mountaineers, mostly unpaid volunteers, who serve in ground-based mountain rescue services swing into action as they would to help another mountaineer, walker or skier. Frequently it is a combination of airborne and ground-based teams that go to a rescue and sometimes it is impracticable to carry out a speedy and efficient rescue without the support of both.

Examples have been given to show that aviation in the mountains is always beset by risks over and above those that attach to most other forms of flying. It would be pointless to try to assess whether those risks are greater or less than those accepted by mountaineers as an integral and unavoidable part of their sport. The risks inherent in tackling any given climb have been significantly reduced by the development of climbing techniques and equipment but, as these have occurred, so ever more difficult climbs have been brought within the ambit of what is considered by mountaineers as justifiable risks. Routes which were once attempted only in summer are now routinely climbed in winter. Objective dangers such as avalanches and falls of rock remain a threat on many routes and the chances of incurring hypoxia are now accepted by hundreds of climbers who attempt Everest and other high peaks every year – a risk formerly confined to a small number of members of expeditions mounted only by experienced and dedicated mountaineers.

It is, however, undeniable that the risks taken by climbers are now only occasionally incurred in giving help to people other than fellow climbers whereas many aviators are incurring risks and providing services to all mountain users on a daily basis.

CHAPTER 15

When Skies and Peaks Entice

The preceding chapters have attempted to survey, if only in brief outline, the manner in which aviation and mountains – respectively human accomplishment and the results of natural geological evolution – have affected each other over the past two and a half centuries. Interwoven with this thread has been the interaction and interrelationships between aviators and mountaineers. The review has spanned only a fraction of the time that human beings will have watched the flight of birds and objects carried by the wind and sought to discover their secrets, so that they could fly themselves. Similarly it has covered only a small portion of the time that humans have been involved with mountains as travellers, worshippers and refugees. It has, however, been concerned with virtually the whole of the period during which there have actually been aviators and during which mountaineering has evolved as a sport.

When this period began knowledge of the globe was still limited and sporadic. Thousands of years of exploration had resulted in some practical knowledge of most areas, relatively detailed in the case of long settled areas such as the whole of Europe and the lands that bordered the Mediterranean Sea, most of the world's coastal lands and some of the inland regions of Asia and America. Geographical knowledge of the central parts of Africa, however, was very limited and that of the polar regions was restricted to their more accessible fringes. Mapmaking still depended on access to the area concerned or at least survey from commanding heights.

The conquistadors had ascended Popocatépetl, a volcano of

5,452m in Mexico, in 1519 and 1522 and brought down sulphur for making gunpowder – the name means 'smoking mountain'. Lesser but still impressive mountains in the Alps had been climbed by the brave and curious, such as the poet Petrarch, who walked up the great rounded ridge of Mont Ventoux (1,909m) in 1336, (now one of the great tests for racing cyclists on the Tour de France) and Leonardo da Vinci who climbed high on Monte Rosa – and also sketched designs for a helicopter. Until the second half of the 18th century Man was still earthbound and penetration of the snow-clad peaks had not been attempted though when necessary glaciers in the Alps were traversed and passes were negotiated. Often, where seasonal transhumance was a way of life, it was in the droving of flocks that glacier crossings were undertaken and occasionally lives of herders as well as of animals were lost in the process. The peaks were avoided until they began to interest and attract the first adventurous mountaineers; effectively beginning almost contemporaneously with the first balloon ascents.

When the balloonists first soared above the peaks they no doubt marvelled at the scientific progress that had made it possible actually to look down upon the giant snow-capped peaks. Perhaps they envisaged the day when the passage of a balloon over the mountains would become commonplace. Then, however, came the aeroplane, and the advances that made possible much more controlled and safer flight and balloons lost much of their relevance. Even in the 1960s it probably seemed unlikely that manned balloons would again be seen over the mountains – or in any other environment – for other than military or scientific purposes such as ascents to extreme altitudes. Yet now they are to be seen in their scores, even hundreds, at balloon festivals worldwide. Meanwhile aeroplanes have moved on in the past fifty years to become one of the basic everyday means of transport, making the whole world accessible to the vast majority of people in the developed world and, increasingly to the more wealthy segments of the populations of less developed countries.

So when fast and modern transport is available and a relatively safe flight will reveal to the curious at least a good sample of the secrets and beauties of mountain landscapes, why struggle on foot to snowy summits or scale precipitous cliffs?

Why do people climb mountains?

This is a question that has received earnest and often prolonged treatment in many books about mountaineering. It is also often asked both by non-participants and by the committed (perhaps over-committed) climber. A question of why does anyone fly is much simpler to answer – time, cost, enjoyment, necessity – the reasons vary but are mainly self-explanatory. Not so climbing. It is hard, uncomfortable, dangerous, and irrational in most cases. The many and involved philosophical explanations that are put forward by devotees will not be discussed here, just one reason, given nearly a century ago – the well known 'Because it is there!' These words were attributed to George Mallory, subsequently lost in the 1924 Everest expedition, by a journalist who interviewed him in the USA and asked why he wanted to climb Everest. It has been suggested that the interviewer invented the response but whether true or not the reply fitted Mallory's aim. As long as there was a higher mountain to climb, mountaineers would intend to climb it as surely as an ambitious explorer would want to reach the North or South Pole – and be part of the first expedition to do so.

In the 1920s, as in the 19th century, mountaineering was still largely the prerogative of academic, clerical and medical men who could take time off to indulge their passionate desire to climb in the Alps and other ranges. Climbing mountains to provide a livelihood was limited to the more adventurous men who lived among them and became the guides and porters of the mountaineers with money. Women featured in small numbers among the 19th century climbers, many of them relations of the gentlemen climbers. Remarkably, however, a young Savoyarde woman had shown as early as 1809 that it was possible to enter into what was then essentially a man's world when she became the first woman to ascend no less a mountain than Mont Blanc.

269

She gets hardly more than a mention in many mountaineering histories and any elaboration usually belittles her achievement. A more positive account given to Alexandre Dumas by his guide, Pierre Payot, when Dumas went to Chamonix in 1832, is worth recounting. Payot had stopped to speak to a woman and explained to Dumas that she was the first woman to make the ascent. Payot said her name was Marie but thereafter called her Maria as he recounted her experiences.

Jacques Balmat who had made the first ascent of Mont Blanc with the local doctor, Michel-Gabriel Paccard in 1786, invited Maria Paradis, then only 18 years old, to accompany a party on an ascent; this in response to a question as to why, when many foreign tourists had been taken up the mountain, few local people had had the opportunity. Balmat turned down another woman because she had a small child but, taking both Maria's hands, said she could accompany them as long as she thought she could cope. 'I'll laugh all the way' she replied. Not surprisingly, though, she found it hard going. However it was one of the six men of the party who at one stage sat down and declared he could go no further. Encouraged by Balmat he struggled on and they all reached the top. As they rested on the summit Maria did laugh again and asked if she could have all that she could see around her as her dowry. Balmat exclaimed 'Then who will marry her?' Michel Terraz said he would, but the opportunity was lost because the sun told them that it was essential to begin the descent. Payot said that she was the heroine of Chamonix. (Iker, Collection, 1980) She drew on her fame as the first woman to climb Mont Blanc to advertise a tea-room she later ran in Les Pèlerins.

Courage in the air

Just over two centuries later, it was similar courage and determination that led Amy Johnson to complete a course of flying lessons and engine maintenance – virtually unheard-of for a woman – at Stag Lane near London, where she secured her 'A' flying licence and her 'B' engineer's licence. In May 1930, when she was 29 years old, she embarked on a solo flight to Australia, not yet attempted by a woman. In her second-hand De Havilland Gipsy Moth, a light biplane, she dared the mountains, the deserts and the oceans. Amy had no experience of flying over mountains or sea – indeed she had very little flying experience beyond her training at the London Aero Club. It was her first flight beyond the English coast yet she hoped also to beat the record to India, which she did despite many setbacks and near disasters in landings en route. To do this, rather than go the long way round, avoiding the mountains, as others had done, she took the direct route across the Taurus range following Cobham's 1924 route.

As she approached the peaks, Amy saw a great bank of cloud obscuring them and tried to climb above it but the Moth could not climb above 11,000ft and the engine began to falter, so she had to descend. She managed to locate the railway line and decided to follow it through the winding gorges, trying not to lose it when it was in tunnels. In an exceptionally narrow gorge with the mountains rising sheer and high above on both sides, only a few feet from the wings:

'Rounding a corner I ran straight into a bank of low clouds, and for an awful moment could see nothing at all. In desperation I pushed down the nose of the machine to try to dive below them, and in half a minute – which seemed to me an eternity – I emerged from the cloud at a speed of 120 with one wing down and aiming straight for a wall of rock. Once I could see where I was going it was easy to straighten the machine, but I was rather badly shaken, and not at all sorry to be through the range . . .' (Smith, 1967, 1988, 194–95)

Sadly, despite setting up more records for inter-continental flights, Amy suffered many disappointments as she failed to find regular employment in aviation. At last in June 1939 she was taken on as a transport pilot but then came the war. She served with the Air Transport Auxiliary (ATA) as a ferry pilot but was lost over the Thames estuary in January 1941, flying an Airspeed Oxford. She was seen from a naval vessel to come down by parachute into the sea and an officer dived in to try to save her but was also drowned. It was, however, most probably high ground that initiated the sequence leading to her death. When she took off from Blackpool she would have had very much in mind that in the very middle of her route to Kidlington, near Oxford, lay the Peak District, rising in the south to Kinder Scout, 2,088ft. ATA's rules were that she should keep clear of cloud and turn back if in doubt. In the end, however, the pilot had to decide and would always be very anxious not to disrupt the daily complex network of movements involving deliveries of fighters, bombers and trainers from factories to airfields all over the war-torn country and air taxis to get ferry pilots back to base. She would have tried to reassure herself that after the midlands she would be heading into the usually better weather of southeast England. So she took a chance and climbed above the cloud, relying for her course on compass and dead reckoning, no doubt confident that she would find a window in the cloud to come down through. She had made exactly the same decision as described, stage by stage, by St. Exupéry, ten years earlier, in *Night Flight* and the fading daylight was no more help to her than the night sky faced by the Aéropostale pilots.

Jean Batten followed Amy Johnson in obtaining her licence at Stag Lane after she had moved, with her mother, from New Zealand in 1929 for that purpose. It was May 1934, before, after overcoming immense financial problems and two failed attempts, she succeeded in the first of her series of record-breaking flights in a 5-year-old Tiger Moth. In 1935 she flew back to England from Australia in the same ageing Tiger Moth – she could not afford another machine. After this, having become the first woman to complete there-and-back England-Australia flights, she decided to attempt the crossing of the South Atlantic. In a new aircraft, a Percival Vega Gull, she flew in November 1935 from England to North Africa and on to Brazil and Argentina. In 1936 she achieved her ultimate goal, the first complete flight from England to New Zealand, which she accomplished in just under eleven days. She set up another new record in a return flight to England. (Boase, 1979, 157–76) Having in between also extensively flown around New Zealand and become familiar with flying over mountainous terrain, she had realised the potential for opening up the country that the aeroplane offered. She became a keen advocate of the development of aviation in New Zealand, in the realisation of which Harry Wigley, whose participation in the rescue of Ruth Adams was described in Chapter 4, was to play a large part.

In the 1930s women were not expected to compete with or even simply share the adventurous life of the pilots and those who did, like Amy Johnson and Jean Batten, received great attention from the media and the general public. There were others who worked quietly away in remote areas and taxing conditions. Aéropostale benefited immensely from the courage and resourcefulness of Lydie, the wife of the South American area manager Paul Vachet, who regularly accompanied him on his pioneering flights. Given the task of preparing one major link without the necessary finance or even the aircraft to do it, Vachet traced one of the first Bréguets sent out to South America, now a wreck, left to rust away exposed to the elements. An ex-mechanic agreed to travel with him to attempt to repair the engine. As usual, Lydie also went along and used her sewing skills to repair the fabric of the wings and fuselage. It was not the only time she did this, when necessary getting hold of household linen to repair cuts and tears in the original material. Like her husband, she later served with the French Resistance and received notable honours, including the Croix du Légion d'Honneur. (Angel, 2004)

The heroism of modern rescuers

The mantle of the pioneers of both mountain exploration and mountain aviation has fallen in no small measure on the men and women of the mountain rescue services. The same spirit of adventure and dedication is found in them today, together with the addition of unstinting dedication to help others, despite the cost to themselves and their own families. To those who were

273

previously unfamiliar with the tasks run by mountain rescue teams it should now be a little clearer what risks they undertake. The role of the doctors who undertake to work in this field, however, has been inadequately treated. Fortunately this can now be remedied by reference to the fascinating, frank and sometimes rather shocking account of his involvement with rescue work at Chamonix written by Emmanuel Cauchy, a qualified mountain guide and climber of worldwide experience as well as a mountain rescue doctor. He does not seek to gloss over the fact that it is not always possible to give immediate relief to the pain and mental suffering of a casualty and the difficult decisions that often have to be taken by the doctor at the scene of the accident, with limited resources available. He does, however, also comment on the immense improvements that have been made in the treatment of mountain casualties since the 1970s and 1980s even though rescue by helicopter was then already well established.

One example of the difficulties and risks faced by the doctor and other rescuers must suffice to illustrate the demands of the job. A climber had fallen on the Dent du Requin within sight of the hut and the accident was reported by the hut guardian mid-afternoon as the weather was deteriorating. The helicopter (codenamed 'Dragon') was scrambled and the pilot deposited the doctor at the hut while he took two rescuers to make preparations at the accident site. Then Cauchy was lifted in:

'The door opened over nothingness. I was jettisoned into the void on the end of a five millimetre cable. Everything was spinning, the wind, the rock, the gusts of air . . . Nanard caught me by the hand. I had all the gear clipped to me: the 20 kilo stretcher, the KED to immobilize head, neck and spine, my backpack. The slab was as smooth as a baby's bottom and I couldn't find the slightest hold for my feet . . . Matteo was above us with the victim's girlfriend . . . Nanard clipped me in, I unhooked from the winching cable and the helicopter flew off with the female climber.'

The fallen climber was in great pain. He had a fractured pelvis and was in a critical state. If he were to be moved in that condition it would probably finish him. Cauchy was by no means sure that he was doing the right thing but he had to make up his mind quickly. He administered a powerful analgesic and got a saline drip connected. It was clouding over and it was doubtful if Dragon could get back in. They had been unable to use the stretcher and so the casualty would have to to be winched in upright, despite risking cardiac arrest from the pooling of blood in the flaccid lower limbs. The helicopter was flying around in the cloud. Thunder rumbled. Then the helicopter appeared and the message came from the mechanic:

' "Hand him over pronto. It's pretty dicey out here. We can't stay long!" . . . The hook had already been lowered down . . . Bernard [the casualty] flew off into the clouds, spinning as he went, which can't have helped his state of shock.'

Unfortunately for the rescuers, the helicopter could not get back in for them. They had to get down by themselves, climbing down four pitches encumbered by the stretcher that they had been unable to use. A wet snow was falling:

'It took us a good hour to get to the bottom of the face. The snow at the bergschrund was rotten and we fell up to our knees in a sorbet of coarse salt-like crystals.'

They decided to leave the stretcher and other equipment and return for it when the weather had improved. Matteo decided to place it under a small overhang, reaching which involved crossing the gaping bergschrund. The others cautioned him, but he persisted and then the snow above gave way and he was precipitated into the crevasse. For two hours the others dug with their hands and the one small shovel they had to try to rescue him. The helicopter could not get in to bring reinforcements. They heard it circling above them with their friends and an avalanche dog aboard. Eventually the pilot put them down at the Requin hut. It was, in any case, too late by then. Finally they got Matteo out but he had been two hours under the packed snow. Cauchy knew it was hopeless but still got out his resuscitation kit. He was utterly exhausted and his hands were frozen. The knowledge that he was dealing with a friend coloured everything he did, but, of course, he persisted long after it was clear that there was no hope. (Cauchy, 2005, trans. Cleere, 2009, 196–209)

Fuelling frustration

The Chamonix rescuers try to avoid using the emergency telephone channel. Apart from the voyeurs and spreaders of gossip there are also those who set off false alarms. Cauchy recalls ten or so rescuers being mobilised and spending two days searching with the helicopter at over 4,000m for someone who claimed to be calling on his mobile phone because he was in trouble not far below the summit of Mont Blanc. By the time they had rumbled the hoax and brought in specialist equipment from Lyon to locate the caller he had stopped. (Cauchy, 2005, trans. Cleere, 2009, 244) During that time many genuine missions would have been compromised, to say nothing of wasting resources, always stretched.

The problem with mobiles, noted Cauchy, is that although they can save lives they can also be used for trifling matters. 'Soon enough we'll get called out before the accident has happened.' (Cauchy, 2005, trans. Cleere, 2009, 179) In fact, at least one case that would meet that description had been reported by the Swiss Rega rescuers by that time. A helicopter had been called out and the pilot found a walker resting comfortably on easy ground as he awaited its arrival. Perhaps he had thought he might stumble if he walked down to the valley. At any rate he had felt too tired and seemed to think his insurance entitled him to the lift.

Should helicopter rescue be free?

There are now a huge number of mountaineers and even more hill walkers, trekkers, skiers, hang-gliding and paragliding enthusiasts and others who find sport and recreation among the mountains. Inevitably the demand for rescue services to go to the aid of any of these people as well as to those who dwell and work in the mountains has also grown exponentially. Not surprisingly there are many people who consider that such services should not be a charge on public funds but should be met out of insurance policies or by the user if no insurance is in force.

The saving of life or rendering assistance to the injured is deeply enshrined in the traditions of mountain rescue. In France it is widely considered to be an unassailable aspect of the concepts of the republican state. In the United Kingdom equally it has always been a part of the approach to rendering help where and when it is needed. In recent years, however, these traditions have come under attack. In France there has been an adjustment to the approach as noted earlier.

Government intentions for the future SAR services in the United Kingdom were examined in 2007 in a symposium held by the Royal Aeronautical Society entitled 'The future of Public Service Helicopters.' (RAeS, 2007) It was noted that the SAR-H Private Finance Initiative (PFI) was expected to begin to operate in 2012. A revised national service was to be jointly managed by military and civil crews. The intention was to bring all SAR helicopters in the UK under one contract with private investment facilitating the replacement of ageing RAF/RN Sea Kings by more modern aircraft. Some delegates to the conference supported this solution but there was known to be some doubt among service personnel as well as others about the wisdom of ceding to a private contractor what is widely recognised as a significant public relations tool. One delegate referred to the familiar yellow Sea Kings as 'The largest piece of positive PR for the RAF.' The possible difficulty for private contractors in finding the essential skilled helicopter crews, at a time when the military pilot pool is diminishing, was also a question for concern. It was further pointed out that while common perception sees SAR as mainly an over-water or coastal activity, 51% of RAF missions were overland, 35% being coastal and 14%

maritime. (Robinson, 2007) In an interview, Air Chief Marshall Sir Glenn Torpy, Chief of the Air Staff, said that the new SAR organisation would consist of a mix of military and civil helicopter crews, with the military element providing skills not currently available within the civil sector. (*Aerospace International*, Vol. 34, No. 9, 2007) The rescue services would, it was understood, remain free of charge to the rescued. The proposal to contract out the service has been controversial and acceptance of the preferred bid was cancelled in February 2011. The approach to reorganisation of Search and Rescue and modernising the helicopter fleet is to be reconsidered.

Difficulties in recouping their fees can be experienced by the rescue services in a number of different ways, for example if a helicopter has been called out by anxious friends and family but the person involved denies he had wanted to be rescued, or if an insurance company disputes responsibility. It is, however, unacceptable for countries that have limited funds available to meet rescue demands to attempt to provide free rescue services and quite unreasonable that trekkers and climbers who are immensely wealthy by comparison with local mountain dwellers should not have adequate insurance to meet emergencies. This is now commonly made compulsory and deposits to cover possible rescues should be made mandatory wherever enforcement is possible, as is the case of countries that can control access and do so by means of climbing and trekking permits. Such a solution would not be practicable to cover areas such as the British hills where going walking or climbing can be undertaken by people without the possibility of tight control even if this were thought to be desirable.

Two and a half centuries on

From the centre of Chamonix the enduring figures of Michel-Gabriel Paccard, Jacques Balmat and Horace de Saussure gaze day and night at the heights of Mont Blanc, Balmat pointing out the route over the Montagne de la Côte to the summit snows. What would they have thought if they could have visualised, as perhaps Jules Verne might have to some extent imagined, that one of the buzzing blue or red insects flying past them every day could land within metres of them and whisk them to the very summit in a matter of minutes? What would they think when they stepped out on to the ice and found that many had preceded them that very morning on to the summit and saw below them the column of climbers wending its way up along the narrow ridge, each close on the heels of the one in front and being passed by yet others on the way down? Then might come a call to the pilot still in his cockpit to pick up an elderly climber with a suspected heart condition from the Vallot hut just below and take him in a few minutes to the hospital where doctors with resources unimaginable to Dr Paccard could probably restore him to health.

Beyond the peaks of the Central Alps, magnificent tilting trains convey thousands of passengers swiftly and luxuriously from the north under the Simplon Pass to Domodossola and the Italian sun. In Brig, at the foot of the pass, on his pedestal in the town square, Georges Chavez the birdman looks out to the scene of the challenge to fly over the pass, which he successfully accepted but did not survive. Little could he have thought that one day his successors would fly over the summits with ease and even do so floating freely under inflatable wings, supported solely by the air currents they exploited. If they were forced down or chose to land in the pass, the paraglider pilots could have a coffee in the same building that in 1910 he had flown over.

What may the future bring?

Adventure, at least for a high percentage of the population of the developed world, is no longer only to be attained by proving one's ability to serve in an expedition being formed to undertake the challenge of some unclimbed mountain, major new route or unexplored desert or jungle. Few expeditions now require absence from home for long periods. Expeditionary experience can be bought from a bespoke provider by those who can afford it, and many can. This is not to belittle the achievements of those who push themselves to the limits of the attainable, but the sacrifices are not normally as great as they were in the past. If things go wrong, rescue is usually possible, as long as a mobile phone is available and weather permits. Even the cost of a long-range rescue may be covered by prudent insurance.

It is unfortunate that the consequences of these increased opportunities and activities include dangerously high demands on the natural systems that have evolved for the endurance of our planet. There is need for ever-increasing awareness and some degree of moderation of the demands made on mountains, forests and seas if they are to be preserved and permit the survival of the species that inhabit them, including mankind. The view from the summit of Mont Blanc may seem virtually the same as caused Maria Paradis to laugh and ask for it for her dowry, but far below where the Glacier des Bossons and Mer de Glace lead to Chamonix and the Valley of the Arve it is very different. Rivers of stone tumble down where in the 17th century the villagers paid for bishops to come and sprinkle holy water and pray that the encroaching glaciers should withdraw from where they threatened their homes and retreat to the higher mountain fastness. They thought that a retreat of 18–20 metres had been observed after one visit so offered to pay for another. (Joutard, 1986, 21–28, Engel, 1965, 52) They also petitioned the king to help. Neither religion nor royalty, however, produced significant results. Centuries later the problems are quite different and the solutions, if solutions there are, clearly must also be different and more radical.

References

AAIB Bulletin, Air Accidents Investigation Branch, Aldershot, Department of Transport, monthly

Acton, J. *The Man who Touched the Sky*, Hodder and Stoughton, London, 2002

Aerospace International, Vol. 33 No. 4, 2006, 28–30

Aerospace International, Vol. 34, No.9, 2007

Aerospace Professional, May, 2008

AFPM: Association Française des Pilotes de Montagne, Bulletin No. 64, 2006

Agresti, B, and Andrew, J. 'Rescue on the Droites' in MacInnes, 2003 (ed)

Air Historical Branch, Ministry of Defence; RAF Search and Rescue records. (Personal communication)

Air Zermatt, *Ready-round-the-clock*, Frehner, St. Gallen, 2001

Air-Glaciers *Fluggesellschaft 1951 Sitten*, B. Siegenthaler, Lauterbrunnen, 2002

Allen, J. with Davidson, R. *Cairngorm John, a Life in Mountain Rescue*, Sandstone Press, Dingwall, 2009

Alpine Journal, Vol. 17, 1895, 41–42

Alpine Journal, Vol. 28, 1914, 95

Andrew, J. *Life and Limb; a True Story of Tragedy and Survival Against the Odds*, Portrait, London, 2003

Angel, R. *Pierre Deley, Pionnier de l'Aéropostale*, Loubatières, Portet-sur-Garonne, 2004

Anker, D, (ed) *Eiger; the Vertical Arena*, The Mountaineers Books, Seattle, 2000

Archer C. and Norman, D. 'EMS: Environmental Management System or Expert Money Saving', *Aerospace Professional*, June 2010, 22–23

Bagnoud, B. in Spahr et al, *Hermann Geiger, 1914–1966,* Librairie Marguerat, Lausanne, 1967

Bailey, N. *Helicopter Pilot's Handbook of Mountain Flying and Advanced Techniques,* Airlife, Shrewsbury, 2002

Band, G. *Everest, 50 years on Top of the World, the authorised MEF history,* Harper Collins, London, 2003

Band, G. *Everest Exposed, the authorised MEF history,* Collins, London, 2005

Beaud, E. *De l'Alpinisme au Paralpinisme,* French Base Association, Internet site, 2004

Begg, J.A. *Burning and Turning,* Mercat, Edinburgh, 2006

Begg, J.A. *Rescue 177: A Scots GP flies Search and Rescue with the Royal Navy,* Mercat, Edinburgh, 2003

Bender T. ARTE/Bayerische Rundfunk, 2005

Benoit, General, *L'Aviation de Montagne, étude alpine,* Arthaud, Grenoble, 1935

Berg, A.S. *Lindbergh,* Putnam, New York; Macmillan, London, 1998

Berry, I. 'A bit of mountain magic', *Aerostat,* Vol.37, No.2, April 2006, 14–15

Bierbaum, P.W. *Im Aeroplan über die Alpen : Geo. Chavez Simplonflug,* Art, Institut Fussli, Zurich, 1910, Rotten-Verlag, Brig, 1985

Biolaz, A. *L'Histoire de l'Aviation en Valais,* Editions Haut de Cry, Sion, 1980

Boase, W. *The Sky's the Limit, Women Pioneers in Aviation,* Osprey, London, 1979

Bonington, C. 'Antarctica – Mount Vinson,' *Alpine Journal,* Vol. 89, No. 333, 1984, 220

Borrel, J. 'La voie des airs', *Mont Blanc Magazine,* No.11, Aug., 1983

Bradbrooke, J. *The World's Helicopters,* The Bodley Head, London, 1972

British Mountaineering Council, *Mountaineering,* No 1, 1947

Bucher, R. *Fliegen Retten Helfen; Werden, Aufbau und Bewährung der Schweizerischen Rettungs-Flugwacht von der Pionieren des Alpenfluges bis ins Jahr 1919,* Verlag Lüdin AG Liestal, 1961

Buckley, M. *Absolute Altitude: a Hitch-hiker's Guide to the Sky,* Hutchinson, London, 2003

Bugayev, B.P. (ed) *Istoriya Grazhdanskoy Aviatsii SSSR,* Vozdushnyy Transport, Moscow, 1983

Burkard, M. 'A cauldron of wind' in MacInnes, H., 1980, 75–81 and MacInnes, H. (ed), 2003, 178–87

CAA, *Aviation Safety Review, CAP780*, Civil Aviation Authority, London, 2008

Cameron, D. *Ballooning Handbook*, Penguin, London, 1980

Card, F. *Whensoever; 50 years of the RAF Mountain Rescue Service 1943–1993*, The Ernest Press, 1993

Carroll, D. 'A long way to Kinabalu' in MacInnes, H. (ed) 2003, 269–79

Cauchy, E. *Hanging by a Thread*, Constable and Robinson, London, 2009, trans. by J. Cleere from the French *Docteur Vertical – mille et un secours en montagne*, Glénat, Grenoble, 2005

Chapman, F. Spencer et al, *Northern Lights; the official account of the British Arctic Air-Route Expedition, 1930–31*, Chatto and Windus, London, 1932

Christopher, J. *Ballooning; from Basics to Record-breaking*, Crowood, Marlborough, 2001

Christopher, J. *Riding the Jetstream; the Story of Ballooning: from Montgolfier to Breitling*, Murray, London, 2001

Clayton, D.C. *Handley Page, An Aircraft Album*, Ian Allan, London, 1970

Clydesdale, Squadron Leader The Marquess of Douglas and; and McIntyre, D.F. *The Pilot's Book of Everest*, Hodge, Edinburgh, 1936

Cobham, Sir Alan, *A Time to Fly*, ed. C. Derrick, Shepheard-Walwyn, London, 1978

Coffey, M. *Where the Mountain Casts its Shadow: the personal costs of climbing*, Hutchinson, 2003, Arrow, 2004

Collier, B. *The Airship; a History*, Hart-Davis MacGibbon, St. Albans, 1974

Cruddas, C. *Highways to the Empire, Long-Distance Flying Between the Wars*, Air Britain (Historians) Ltd, Tonbridge, 2006

Cruddas, C. *Those Fabulous Flying Years: Joy-riding and Flying Circuses Between the Wars*, Air Britain (Historians) Ltd. Tonbridge Wells, 2003

Curran, J. *K2, Triumph and Tragedy*, Hodder and Stoughton, London, 1987

Cuvelier, L. 'La princesse brisée,' *Alpinisme et Randonée*, No.251, 2004

D'Aeth, N.H. Appendix 1, Report on Flying Work, in Chapman et al, 1932, 265–75, reprinted from *The Geographical Journal*

Deck, C. 'La tragédie Vincendon et Henry', in Romet, 1990

Defence Analytical Services Agency; Search and Rescue Statistics (including personal communications)

Desmaison, R. *342 Heures dans les Grandes Jorasses*, Flammarion, 1973

Desmaison, R. *La Montagne a Mains Nues*, Flammarion, 1971

Desmaison, R. *Total Alpinism*, Granada, London, 1982, trans. J Taylor (from the above)

Desmaison, R. 'The climb,' in *The Mammoth Book of the Edge, an anthology of climbing adventures*, ed. J.E.Lewis, Robinson, London, 2001, 230–78

Dickinson, L. *Ballooning over Everest*, Cape, London, 1993

Dickinson, M. *The Death Zone: Climbing Everest through the Killer Storm*, Hutchinson, 1997, Arrow, London, 1998

Dittert, R. 'The tragedy on Mont Blanc,' *The Mountain World, 1958–59*, Allen and Unwin, London, 1959

Dollfus, W. 'Die Geschichte der Alpentraversierungen und Hochgebirgslandungen' in *Alpenflug, Geschichte, Geographie, Erlebnis*, Kümmerly & Frey, Bern, 1969

Driant, le Commandant, *Au-dessus le Continent Noir*, Librairie Flammarion, Paris, 1911

Dunkerley, J. *Sometimes Eagles Wings: the Saga of Aéropostale*, published by the author, 2010

Earl, D.W. *All in a Day's Work; RAF Mountain Rescue in Snowdonia 1944–1946*, Gwasg Carreg Gwalch, Llanrwst, 1999(b)

Earl, D.W. *Hell on High Ground: a guide to aircraft hill crash sites in the U.K. and Ireland*, Airlife, Shrewsbury, 1995

Earl, D.W. *Hell on High Ground, Vol. 2, World War II air crash sites*, Airlife, Shrewsbury, 1999(a)

'En planant sur les Cimes Neigeuses' *Lectures pour tous, No 4*, January, 1913, 299–300 [Alpine Club Library]

Engel, C.E. (compiler) *Mont Blanc, An anthology*, English edn. Allen and Unwin, 1965

Engesser, F. and Kurz H-P, *La Rega: Destination patient*, Staempfli, Berne, 2002

Falke, C. *Im Ballon über die Jungfrau nach Italien*, Braumbech, Berlin, 1909

Fellowes, P.F.M. et al, *First over Everest*, John Lane, London, 1933

Frison, G. . . . *et le Ciel t'Aidera* Edns. France-Empire, Paris, 1985

Frison-Roche, R. *Le Versant du Soleil*, Flammarion, Paris, 1982

Gauderon, R. *Alarm am Matterhorn. Bruno Jelk: ein Leben fûr die Bergrettung*, Matterhorn Verlag, Roger Gauderon/Kandersteg +Bruno Jelk, Zermatt, 2006

Geiger, H. *Pilote des Glaciers*, Arthaud, 1955; trans. as *Alpine Pilot*, Cassell, London, 1956

GIACC: Group on International Aviation and Climate Change, 'Aviation and climate change' Appendix A. 4th Meeting, Montreal 25–27 May 2009.

Gibbs-Smith, C.H. *Aviation; an Historical Survey from its Origins to the end of World War II*, Science Museum, London, 1970

Gilbert, D.I. 'The first documented report of mountain sickness. The China or Headache Mountain story,' *Respiration Physiology*, Vol. 52, 1983, 313–26

Gilmore, P (ed) *Everest; the Best Writing and Pictures from Seventy Years of Human Endeavour*, Little Brown, London, 1993

Grazhdanskaya Aviatsiya, Moscow, monthly Soviet publication.

Gregory, G.R. *Alaska, My Alaska*, Trafford, Victoria, 2006

Grierson, J. *Challenge to the Poles, Highlights of Arctic and Antarctic Aviation*, Foulis, London, 1964

Griffin, L. 'Events and trends in the Alps,' *Alpine Journal*, Vol. 88 No.332, 1983, 185–89

Griffin, L. 'The Western Alps 1991,'*Alpine Journal*, 1992/93

Hamel, G. and Turner, C.C. *Flying: Some practical experiences,* Longmans, Green, London, 1914

Hardie, N. 'Long haul on La Perouse,' in MacInnes, 1980, 134–45

Harrer, H. *Die Weisse Spinne*, Ullstein, Berlin, *The White Spider*, trans. by R. Hart-Davis, 1959, 2nd rev. edn., Granada 1976, Paladin, London, 1989

Harvey, H. 'Jet streams and mountain waves', *Shell Aviation News*, No.204, June 1955, 5–8

Haveron, A. 'Kinabalu 1994' *On the Hill, Jnl. of the RAF Mountain Rescue Association*, No. 12, 2004, 18–20

Hempleman-Adams, D. *At the Mercy of the Winds*, Bantam, Transworld, London, 2001, 2002

Hildebrandt, A. *Balloons and Airships*, EP Publ, 1973, facsimile of *Airships Past and Present*, Constable, 1908

Hillary, Sir Edmund, *Schoolhouse in the Clouds*, Hodder and Stoughton, London, 1964

Hillary, Sir Edmund, *View from the Summit*, Doubleday, London, 1999

Hinckes, A.' Challenge 8000', *Alpine Journal*, Vol. 103, No. 347, 1998, 83–88

Hunt, J. and Gray, D. 'The future of Himalayan expeditions', *Alpine Journal*, Vol. 88, No. 332, 1983, 59–64

Hunter-Jones, G. 'Test flying the Erikson Air-Crane, '*Helicopter Life*, Summer, 2005

Hürzeler, H. 'Atterissage interdit,' in *Les Alpes*, Readers Digest, 1969

Iker, Olivier, Collection dirigée par, *Sur les traces de . . . Alexandre Dumas de la Grande Chartreuse à Chamonix; 'La première ascension du Mont Blanc,' raconté . . . à Alexandre Dumas père*, Les Oevres Libres Encre, Paris, 1980

Il Soccorso alpino Valdostano, Montagna e Vita/Le secours Alpin Valdotain, Musumeci Communicazioni, 2002

Inglis, M. *No Mean Feat*, 2002

International Civil Aviation Organization, Information Paper, *see* GIACC.

Irving, R.L.G. *The Alps*, Batsford, London, 1939

Itin F. and Rutschmann, P. with Odermatt, W. *Zur Gesachichte der Schweizerischen Rettungsflugwacht bis 1979; Histoire de la Garde Aérienne Suisse de la Sauvetage jusqu'en 1979; La storia della Guardia Aerea Svizzera di Soccorso fino al 1979*, Verein SRFW, Zurich, 2002

James, O.G. 'Fertilizer application – large-scale operations in New Zealand,' *Proceedings of the Fourth International Agricultural Aviation Congress*, Kingston, Canada, 1969, 496–500

Jane, F.T. (ed) *All the World's Air-craft*, Sampson Low, Marston & Co, London, 1913, reprinted as *Jane's All the World's Aircraft*, David and Charles, 1969

Jane's All the World's Aircraft 1945–6, compiled by L. Bridgman, Sampson, Lowe Marston, 1946, reprinted by David and Charles, 1970.

Jones, H.A. *The War in the Air*, Vols. 2–5, Oxford, 1928–35

Joutard, P. (Présenté par) *L'Invention du Mont Blanc*, Collection Archives Gallimard Julliard, 1986

Kamler, K. *Doctor on Everest*, Lyons, New York, 2000

Kellas, A.M. 'A consideration of the possibility of ascending the loftier Himalaya,' *The Geographical Journal*, Vol.49, 1917, 26–48

Kellas, A.M. 'The possibilities of aerial reconnaissance in the Himalaya,' *The Geographical Journal*, Vol. 51, 1918, 374–80

Kossa, M. *Le Vol en Montagne; Technique et Entrainement*, Editions Chirons, Paris, 1971

La 'chamoniarde' et le secours en montagne 1948–1998 SCSM, Chamonix, 1998

Laskina, E. 'MAKS' A report from the 7th International Aerospace Salon, 2005, *Aerospace International*, Vol. 32, No. 10, October 2005, 30–35

Lee, D.S. et al, 'Aviation and global climate change in the 21st century, GIACC/4–IP/9 Appendix B, 2009

Lewis, J.E. (ed) *The Mammoth Book of the Edge, an anthology of climbing adventures*, Robinson, London, 2001

Lobik, D.P. *Power available vs. power required*, School of Aviation Safety, Monterey, 2003, via Internet.

Lumpert, R. *Les Compagnons de l'Alouette*, Arthaud, Paris, 1973

Lunn, A. *The Mountains of Youth*, 1925, 138

Léon, D. 'Le sale air de la pale,' *Alpinisme et Randonée*, No. 253, 2004, 72–74

Macfarlane, R. *Mountains of the Mind*, Granta, London, 2003

MacInnes, H. *High Drama; Mountain Rescue Stories from Four Continents*, Hodder and Stoughton, London, 1980

MacInnes, H. *International Mountain Rescue Handbook*, 3rd edn. Constable, London, 1998

MacInnes, H. *The Mammoth Book of Mountain Disasters*, Robinson, London, 2003

Mackay, J. *Airmails, 1870–1970*, Batsford, London, 1971

Mahon, P. *Verdict on Erebus*, Collins, Auckland, 1984

Maslen-Jones, Bob *Countdown to Rescue*, The Ernest Press, 1993

McIntyre. D. *Prestwick's Pioneer, A Portrait of David F. McIntyre*, Woodfield, Bognor Regis, 2004

Mensink, D. *Around the World by Zeppelin*, Peter van Huystee /NPS film, in association with Arte, France, 2009

Meredith-Hardy, R. 'Over Everest, 2004,' Internet.

Miller, D.S. (ed) *Rescue: Stories of Survival from Land and Sea*, Mainstream Publishing, Edinburgh and London, 2001

Ministère des Travaux Publics, *Expériences de sauvetage en montagne au moyen d'hélicoptère*, Bulletin No. 76, 1954

Moffat, G. *Two Star Red; a book about RAF Mountain Rescue*, Hodder and Stoughton, London, 1964

Moore, K. Hinckes, *Berestone to Bering Strait*, 1999

Moore, T. and Andasco, K. 'Shining mountains, nameless valleys:

Alaska and the Yukon – Pt.II,' *Alpine Journal*, Vol. 83, No. 327, 1978, 23–28

Munro, Bob 'Middle Peak Hotel' in MacInnes (ed) 2003, 437–52

Mure, B. *L'Histoire de l'Aviation au Passy; l'Aerodrome du Mont Blanc*, Vatusium, Passy, 2002

Neale, J. *Tigers of the Snow*, Dunne, 2002, Abacus, London, 2003

Noel, J.B.L. Appendix 'Science versus Nature' in *Through Tibet to Everest*, Arnold, 1927

Norris, A. 'Eurocopter X3,' *Helicopter Life*, Winter, 2010, 18–19

Norris, A. 'From the mountain top,' *Helicopter Life*, Spring, 2006, 26–31

Norris, A. 'The mystery chopper,' *Helicopter Life*, Summer, 2006, 38–47

Oelz, O. Chambers, R. and Margreiter, R. 'Snow on the equator', in MacInnes, 2003, 406–26

Parsons, P. 'The Gimmigela adventure', *Alpine Journal*, Vol. 103, No. 347, 1998, 126–32

Piccard, B. and Jones, B. *The Greatest Adventure: the Balloonists' Own Epic Tale of their Round-the-World Voyage*, Headline, London, 1999

Pickford, D. 'Small world,' *Summit*, 48, Winter, 2007, 22–29

Pilatus AG, 'PC-6 Porter seit 40 Jahren im Produkteprogramm', *Pilatus Post*, 3.99, 1999, 20–26

Pilatus Aircraft Co. *Pilatus Flugzeuge 1939–1989*, Pilatus AG, Stans

Potelle, J-M. 'Un helicoptère sur le Mont Blanc', *Helico Review*, No.8, 1990, 57–59

Potterfield, P. *In the Zone*, The Mountaineers, Seattle, 1998

Poulet, P. and Raylat, C. *Secours en Montagne*, Didier, 2001

Pyatt, E. *Mountains and Mountaineering: Facts and Feats*, Guinness Superlatives, Enfield, 1980

Pyatt, E.C. *The Passage of the Alps*, Hale, London, 1984

Rega, *1414*, Zurich, (Newsletter)

Report of the R101 Enquiry, 1931, *R101; the Airship Disaster*, The Stationery Office, London, 1999

Rey, F. *Crash au Mont-Blanc, les Fantômes du Malabar Princess*, Glénat, 1991

Roberts, D. *Escape from Lucania*, London, 2002

Roberts, D. *True Summit: What Really Happened on the Legendary Ascent on Annapurna*, Simon & Schuster 2000

Robinson, D.H. *The Zeppelin in Combat; a History of the German Naval Airship Division, 1912–1918*, London, 1962

Robinson, T. 'Red hot Russians,' *Aerospace International*, Vol. 37, No.9, 2010, 18–19

Robinson, T. 'SAR looks to the future,' *Aerospace International*, Vol. 34, No. 9, 2007

Rolt, L.T.C. *The Aeronauts: a History of Ballooning, 1783–1903*, Longmans, 1966

Romet, R. *L'Helicoptère et la Montagne*, Majuscule, 1990

Ronne, F. *Antarctica My Destiny*, Hastings House, New York, 1979

Royal Aeronautical Society, *'The future of public service helicopters,'* London, 2007

Rutschmann, P. and Itin, F. with Odermatt, W. *Zur Gesachichte der Schweizerischen Rettungsflugwacht bis 1979; Histoire de la Garde Aérienne Suisse de la Sauvetage jusqu'en 1979; La storia della Guardia Aerea Svizzera di Soccorso fino al 1979*, Verein SRFW, Zurich, 2002

Sabitonni, A. and Halet, D. 'Secours en montagne, ceux qui le font et comment,' *Mont Blanc Magazine*, No. 2, 1982, 40–43

Samivel/Norand, S. *Les Grands Cols des Alpes, Histoires et Aventures*, Glénat, Grenoble, 1996

Sauvy, A. *Mountain Rescue Chamonix – Mont Blanc: Close Observation of the World's Busiest Mountain Rescue Service*, Bâton Wicks, London, 2005 (trans. from *Secours en Montagne*, Arthaud, Paris, 1998 with additional material, by John Wilkinson and Anne Sauvy)

Sherwonit, Bill (ed), *Alaska Ascents*, Alaska Northwest Books, Anchorage, 1996

Simpson, J. *Dark Shadows Falling*, Cape, 1997; Vintage, London, 1997

Simpson, J. *This Game of Ghosts*, Cape, London 1993

Simpson, Joe, *The Beckoning Silence*, 2002, 2003

Smith, C.B. *Amy Johnson*, Collins, 1967, 3rd edn. Patrick Stephens, Wellingborough, 1988

Soroka, W. Annapurna North-West Ridge, trans. by I. Dubrawa-Cochlin, *Alpine Journal*, Vol. 103, No.347, 1998, 89–92

Spahr et al, R. *Hermann Geiger, 1914 – 1966*, Librairie Marguerat, Lausanne, 1967

St. Exupéry, A. de *Vol de Nuit (Night Flight)*, Gallimard, 1931

St. Exupéry, A. de *Wind, Sand and Stars*, trans. from the French *Terre des Hommes* by L. Galantière, Heinemann, London, 1939, Guild Books 1943.

Stangier, *Retter die von Himmel kommen*, Scherz Verlag, Berne and Munich, 1981; trans. *Ces secours qui tombent du ciel*, Arthaud, 1982

Steele, F.J. 'The control and regulation of agricultural aviation in New Zealand', *Proceedings of the Fourth International Aviation Congress*, Kingston, Canada, 1969, 367–73

Stephen, L. *The Playground of Europe*, Longmans, Green, London, 1871

Strahan, D. 'Climate criminals,' *Summit*, 45, Spring, 2007, 20–25

Symons, L. *Russian Agriculture*, Bell, London, 1975

Symons, L. 'The Soviet approach to agricultural aviation', *Proceedings of the Fifth International Agricultural Aviation Congress, 1975*, International Agricultural Aviation Centre, 1976, 280–96

Symons, L. 'Weather-influenced accidents to UK transport aircraft,' *Aviation Safety Review*, CAP 673, Civil Aviation Authority, London, 1997, 42–46

Tabin, G. 'Records and Tragedies' in Gilmore, 1993

Taylor, L. *Air Travel, how safe is it?* BSP Professional, Oxford, 1988

Terrancle, P. 'Léon, saute-montagnes', *Pyrénées Magazine*, No.20, March-April, 1992, 33–39

Transport i Svyaz' SSSR, Moscow, 1972

Transportation Safety Board of Canada, *Safety Study of VFR Flight into Adverse Weather*, Report No. 90–SP002, 1990

Trewby, M. (ed) *Antarctica, An Encyclopedia*, Natural History New Zealand and D. Bateman, Auckland; Firefly Toronto and New York, 2002

Unsworth, W. *Everest: the Mountaineering History*, 3rd edn., The Mountaineers, Bâton Wicks, 2000

Valenti, S. 'Base-jump, la montagne autrement?' *Alpinisme et Randonée*, No. 2004, 72–74

Vehrkehrshaus (Swiss Transport Museum) Luzern, archives

Venables, S. *A Slender Thread*, Hutchinson, 2000; Arrow, 2001

Vette, G., with Macdonald, J. *Impact Erebus*, Hodder and Stoughton, Auckland, 1983

von Richthofen, M.F. *Der rote Kampfflieger*, Berlin, 1917

Walker, P.B. *Early Aviation at Farnborough: Volume II, the First Aeroplanes*, Macdonald, London, 1974

Ward, M.P and Clark, P.K., 'Everest, 1951: Cartographic and photographic evidence of a new route from Nepal,' *The Geographical Journal*, Vol. 158, No. 1, March 1992, 47–56

Ward, M.P. *Everest, a Thousand Years of Exploration*, The Ernest Press, Glasgow, 2003

Ward, M.P., Milledge, J.S. and West, J.B. *High Altitude Medicine and Physiology*, Chapman and Hall, London, 1989, 1995

Ward, M.P. 'Mountain medicine and physiology,' *Alpine Journal*, Vol. 95, 191–98

Washburn, B. with Smith, D., *On High, the Adventures of Legendary Mountaineer, Photographer and Scientist Brad Washburn*, National Geographic, Washington, 2002

Weathers, B. *Left for Dead; my journey home from Everest*, Villard, 2000; Warner, London, 2001

Webster, P. *Antoine de St. Exupéry, the Life and Death of the Little Prince*, Macmillan, London, 1993, 1994

Wedtgrube, G. *Retter aus der Luft: ein Rega-Pilot schildert seine dramatischen Einsätze*, Schertz, Bern, 1997

Welch, A. *Accidents Happen: Anticipation, Avoidance, Survival*, John Murray, London, 1978

Welch, A. *Happy to Fly, an autobiography*, Murray, London, 1983

Wenger, H. and P. *Geo Chavez: Der erste Flug über die Alpen: The First Flight across the Alps: La Prima Trasvolata delle Alpi: Le Premier Survol des Alpes*, Rotten-Verlag, Visp, 2001

Wheeler, S. *The Magnetic North: Notes from the Arctic Circle*, Jonathan Cape, London, 2009

Whittall, N. *Paragliding: the Complete Guide*, Springfield, Huddersfield, 1995

Wick, Emil. 'Over Everest,' Internet, 2005

Wigley, H. *Ski-plane Adventure Flying in the New Zealand Alps*, Reed, Wellington, 1965

Winton, J. *For Those in Peril: 50 years of Royal Navy Search and Rescue*, Robert Hale, London, 1992

Wohl, R. *A Passion for Wings; Aviation and the Western Imagination*, Yale, New Haven and London, 1994

Wohl, R. *The Spectacle of Flight; Aviation and the Western Imagination*, Yale, New Haven and London, 2005

Young, G.W. *Mountain Craft*, London, 1920

Index

Photographs are shown in bold type